Selling Out a
SUPERPOWER

Further praise for *Selling Out a Superpower*

"Economist Ronald Pollina is a well-respected voice in the world of real estate and economic development. His tell-it-like-it-is approach makes for an eye-opening and interesting read."

Jeffrey M. Anderson
President and CEO, Virginia Economic Development Partnership

"The book provides great insight into the causes behind the global shifts in international economic power and the erosion of US economic supremacy. There's enough blame to spread around among our political, educational, and corporate leaders—and even the American people. Pollina notes that a coordinated, strategic approach is necessary to reverse this decline, starting with a citizenry that participates in electing responsible leadership and holding those leaders accountable."

Geraldine Gambale
Editor, *Area Development* magazine

"In *Selling Out a Superpower*, Ronald Pollina has provided a great synopsis of where we are, how we got there, and what we can do to change the situation. I just hope enough people listen to what he has to say."

Mark S. Willis
Chief operating officer, Wyoming Business Council

"Pollina's unique perspective adds an important dimension to the national economic debate. It should be required reading."

Dr. Ron Swager
Senior research professor, University of Arkansas at Little Rock

Selling Out a
SUPERPOWER

Where the US ECONOMY WENT WRONG
and HOW WE CAN TURN IT AROUND

RONALD R. POLLINA

 **Prometheus Books**

59 John Glenn Drive
Amherst, New York 14228–2119

Published 2010 by Prometheus Books

Cover design by BMF Promotions, Inc. Cover images © 2010 Media Bakery.

Inquiries should be addressed to
Prometheus Books
59 John Glenn Drive
Amherst, New York 14228–2119
VOICE: 716–691–0133
FAX: 716–691–0137
WWW.PROMETHEUSBOOKS.COM

14 13 12 11 10   5 4 3 2 1

Library of Congress Cataloging-in-Publication Data

Pollina, Ronald R., 1944–.
    Selling out a superpower : where the US economy went wrong and how we can turn
it around / by Ronald R. Pollina.
        p. cm.
    Includes bibliographical references and index.
    ISBN 978–1–61614–215–5 (cloth : alk. paper)
    1. United States—Economic policy—2009– 2. United States—Social policy—21st
century. 3. Free trade–United States. 4. Recessions—United States—History—21st
century. I. Title.

HC106.84.P65 2010
330.973—dc22

                                                                    2010020542

Printed in the United States of America on acid-free paper

This book is dedicated to my grandparents, who came to the United States at the beginning of the last century, and to all other immigrants who, for over two centuries, have come here in search of the American dream, with hope of a better life for their children and their children's children.

CONTENTS

PREFACE   13

ACKNOWLEDGMENTS   19

1. SUPERPOWER NO MORE?
   THE SHIFT IN INTERNATIONAL ECONOMIC POWER   21
       Declining Middle Class—Declining Superpower   21
       Government Complicity in Offshoring   26
       Reality Check   28
       A Shift in International Economic Power   33

2. WHERE HAS ALL OUR VISION GONE?   37
       The Ruling Class   37
       Lobbyists—Our Third Political Party   41
       Pay to Play   49
       Leadership Vacuum   51

3. EAST IS THE NEW WEST
   THE SHIFT IN THE BALANCE OF POWER   55
       Emerging Superpowers   55
       Shifting Technological Supremacy   59
       Keeping Our Entrepreneurial Spirit   63
       Difficulties to Overcome   64
       Building a New China?
          Do Not Restrain Your Expectations   67

Contents

4. **To the Victor Go the Spoils**   71

Hot War vs. Economic War   71
India: Our Other Competitor   76
A Marriage Made in Heaven?   77
Yuan vs. US Dollar   80
Decoupling China and the United States   81

5. **Twentieth-Century Education Does Not Produce Twenty-first-Century Jobs**   85

Importance of Education to Economic Development   85
The R&D Black Hole   90
The K–Undergraduate Disaster   93
Staying Competitive in the Twenty-first Century   95

6. **Outsourcing National Security**   103

Outsourcing the Military and CIA   103
The Free American Press of India   108

7. **Driving American Companies Offshore It's More Than Cheap Labor**   117

Returns on Assets—Core Competence Death Spiral   117
US Tax Code—Designed to Be Avoided   120
Choking on Red Tape and Litigation   127

8. **The Great American Job Purge We're Making Little Effort to Stop It**   133

Offshoring Our Workforce   133
Government, Unions, and Cars   139
Reversing the Loss of Jobs   144

Contents

9. TAKING RESPONSIBILITY FOR
   ECONOMIC DEVELOPMENT   153
   Helping the Small and Midsize Companies   153
   Most States Receive Failing Grades   154
   Holding Corporations and Politicians Responsible   163

10. OUR REPRESENTATIVES AREN'T
    REPRESENTING US
    FEDERAL AND STATE LEADERS
    JUST DON'T GET IT   167
    Disconnect between Government and Business   167
    Witches' Brew—Congress, Lobbyists, and Pork   173
    Agricultural Subsidies—More Pork Than Bacon   177

11. A NATIONAL ADDICTION TO
    DEFICIT SPENDING   181
    Federal Budget Deficit   181
    National Debt's Impact on Americans   185
    Unraveling of Our Economy   189

12. WHY FREE TRADE DOESN'T MEAN FAIR TRADE   197
    Federal Trade Deficit   197
    Phantom GDP   201
    Clinton's and Bush's Free Trade Policies   203
    Free Trade's Impact on America   205

13. THE ELEVENTH COMMANDMENT
    FOR SOME PRESIDENTS,
    IT'S A MATTER OF FAITH   211
    Ricardo's Eleventh Commandment vs. The Soothing Scenario 211
    Free Trade Reality   216
    Theory vs. Empirical Evidence   221

Contents

14. THE HIGH COST OF FREE TRADE   225
     Free vs. Fair Trade Policy   225
     Sixteen Years of Ping-Pong Trade Policy   227
     Steel Industry Tariff   229
     Isolationist Temptation   233

15. THERE'S NO SUCH THING AS WIN-WIN NEGOTIATING   239
     Lose-Lose Negotiations   239
     Win-Win Negotiations   242
     Our Trading Partners Are Brilliant   245
     "Qui se Fait Brebis le Loup le Mange"   247

16. EASY CREDIT, FAMILY DEBT, AND TAX CUTS WHY YOU CAN'T GET AHEAD   251
     Family Debt—Maxing Out Credit Cards   251
     Bankruptcy Abuse Prevention and Consumer Protection Act   255
     Personal Tax Cuts—Who Benefits?   259
     Dangers of Easy Credit   261

17. THE MORPHINE SOLUTION TO ECONOMIC PROBLEMS   267
     The Morphine Solution   267
     You Could Always Depend on Aunt Fannie and Uncle Freddie   269
     Bush's $1.1 Trillion Bailout   272
     Bailout Ramifications   276
     Obama's $787 Billion Bailout   279

18. TWENTY-FIRST-CENTURY ECONOMIC WARS   287
     What Does the Future Hold?   287
     America Is Not Rising to the Challenge   290
     Twenty-first-Century Economic Warfare   293

Contents

Easy to Elect, Hard to Keep on Course   297

Do We Have the Leaders We Deserve?   300

ENDNOTES   303

INDEX   325

PREFACE

As a member of the baby boom generation, I have had the plea-
sure of growing up and spending most of my career in one of
the greatest periods in United States history—the twentieth
century. During this period, the United States became the richest and
freest nation in the world. It attained this status in part by the immigrants who have been coming to this country for over two hundred
years. It is these Americans and their descendants who contributed to
making what many consider to be the greatest country in the world. But
the nation's current state of decline is a dishonor to these past generations of Americans who worked so hard to make this country a global
superpower.

In part, this book illustrates the changes I have witnessed over the
past thirty-five years, while I helped corporations select locations for
their manufacturing, distribution, research and development, and corporate office facilities. I have been to places where tourists do not go—
from small towns in rural Mississippi to the aging industrial neighborhoods of the nation's largest cities. I have talked to laborers and some
of the nation's most senior corporate executives, as well as numerous
small-town mayors, governors, and members of the United States Congress. I was often charged with digging deeply to identify communities,
states, and countries that would provide the most desirable location for
my corporate clients' specific needs. These comparative investigations
examined factors such as labor, taxation, education, infrastructure,
transportation, health care, and quality of life.

Earlier in my career, I witnessed, researched, and wrote about the
outward migration of manufacturing from the Rust Belt states of the
North and Northeast to the South and West, and the movement of
office and manufacturing from central cities to suburban and rural loca-

tions. Essentially, these migrations have had negative repercussions on parts of the nation while benefiting other parts. In recent years, I witnessed another economic migration characterized as "globalization" or "offshoring," a phenomenon of the twenty-first-century global economy. There are forces causing this migration that are inevitable. Like all economic forces, they can be managed poorly or they can be managed in such a way that we as Americans can benefit from them. This book will show that we as a nation have been dealing with these economic forces in a disastrous manner. The brunt of this disaster is being felt today primarily by the middle and lower classes throughout the nation—it would be felt whether we had been in a recession or not.

The recession, while helping us focus on some of the causes of economic problems, distracted our attention from others. Unfortunately, the cause of the recession was not simply the collapse of the housing market or a greedy and unregulated Wall Street. These were recessionary triggers for an economy that has been wracked with problems and spiraling downward for decades. Pulling ourselves out of the recession with quick-fix solutions such as TARP, the American Recovery and Reinvestment Act, or the reregulation of Wall Street are not going to reverse our economy's long-term trend. A rebound from the recession based on stock adjustments or government stimuli alone will not last. Without addressing the other crucial factors eating away at our economic strength, we will not be in a position to regain our economic stature or maintain our role as a superpower as we progress further into the twenty-first century. We are simply applying Band-Aids to mortal wounds.

For most of my career, I saw optimism among the population, as incomes rose and the number of jobs grew. But over the last two decades, and especially since the turn of the century, attitudes have started to change. I have witnessed a rapidly changing attitude in Americans toward their future and that of their children as well as that of the nation. Today, most Americans see their incomes eroding, their personal debt rising rapidly, and the prospects for a better job and standard of life disappearing. Especially troubling, many people do not see the situation improving for their children.

I wrote this book out a love for my country and for my family. I did not write it for any particular audience but rather for the general public. My objective has been to identify many of the issues that most Americans are aware of but may have a difficult time tying together. I have tried to answer the following questions: Why is it so hard for my family to stay out of debt? Why did the housing and financial markets melt down? Why can't my state or community attract more and better jobs? Why are so many of our best jobs lost to China, India, and Mexico? Why can't I find American-made products to buy? If America is so wealthy, why is the value of the dollar so low? Why do politicians promise so much before the elections and deliver so little after elected? How do special-interest groups control our political system? How can the richest nation in the world be so much in debt?

I am neither a liberal nor a conservative, although there are those on both sides of the political spectrum who will read this book and feel compelled to label me one or the other. I am an American who sees politicians on both sides, Democrats and Republicans, mismanaging the country. Perhaps we, the American people, really are at fault, considering that nearly 40 percent of us did not take the time to vote in 2008, when we had that right.

At best, some may argue that our political leaders have us on a path of "managed decline," similar to what the British experienced at the end of World War II. I would argue that to assume that our government is managing the decline may be overly generous. I see the nation more in a free fall. What is most frightening is that our leaders do not appear to be making any effort to even open a parachute to slow our descent.

Throughout the book, I give many case studies that illustrate examples of political mismanagement that have resulted in the loss of jobs. The case studies presented are based on projects in which I was involved over the last fifteen years. Readers will note that I did not identify the names of the communities and states or the local and state political leaders who were responsible for these job losses.

There are two specific reasons why names, dates, and locations have been withheld. First, because of the business I am in, I am often required to sign confidentiality agreements relative to the projects I work on. These agreements legally prohibit me from disclosing identities. The veiled case studies were also selected based on the fact that the individuals discussed are, to my knowledge, no longer in decision-making positions. Second, to name names and attribute guilt or chastise a state, community, corporation, or union based on performance of former leaders would be counterproductive and unfair. To identify the governor, mayor, or union official who might have been responsible for the loss of hundreds or thousands of jobs would have the effect of unfairly stigmatizing a state, community, or union that may have long been rid of its incompetent leader. This is not to say that some states and unions do not continue to elect leaders who have no concept of economic development or of the global competition for jobs. It happens and it is not uncommon.

Certainly, it would be unfair to attribute all job losses to political and union leaders. I have also witnessed some decisions made by corporate leaders who may have been too quick to give up on discussions with political or union leaders and decided to close an operation and relocate it offshore.

Even with the restrictions of confidentiality under which I must write, I thought the case studies allowed essential insight into one of the reasons unemployment is so high and so many jobs have been lost to offshore locations. We should be aware that the type of behavior described in the case studies is likely taking place somewhere in the United States right now.

Here in the twenty-first century, you might want to believe that every political leader understands that the most critical component of economic prosperity is good, high-paying jobs. Whether we are talking about a community, state, or nation, a strong economy means government can afford to provide good schools, healthcare, infrastructure, security, low taxes, environmental protection programs, and all the other elements of a good quality of life. If the population has good job opportunities, the entire society prospers, whereas without jobs, it falters. I am continually shocked at how few political leaders appear to understand this most basic concept.

While incompetence and ignorance is understandable and, in small doses, may even be forgivable in a political leader, corruption is not. Political corruption is not new to this or any other nation. One of the primary premises of this book is that we have a system for electing our leaders that contributes to their being controlled, and thereby corrupted by, powerful special interests. These special-interest groups are not motivated by the best interest of the nation; in many cases, their interests are in direct conflict with the best interests of the American people. Unfortunately, these special-interest groups and their lobbyists provide the funding our political leaders depend on to get elected, and these funds come at a very high price to the public.

ACKNOWLEDGMENTS

I could not have written this book without the support and critical editing of my most respected and roughest critic, my wife, Mary. Without Mary's support, acting as my North Star, encouraging me and keeping me on track, I could not have finished this book. My daughter Kristen and son Brent also provided encouragement and suggestions. Brent has been a very dedicated researcher for this book and has been invaluable in keeping our company running while I was distracted by my writing. Thanks also to my brothers Denis, Lee, and Ray, and my brother-in-law, Phil Dlouhy, who offered suggestions on early drafts. My sister-in-law, Elizabeth Dlouhy, also deserves thanks for providing much-needed editorial comments. My friend, Dr. Phil Phillips, an expert in the field of economic development, offered many helpful suggestions on an early draft. The tireless efforts of my two invaluable assistants, Lois Blood and Terri Barreras, are greatly appreciated for their research expertise and for suffering through untold drafts of this book and countless hours of typing and editing.

I have had two mentors that greatly influenced my ability to write. My first real education in writing came from my graduate school adviser, Professor Howard Roepke. I learned a lot from Howard, including how to think logically, research, and write. My second education in writing came at my first job after graduate school—Continental Bank. My boss, Charlie Wilson, upon reading my first report, told me that I had to stop writing like I was writing for an academic journal and understand that my audience was now business executives. He said I needed to summarize and rely more on my opinions. Most executives were not terribly interested in details as long as my opinions proved consistently correct. Charlie and Howard also taught me a great deal about ethics, honor, and hard work.

Acknowledgments

Jim Wade was instrumental in helping develop an early draft of this book. A retired vice president and executive editor with Random House, Jim was a valuable asset. I was fortunate to find an excellent guiding hand in my agent Cynthia Zigmund of Literary Services, Inc. Before Cyndi agreed to be my agent and guardian angel, I felt like Dante on his journey through the three realms of the dead. Writing the book was the easy part of the process. Cyndi found Linda Greenspan Regan, of Prometheus Books, who helped me with the final editing of the manuscript and preparation for publication.

Certainly, most influential of all were my parents. It is to them that I owe my desire to learn, although it did not come to me until after high school. Working-class parents who could not afford to send four sons to college, they provided something more valuable in the form of encouragement, desire, and drive to achieve the education they knew was critical to their sons' success. Children of the Great Depression, my parents understood hardship, the need for education, and the need to work hard to achieve the American Dream. Somehow, among the four of us, we racked up nearly thirty years of higher education and four successful careers.

CHAPTER 1

SUPERPOWER NO MORE?
The Shift in International Economic Power

America will never be destroyed from the outside. If we falter and lose our freedoms, it will be because we destroyed ourselves.

—Abraham Lincoln
US president, 1861–1865

DECLINING MIDDLE CLASS—DECLINING SUPERPOWER

Myth Number 1: The United States is the preeminent global super-power in economics, political influence, and military dominance, and that is not going to change, certainly not in my lifetime or that of my children. In the 1980s, as a nation we were riding high—we were risk takers, inventing new ways to make money and new things to spend it on. As a nation we were prospering and we felt secure. From 1980 to the financial crash of late 2007, the Dow Jones industrial average continued a rapid climb, hitting 14,165,[1] and median new home prices quadrupled.

With the beginning of the new century, we began to hear more about jobs going offshore and the decline of manufacturing. At the same time, we were being told by our political leaders and the press that this was all part of the wonders of the twenty-first-century global economy, and America was going to benefit from these changes. Many Americans found these benefits difficult to see.

Soon, all was not well for an increasing number of Americans. Factories were closing in all parts of the nation, not just in the Rust Belt of the North and Midwest. Unemployment began to rise in certain areas of the nation and in certain industries. The overall unemployment rate was still relatively low, averaging about 5.7 percent for the 1990s, although many thought the situation was worse than this statistic reflected. Employment experts were concerned that many who had lost their jobs were forced into being underemployed (in a job below their skill level), into early retirement, or gave up on finding a job. With the advent of the recession in December 2007, the unemployment rate jumped to over 10 percent by the end of 2009. We were in the worst financial downturn since the Great Depression.

The American public and their governments—federal and state—were on a huge spending spree. Americans were financing a lifestyle that they could no longer afford. We had become addicted to borrowed money. Other countries like China and India were taking our jobs and technology, but, hey, we were getting cheap TVs, cell phones, and iPods. Interest rates were low, so when we couldn't afford what we wanted, we borrowed.

By the beginning of the new century, the nation's deficit was rising rapidly, as was the trade deficit. For the first time, median household income began a consistent decline, while inflation continued to rise. In spite of these signs, we were being told we were doing great, and many thought we were, because our investments were still riding high and our home values were soaring. We were confident in Wall Street and our political leaders when they explained away the danger signs.

By 2000, we were in the twenty-first-century world of globalization. The term *globalization* has become a common buzzword covering a wide range of political, economic, and cultural trends. For our purposes, it describes a process by which national and regional economies and cultures have become integrated through global systems of communication, trade, capital flows, migration, and the spread of technology into the international economy. With globalization, words like *outsourcing, offshoring, downsizing,* and *rightsizing* began to be used more frequently than ever before. Millions of American workers, not just in manufacturing, lost their jobs and were unable to find new jobs. For these Americans, it made no difference what jargon was used—the results for them and their families was the same. But it is not just these workers and their families that were being affected—the nation as a whole began to feel the repercussions of globalization. We didn't pay much attention, if any at all, to the fact that with the turn of the century, the US economy began growing slower than the global economy.

We heard of the wonders of globalization and how rapidly it was advancing countries like China, India, and Brazil, where hundreds of millions of people were rising from poverty into the middle class. American families increasingly found that in spite of a flood of low-cost products from offshore, their standard of living was not improving, their incomes were not rising (see chapter 11), and they were sliding increasingly into debt (see chapter 16).

It is important to recognize that the factors leading to America's economic troubles existed long before the downward spiral of the housing market after its peak in early 2005, the start of the recession in December 2007, or the collapse of the financial markets in 2008. These were the slap in the face the public needed to awaken us from our spending binge. We began to come to the realization that our economy was losing its ability to generate the income necessary to maintain the lifestyle we sought. The American public has since begun to adjust by attempting to decrease its household debt and consumption. However, the federal government continues to borrow, tax, and print money— showing no indication that it is making enough of a similar effort.

Globalization, once promoted as the path to economic growth, is no longer regarded in the same way by populations in advanced nations. In Europe, polls report that two-thirds of EU citizens see globalization as profitable for large global companies but not for citizens. A 2002 Pew poll showed that in the United States, 78 percent of its citizens thought foreign trade was beneficial to the country; by 2007 (prerecession) the percentage had dropped to 59 percent.[2] By 2008, a CNN poll showed that a majority of Americans saw trade as a threat, not an opportunity.[3]

For the first time, Americans began to feel a threat to our status as the world's superpower. Try to imagine what life would be like in America if it were the third-ranked global superpower behind China and India. How would it affect us socially and economically and from a security perspective? Picture this change reflecting a substantial improvement in the economies and standard of living in China and India, with a commensurate weakening of the United States economy and standard of living. Envision that this will occur in your lifetime, or at least within your children's lifetimes. Finally, imagine that this situation is, in large part, the result of mismanagement by our political leaders.

The worst part of this scenario is that it does not need to occur. Populists and protectionists tend to blame the growing apparent United States disadvantage on "unfair" trade practices by other countries. Most of our political leaders understand the direction in which the nation is traveling, but they are not taking the necessary action to make a course correction. Historically, this is not unusual; many great superpowers have been largely responsible for their own demise.

The economic, social, and political implications of America's mis-managed globalization threaten to shake our society to its foundations. The middle class is at war, engaged in an international battle to keep its jobs and standard of living—and the battle is not going well. For the first time in our history, the size of the middle class is diminishing and its income is not rising to keep pace with inflation (see figures 6 and 9, on pages 186 and 223, respectively), and this trend began long before the 2007 recession. Many of the same forces causing the middle class to shrink are causing Americans with the lowest economic prospects to grow in number.

How did we get to this point? During the housing boom that kicked off the twenty-first century, middle-class Americans who could no longer improve their earning power refinanced their homes, pulling out billions of dollars in equity to protect a lifestyle they could no longer afford. By turning their homes into ATMs and increasing their credit card debt, most middle-class Americans are now paying interest on their groceries, making the possibility of retirement or paying for medical emergencies or college tuition impossible. Never before has the American public and its government been so deeply in debt, and never before have the economic prospects for our children and our children's children to have a better standard of living than we have been so dismal. For many Americans, their last job was the best job that they will ever have.

Our economy was built on the fact that we as a nation made excellent products and provided exceptional services that were in demand worldwide. We have been rapidly surrendering our position of leadership in these areas where we truly excelled, which were responsible for making the United States a superpower. In the last two decades, we have shifted to a nation that can claim that one of its biggest growth sectors is providing financial services. Thus far in the twenty-first century, we have shown that this is not a business we are very good at. In fact, we are so bad at it that we triggered a worldwide recession.

Our nation became a superpower because we invested in manufacturing, research, and development. We were innovative and we made things. However, we are rapidly becoming a nation that makes nothing, and we now spend more money on lawsuits than on research and development. The United States now has the largest national and personal debt of any nation. Most important is that this debt has not been caused by financing investments but rather by government spending and high levels of private consumption of goods produced offshore.

When the public first began to recognize that the nation's financial industry was beginning to implode in September 2008, the government responded by flooding the industry with $700 billion. This money did not come from a government rainy-day account but rather was added to the national debt.

The federal government acts like it has a credit card with no spending limit. Credit extended to the government comes through the sale of United States treasury securities. These securities are backed by the "Full Faith and Credit" of the United States government. Over 25 percent of these treasuries are owned by foreign governments—mostly China and Japan (the oil-exporting countries) and the United Kingdom.

When as a senator Hillary Clinton was asked why the federal government does not get tougher on trading partners like China, she stated, "How do you get tough on your banker?" She also stated that she sees "a slow erosion of our economic sovereignty."[4] It is difficult to comprehend that our political leaders acknowledge that they see our economic sovereignty eroding, yet they do little or nothing to stop it. Indeed, they have created the situation and are perpetuating it as a result of their unbridled spending and poorly conceived legislation, regulation, and trade policies. Our government's policies have led the United States toward a future of diminished economic and political power that has left us vulnerable to external economic forces.

GOVERNMENT COMPLICITY IN OFFSHORING

A leading cause for the United States' weakening financial position is our tax structure that encourages companies to move offshore. Unlike most advanced nations that have reduced corporate taxes in order to become more competitive with countries with low labor costs, the United States has maintained a tax system with the second-highest (Japan is first) corporate taxes in the world.[5] We regulate certain industries to the point that we drive them offshore, while we deregulate others, allowing them to drive personal bankruptcies to record highs and the nation into recession. For example, after twenty years of deregulation in the lending industry, in 2005 (pre–housing bubble), home foreclosures had more than tripled in less than twenty-five years.[6]

Offshoring of the nation's high-tech and manufacturing jobs is continuing at a rate that is growing in intensity. In spite of this, the federal government and many state governments continue to offer little or no assistance to businesses to promote job growth at home.

During my career, I have assisted in relocating numerous manufacturing operations, research and development facilities, and corporate headquarters from one part of the nation to another. But what is most discouraging is the ease with which executives are able to expand offshore, once a company has established some presence beyond the United States. Making an economic case for expansion in the United States is getting harder every year, and it is not all due to lower offshore labor costs.

It's not just large corporations that are moving offshore; it is increasingly midsize and even small companies that are making the move. Several years ago, we were engaged by a client to approach their local and state economic development organizations. Our client, like many US companies, was having a difficult time competing in the global marketplace. This small company had about 390 employees, most of whom were in manufacturing. Their facility was old and cramped, and they needed to automate to cut costs and to meet the pricing demands of new customer orders. They also had a small operation with about eighty manufacturing employees in China.

The United States officials from the community and state refused to provide financial assistance to retrain existing employees or to provide tax abatements or infrastructure improvements. They claimed that they had no assistance programs for companies already in the state. The other negative was that the company would be adding only twenty-five employees as a result of their expansion and automation program. The company said they would agree to repay any financial assistance provided by the state or community if, during the next ten years, they dropped below 350 employees. We had negotiated with another state that was willing to give them $21 million in state and community incentives to relocate. The third choice of a Chinese location would have reduced their labor costs substantially and some of their other operating expenses.

Without the assistance that would make staying at their current location feasible (substantially less than the $21 million offered by the other state), and with the negative messages from their state and community, the company owner said the governor and mayor made a tough decision easier. He also said that while the offer of $21 million from the competing state made his choice difficult, if they had to relocate and train a new labor force, it would be more profitable long-term to expand their operation in China and phase out the US operation altogether.

As requested by our client, and as is customary, we did not tell the state or community of our client's plan to downsize and eventually close the operation. Companies often do not divulge plans for long-term phaseouts, as they may adversely affect operations in other parts of a state that are doing well. Also, if conditions improve, a phaseout may be stopped or even reversed. When asked by local and state officials about our client's plans, we could only say that they would not be moving to another state. The response of one of the state officials was, "We knew you were bluffing when you said they would move if we didn't help." The governor and mayor put out a press release stating that through their efforts, they had preserved 390 jobs. Within three years, the operation was gone. With a few million dollars and a more positive attitude, these jobs, with an approximately $18 million payroll, could have been saved. Did the state and community win this negotiation or did 390 families lose? Or did neither win?

Unfortunately, based on my experience, this is not an uncommon outcome of globalization for American workers. We often see in the news that a particular company is "downsizing." The reality is that downsized jobs very often are not being eliminated but rather "offshored." This case is not an isolated incident—it is a common scenario that has been taking place throughout the United States since the early 1990s.

REALITY CHECK

Certainly, any global recession will bring out the worst in trading partners. American companies continue to accuse Chinese rivals of dumping products in the United States (selling below market prices). Fair-trade advocates continue to accuse China of using subsidies, currency manipulation, and tax breaks for their industries in an effort to maintain growth for their economy at the expense of the US economy.

President Barack Obama has a dilemma. He has promised to be tougher on China, but he is dependent on Chinese funds to finance a $1.15 trillion federal budget deficit (2010). This is exactly the problem Hillary Clinton warned of. The Chinese know they have the upper hand. In March 2009, *Economist* magazine cited an article in the Chinese think tank publication *Economic Reference*, which stated that the economic crisis will weaken the economic, political, military, and diplomatic power of developed countries. Regarding the United States, the article said China should buy up businesses in order to acquire sophisticated knowledge. If the United States government does not approve, "the Chinese government absolutely can use its American dollar savings as a bargaining chip to force the American government to agree to China's acquisitions" (see chapter 11).[7]

The reality of where this country stands in the global economy, and where it is headed, has been obscured by a cloud of myths—generated by mistaken or unjustified assumptions, political irresponsibility, and special-interest propaganda. These myths obscure the fact that our status as an economic and military superpower is being steadily undermined every day. If we are going to reverse this decline, we must free ourselves from the spell of accepting these myths and come to grips with the interlocking causes of the problems facing us.

Throughout this book, you will see many myths highlighted. During my business travels and my speaking engagements, Americans of various social and economic levels have presented their versions of these myths. They came from cab drivers in Washington, DC, Chicago, and Dallas; a rancher in Wyoming; legislators; reporters; university professors; and CEOs of major corporations. The myths I've identified are those I hear on a relatively consistent basis. This is not to say that all Americans believe all of these myths but that these myths are relatively commonly held beliefs, some certainly more widely accepted than others. In some cases, they are rationalizations or misconceptions created by politicians or the public because they do not want to face the truth. In other cases, they are created out of self-interest by people who know these myths to be untrue but find they soothe the public's concern about their future.

Myth Number 2: Offshoring is simply part of the twenty-first-century globalization, and ultimately America will benefit. Many politicians and special-interest lobbyists argue that offshoring is simply part of twenty-first-century globalization and that ultimately America will reap rewards. In spite of all the positive rhetoric about globalization, the facts do not support the optimism of the myth.

Globalization is a critical component of the twenty-first-century American economy. It's happening, and there isn't anything we can do to stop it, nor should we. America must be an integral part of the global marketplace if it is to remain a superpower. Thus far, as a nation, we have done a terrible job integrating ourselves into the twenty-first-century global market. Many American corporations have done a masterful job and have benefited, but the majority of Americans have not. The fact that many American corporations are successfully integrating into the global economy does not mean that America or the American public is benefiting (see chapters 7–9).

Prior to the recession, corporate profits had been rising worldwide, but these increases were not being reflected in the economic growth of many of the nations in which these companies are headquartered. Generally, for most Western countries, real incomes for workers either have been stagnant or have fallen.[8] The old relationship between corporate profits and national prosperity no longer exists. In the past, big profits meant companies invested more, hired new workers, and paid existing workers higher wages. In recent years, corporate earnings per share have risen for large Western European and American global companies, and are more reflective of the growth of the global economy than their homeland economies.

Myth Number 3: Sure, America has lost a lot of jobs, but as the economy picks up, our companies will be hiring these people back. It's temporary—it's just like the past recessions. To believe that these large companies will rehire Americans when the economy finally starts to rebound is wishful thinking at best. It is in the world's emerging economies that market growth is occurring. It is also where they were hiring the greatest number of employees and offshoring American jobs well before the recession.

Stephen King, chief economist for HSBC in London, found that of the world's forty largest international corporations, 55 percent of their workforces are located in foreign countries and 59 percent of their earnings come from abroad. If the growth in profits is from abroad, it's not surprising that this is where the lion's share of their investment in new plants and equipment will take place.

Over the next decade, the United States would need to create at least another 1.8 million net new jobs per year to keep up with the growing working population. During the 1990s, the United States was creating approximately 2.2 million jobs per year, and this number dropped to less than half that number from 2000 to 2008. It is not just the recession that has caused this decline. As a nation, we simply do not have the ability to create the high-quality jobs we once did. In past decades, we were able to replace good, well-paying jobs lost in industries like consumer electronics, automotive, and textiles with jobs in industries developed in the United States, such as personal computers, cell phones, and Internet and software development. As these jobs have been shipped offshore, no new industries have emerged to replace them.

Superpower No More?

There is no white knight industry that can produce the millions of high-paying jobs needed to replace the jobs lost during the recession. As new energy sources are being developed to replace carbon fuels, or developments are made in other areas, the jobs that go with production are often shipped offshore immediately. Increasingly, the scientific development of new products is also shipped offshore for further development and refinement.

The real threat of moving more manufacturing, research and development, and high-paying service jobs offshore has been used successfully to keep wages down in the United States and has also been felt by employees in terms of their healthcare and pensions. With growing numbers of employees located offshore and an increasing share of investment taking place there, the line between domestic and foreign companies is certainly blurring.

Take American car companies, for example. While they continue to lose market share in the United States, they are doing much better in emerging markets. In recent years, 65 percent of General Motors' sales were generated abroad. In 2009 the US government bought 61 percent of GM and 8 percent of Chrysler to prevent bankruptcy. Early in 2009, GM outraged the United Auto Workers when it said it would be producing the Chevrolet Spark in China for export to the United States. *Automotive News* reported that based on a document circulated among federal lawmakers in May 2009, GM plans to sell 17,335 China-made vehicles in the US in 2011 and 51,546 by 2014. The plan called for a reduction of US workers and more vehicles coming from Mexico and South Korea. The percentage of GM cars manufactured in China, Mexico, and South Korea and sold in the United States will rise from 15 percent to 23 percent over a five-year period, according to the document given lawmakers.[9]

There are political and union leaders as well as journalists who want us to believe Myth Number 4: Corporate greed is the main reason so many jobs are offshored. This book will argue that corporate America is not solely responsible for the offshoring of our nation's best jobs—federal, state, and local political leaders create the laws and policies that often contribute significantly to driving companies offshore.

Contrary to popular belief, companies do not move offshore solely because of lower labor costs. Our federal government and most state governments have created a business environment that has become hostile to business, while other countries have created environments that are considerably more business-friendly. Many states have also created hostile environments for business through the use of overzealous taxation and regulation (see chapters 7 and 10).

The United States is in a global economic war, and we're losing. India and China each have a collective will and strategy to win this economic war (see chapters 3 and 4). As a nation, we Americans appear to have no will or strategy to win (see chapter 18).

Today

- The percentage of middle-class Americans is decreasing, while China's and India's middle classes are growing rapidly.
- We are losing high-paying engineering, medical, business, technology, and manufacturing jobs to our free-trade partners and gaining low-paying service jobs.
- We have a dangerously high and continually rising national budget deficit and trade deficit. Annual interest payments on the national debt are approximately $383 billion, while we spend only $53 billion on education.
- Americans are clinging to a standard of living that they no longer can afford by borrowing money. The average American has over $9,000 in credit card debt and virtually no savings.
- We must sell treasuries to foreign governments to support our national debt, while buying consumer goods from these same countries and paying the interest on these treasuries by taxing Americans.
- In spite of a great deal of rhetoric, the federal government and most state and local governments do very little to encourage quality job growth.
- Special-interest groups who finance political candidates have more control over political leaders than the American people do.

A SHIFT IN INTERNATIONAL ECONOMIC POWER

Myth Number 5: China and India may be growing rapidly now, but the American economy is keeping pace with global economic growth. There appears to be little doubt that the balance of power is shifting away from the United States to the East, as China's and India's economies evolve. What is most important is that these two countries are not complementary economies, growing in unison with the United States, but rather they are to a large extent at the expense of the US economy. In essence, they have pulled millions of jobs from the United States economy with the assistance of our federal and many state governments. For Americans, this means a far different future, one in which our standard of living will be diminished and our military dominance likely challenged.

Myth Number 6: China and India are simply examples of bubble economies in countries with significant social and political problems and therefore will never rise to be threats to the United States' economic supremacy. In just a few years, India has created world-class innovation hubs and China has shifted from a nation that attracted low-cost jobs to one that excels in state-of-the-art manufacturing. Given their young populations' skilled labor, the magnitude of their emerging markets, their high rate of savings, and capital- and business-friendly governments, it's apparent why most economists believe these countries have what it takes to maintain growth rates of 6 percent to 10 percent well into this century. These countries simply have too much going for them to be dismissed as bubble economies.

While the governments of China and India appear to have a vision to achieve economic, political, and military power (China), which they are fulfilling, US political leadership appears to have no such plan. We enter the twenty-first century as a complacent superpower. Our political leaders seem to feel that we, like the sons and daughters of billionaire parents, need not work hard to have a comfortable life. We have this sense of entitlement simply because we are Americans. We entered the twenty-first century at the pinnacle of success, a far different position than the one we were in when we entered the twentieth century.

A Goldman Sachs study estimated that by 2027, China will surpass the United States as the largest economy.[10] The *Economist* stated that, based on estimates of the Economist Intelligence Unit, China's economy could surpass America's by 2030 in terms of gross domestic product (GDP) purchasing-power parity.[11] Whether you want to use 2027 or 2030 as the target date, the fact is, America is headed for a less prominent position in the world order. History tells us that with economic power comes commensurate military power. No nation has ever been able to sustain military power without its own internal economic power or that of another more powerful nation. The decline of our economic status, therefore, signals a major shift, not only in our standard of living, but also in our security. There are forces in play today in the United States that will allow the growth of China to gradually surpass the United States. The forces causing this change are not coming primarily from external sources but rather from internal political mismanagement.

With China's economic growth comes a strengthening of nationalism. With this nationalism comes a need for international recognition and respect, leading to a demand for political and military power. This is occurring in China today.

Many nations delighted in seeing the United States discredited as a result of our 2008 financial market collapse. They would like to see us taken down a few more pegs. What is most frustrating about the financial collapse is that it could have been avoided. It was a disaster created by Wall Street with a good deal of assistance from Congress (Republicans and Democrats) and George W. Bush's administration. Wall Street (the world of money and investment) was, thanks to Congress, running with little regulation and with other people's money. It was an unbridled industry allowed to take huge profits with no fear of the long-term consequences.

But the problem wasn't just with Wall Street—the nation was awash in cheap money. Americans who knew little or nothing about the real estate industry became real estate speculators. There was little fear of buying a house with no money down, or of buying a house you could barely afford. After all, the worst thing that could happen was that you would have to sell the house because you could not make the payments.

The longer you could hold out having to sell, the more you would make, as house prices were skyrocketing. Wall Street (money) and Main Street (regular folk) had cast aside all fear of risk taking. They were both gambling with other people's money.

Throughout our history, we have been dependent on government, both federal and state, to regulate us and to protect us from our own greed and ignorance, but this didn't happen in this situation. Our political leaders were too busy looking for contributors to their next campaign, many of whom were on Wall Street. Nothing pleased Wall Street more than deregulation. Many great new fortunes were being made on Wall Street, and Wall Street lobbyists made sure Congress got a taste of them (see chapters 2 and 10).

While other nations awaken and strive for greater economic strength and political respect, the United States, it would appear, has suffered from its own arrogance and has fallen into a complacent sleep. Has the United States "had its day," and if so, how far will it slide as others push to surpass it? There is a great deal of hope that the Obama administration will change the direction in which the nation is moving. Whether Obama and a Democratic Congress can make this course correction is difficult to predict. Rhetoric alone will not create change, and change will not occur overnight. We have dug a deep hole over many years, and it will take many years to pull ourselves out. This assumes that the leaders both at the federal and state level are bold enough to accomplish this daunting task.

CHAPTER 2

WHERE HAS ALL OUR VISION GONE?

A nation or civilization that continues to produce soft-minded men purchases its own spiritual death on the installment plan.

—Martin Luther King Jr.
1929–1968

THE RULING CLASS

Myth Number 7: The American people still control our political leaders, and they will not allow the United States to slip from first place as an economic superpower. There have been basically three groups that control our government, both at the state and federal level. This "Ruling Class" is made up to a large degree by the extreme right and the extreme left, both of which can be counted on to support their parties financially and to go to the polls and vote. The Democratic and Republican parties like to refer to these groups as their "base." While this base isn't made up solely of each party's most extreme members, it is often these extreme elements that project the loudest voices when determining their party's positions on issues. The third group, special interests, has gained great power by exerting their influence through the use of lobbyists who provide campaign financing.

Writing about the 2004 presidential election, social psychologist Marlowe C. Embree stated, "Winning elections is now increasingly about generating higher and higher turnout in each party's base, rather than reaching out to moderate, centrist voters. As a result, party affiliation is more closely aligned with underlying ideology than at any time in recent memory."[1] What about the independent voter movement of today? It is estimated that approximately 29 percent of voters in the 2008 election were independents. Barack Obama received 52 percent of the independent vote as compared with John McCain's 44 percent. Independents want to be considered the swing voters in today's angry America and thus are wooed by both parties. If all independents were truly nonpartisan, they would be a more formidable force. Care must be taken when estimating independents' influence, as many are traditional Democrats and Republicans who feel their party has not been liberal or conservative enough. These independents are not likely to cross over to the other party when it comes time to vote, but they may refrain from voting if not satisfied with the candidates. Only approximately 60 percent of all eligible Americans went to the polls in the 2004 and 2008 presidential elections.[2] The extreme elements of the left and right are well organized, and they do vote.

Look at the Tea Party, which has touted itself as an independent voters' movement. It was founded by a group of former Libertarian Party members who declared that "Americans deserve and desperately need a pro-freedom party that forcefully advocates libertarian solutions to the issues of today." The party supported reducing the size, scope, and power of government at all levels. It didn't take long for the extreme right of the Republicans to steal the idea and claim it as their own.[3]

The February 2010 national Tea Party convention in Nashville was a parade of Republicans, with former Alaskan governor Sara Palin as keynote speaker and darling of the United States conservative movement. This gave her a national platform to appeal directly to the base of the Republican Party. Fox News reported that activists who put the convention together proposed that "prospective political candidates will be expected to support the Republican National Committee platform, though without any specific litmus or purity test." They went on to propose that candidates who met the proposed Tea Party criteria would be eligible for fund-raising and grassroots Tea Party support.[4] In other words, business as usual.

Special interests, working through their lobbyists, select who will receive the cash necessary to run for office, while the well-organized left and right battle it out as to who will win (see chapter 10). Without the campaign money handed out by the special-interest lobbyists, a politician could not run a campaign. Why should politicians pay any attention to the average American traveling down the middle of the political road when they are not likely to finance campaigns, nor are they likely to vote?

Looking at the 2008 campaign, for the first time, presidential candidates were able to raise significant campaign contributions on the Internet from average Americans. As a result, candidates, with the backing of their base and special-interest financing secured, appeared to be taking more of a moderate view in their campaign rhetoric in an effort to appeal to a wider range of voters and contributors. While presidential candidates can create the necessary hype to develop Internet-based contributions and support, congressional candidates or state and local candidates are dependent on the traditional campaign contribution sources of their parties' base and lobbyists.

Both 2008 presidential candidates initially conformed more to their parties' extreme elements in the primaries in order to win the nomination. After the primaries, they moved to the center to garner more votes in the general election.[5] Party regulars and the press recognize that this movement to the center was only temporary. Once elected, standing presidents need the support of their parties, and the will of these parties is controlled by their extreme elements. It is at this point that they often move back to the left or right. The growing need for campaign funds has brought with it the entrenchment of special interests, which politicians please at the public's expense. Since the greatest amounts of special-interest funds for future elections are given to incumbents during their term in office, this has in the past enhanced the power of incumbency. It also has made it extraordinarily difficult for challengers to mount effective campaigns.[6]

The bitter partisanship that has gridlocked government is not likely to decrease significantly in intensity unless the voting behavior of a majority of Americans profoundly changes and the public mounts a negative campaign against special interests injecting massive amounts of money in politics at all levels. Members of Congress are loath to vote on any bill if they fear it may offend a particular special interest that could be a potential campaign financing source. This continues even when one party controls both the House and Senate. While more legislation may or may not be passed, the amount of party bickering remains intense. There are exceptions to the "gridlock as usual" rule. The 2008 economic stimulus package was approved hastily in the face of a dramatic economic slowdown; both Republicans and Democrats could not risk inaction in an election year.

How did Washington get into this mess? Sarah Binder, a senior fellow at the Brookings Institution, said that "all the things that lead to gridlock are in place," including a partisan pattern of campaign contributions, gerrymandered congressional districts that protect incumbents, and party strategy that heightens the differences and plays to respective political bases. Perhaps most important, she says that "the parties are pretty polarized. Even if you do have a member who has a desire to build bipartisan coalitions, it's very hard to do it if there's no one in the middle."

Myth Number 8: One of Congress's most important jobs is to write legislation that is in the best interests of the American people. At some point, Congress decided that it was in the public's best interest to have lobbyists dictate and actually write our legislation. Gareth Cook, in the *Washington Monthly*, stated, "From behind the Capitol's closed doors emerges a portrait of everything voters hate about Washington: special interests laying down fat campaign contributions to gain a Congressman's ear and, at times, his pen."[7] In 2007, Nancy Pelosi, now Speaker of the House of Representatives, stated in reference to the period in which the house was controlled by Republicans, "The cozy relationship between Congress and special interests has resulted in lobbying scandals, such as those involving Republican super lobbyist Jack Abramoff. Republicans permitted a Congress in which lobbyists write the bills, 15-minute votes are held open for three hours, and entirely new legislation is crammed into signed conference reports in the dead of night."[8] Senator Barack Obama said in 2006, "And people shouldn't lump together those of us who have to raise funds to run campaigns but do so in a legal and ethical way with those who invite lobbyists in to write bad legislation."[9]

As far back as 1995, President Bill Clinton described how Congress was turning increasing levels of power over to lobbyists. "Now this new majority lets lobbyists for polluters write legislation rolling back environmental and public health protections. They've brought them in to explain the legislation. They even gave them a room off the House floor to write the amendments and the statements the members would have to give explaining the bills that the lobbyists had written for them."[10]

Not only do members of Congress not write much of the legislation, but many of them don't even read the legislation after it's ready to be passed. Many political leaders claimed that the Obama administration's 2009 $787 billion stimulus was rushed through Congress without any member having read it. This may be an exaggeration, but it would certainly not be the first time federal lawmakers quickly passed legislation without reading it or giving anyone else time to read it.[11]

LOBBYISTS—OUR THIRD POLITICAL PARTY

The difficult situation we are in today results in large part from a system of government driven by special-interest groups and politicians who must weigh campaign contributions before deciding what causes to support and how to vote. In his book *Selling Out: How Big Corporate Money Buys Elections, Rams Through Legislation, and Betrays Our Democracy*, Mark Green writes that one senator complained that he was lucky to work from mid-Tuesday to Thursday, as he needed to spend the rest of the week fund-raising. He went on to state that members of Congress are "loath" to vote on any controversial issue as it may come back to haunt them when raising money. This constant fund-raising takes a toll physically and psychologically, as he relates through a comment made by President Clinton: "I can't think," the exasperated president bellowed to his staff. "You want me to issue executive orders, but I can't focus on a thing but the next fund-raiser." In essence, Mark Green indicates that a candidate must win two elections, the first in which contributors select candidates that the voters then get to vote on. If you can't win the first election and receive financial support, you don't stand a chance of winning the second among the populace.

Myth Number 9: Our system for selecting political leaders is based on who will do the best job for the American people. It should be the best system the world has to offer, but it has evolved into a less than stellar system. Our political leadership is elected based on who can raise the most money to buy TV airtime, most of which is devoted to discrediting the other candidate, rather than telling the public what the candidate stands for.

When Senators John McCain (Republican) and Russ Feingold (Democrat) introduced the Bipartisan Campaign Reform Act of 2002, commonly known as the McCain-Feingold Bill, it was met with considerable resistance on both sides of the aisle. The bill's three principal objectives were to address the increasing role of soft money in campaigns (contributions to a party in order to avoid federal limits on contributions made directly to candidates), the proliferation of issue ads (discuss an issue without identifying a candidate), and the disturbing campaign practices during the 1996 presidential race.[12] The bill, first introduced in 1997, did not get approval until 2002, and even then it had been revised numerous times and watered down to make it palatable to every special-interest group, lobbyist, and congressperson, in that order. This is a good indication of the control special-interest groups have, and how dependent Congress is on their funding. No sooner was the act put in place than both parties and lobbyists were looking for ways to further circumvent it.

The swift unraveling of the campaign-finance-reform law came as no surprise. Even before it was signed, both parties had plans to thwart its intent. Within hours of the signing, lawsuits were filed to gut the act's provisions. The Federal Election Commission (FEC) was also taking action to weaken the act, encouraged by fierce resistance to it by the Republican and Democratic national committees. Neither party supported the law's changes that cut off soft money necessary for party fund-raising. They didn't want to upset the natural incumbent advantage built into the fund-raising system. "And so they have pulled out all the stops to declaw the new rules: lobbying the FEC to weaken the regulations, filing lawsuits to challenge the law's constitutionality and setting up sham—supposedly unrelated—committees to funnel soft money to the parties."[13]

The Republican and Democratic national committees received much of what they wanted from the regulatory commission. While the new law prevents federal candidates and officeholders from accepting or soliciting soft money, the commission defined "soliciting" very narrowly. For example, federal candidates and officeholders are allowed to solicit soft money at party fund-raising events. In another attack on the law designed to prohibit coordination between candidates and free-standing soft-money committees, the FEC permits candidates to coordinate ads with any third party—corporation, labor union, or foreign national. This is allowed provided the ad runs more than 120 days before the election. The ad may not expressly advocate the election or defeat of a candidate. Thus a candidate can write the ad, run it, and ask a foreign national to pay for it, provided the candidate doesn't touch the money. These issue ads can be written and produced by the candidate. The commission has effectively sanctioned the setting up of "shadow" organizations that can continue to accept soft money, thus undermining the law. Federal Election Commission–issued regulations are vague, are inconsistent with the law, and provide little of the enforcement necessary to make it work.[14]

On January 21, 2010, big corporations and their lobbyists won the Super Bowl of political victories. The United States Supreme Court, in a 5-to-4 decision, ruled that the government may not restrict political spending by corporations, labor unions, and other organizations in candidate elections. The conservative majority of the Supreme Court overturned decades of law and legal precedent with a decision that will inevitably further corrupt our system of government by giving unprecedented power to special interests at the expense of the American people.

Writing for the conservative majority, Justice Anthony Kennedy said the long-standing campaign finance limits violated constitutional free-speech rights of corporations. Justice Kennedy must be living under a rock—if there is any group in the nation that has had the least trouble being heard, it is big corporations. In the 2008 election cycle, more than $1 billion was contributed by corporate political action committees, trade associations, executives, and lobbyists. The 2008 election reconfirmed one truism about American politics and our system of democracy: Money wins elections. In over 90 percent of 2008 House and Senate races, the candidate who spent the most money ended up winning, according to the nonpartisan Center for Responsive Politics. There isn't a politician or lobbyist in Washington who does not understand and live by this truism. Democratic senator Charles Schumer said, "The bottom line is, the Supreme Court has just predetermined the winners of next November's election. It won't be the Republicans or the Democrats, and it won't be the American people; it will be corporate America."[15]

More than a century ago, President Teddy Roosevelt saw that allowing corporations to drench our political campaigns in special-interest money would drown out the voice of the majority. In 1907, he signed the Tillman Act, which banned corporate political spending. Weak enforcement mechanisms made the act ineffective until disclosure requirements and spending limits for House and Senate candidates were imposed in 1910 and 1911. Decades later, Congress extended the ban to unions. Supreme courts have affirmed these limits as legitimate several times since.

Previous courts ruled that spending limits protected the public against corruption or the appearance of corruption. The January 21, 2010, ruling overturned Supreme Court precedents from 1990 and 2003 that upheld federal and state limits on independent expenditures by corporations to support or oppose candidates. The ruling overruled two precedents: *Austin v. Michigan Chamber of Commerce*, a 1990 decision that upheld restrictions on corporate spending to support or oppose political candidates, and *McConnell v. Federal Election Commission*, a 2003 decision that upheld the part of the McCain-Feingold Bipartisan Campaign Reform Act of 2002 that restricted campaign spending by corporations and unions.

The Supreme Court thus has now granted special interests unprecedented power over government at all levels. President Obama said, "The Supreme Court has given a green light to a new stampede of special interest money in our politics. . . . It is a major victory for big oil, Wall Street banks, health insurance companies and the other powerful interests that marshal their power every day in Washington to drown out the voices of everyday Americans."[16]

Justice John Paul Stevens wrote for the minority that corporations "are not members of our society. They cannot vote or run for office." If corporations can't vote, why should they have the ability to crowd out those Americans who can vote? Justice Ruth Bader Ginsburg, who also dissented, asked if foreign companies should have the same free-speech rights as domestic ones, since foreign individuals are allowed to make a speech in this country. Those of the majority had no answer for Justice

Ginsburg. Will Chinese, Indian, Arab, and Russian corporate leaders now have a free hand to buy legislators' loyalty?[17] For large global corporations, the cost of buying loyalty in Washington is certainly insignificant, considering the huge potential returns. How will this impact an already disastrous federal deficit, the trade deficit, the unemployment rate, and our national security?

The Constitution does not say free speech is for "individuals," or "persons," and therefore some argue that corporations are entitled to the same rights of speech and political advocacy as individuals. The argument acknowledges that corporations are not real people, but those who own and manage corporations are. Corporate speech, it is argued, is really just speech by people using corporations to voice their opinion. Is it therefore a mistake to deny free speech rights to people organized as corporations on the grounds that corporations aren't "people"?

If I have joined a union or an organization such as the National Rifle Association (NRA), and that union or organization wishes to help finance a politician's campaign that is favorable to my union's or organization's ideology, I should have the right to be heard and the same rights to finance a campaign as any individual citizen. In this case, I and the other members have pooled our money for the purpose of having specific ideological concerns heard relative to the right to bear arms. Does the NRA leadership then have the right to contribute heavily to one candidate over another based on a candidate's position on abortion or gay marriage, if both favor the NRA's positions relative to gun rights? Could the NRA be accused of misappropriation of funds by members opposed to the contributions based on issues unrelated to gun rights?

In the case of a corporation, the real question should be: Is the corporation representing the voice of its stockholders when it pours millions of dollars of the stockholders' money into particular politicians' campaigns? Let's say I own stock in a major Wall Street financial institution that wants to oppose pending legislation that will require very strict lending standards and other consumer protection regulations, which will have a mildly adverse affect on stock price, profits, and dividends but most significantly on executive bonuses. The president of the company and board decide that it would be worth pouring millions of dollars into the campaigns of friendly politicians who will kill the legislation or water it down to an acceptable level. Having witnessed the effect of an unregulated Wall Street, I, as a stockholder, favor the legislation and believe that slightly lower dividends or stock price are better than exposing the nation to another financial crisis or to exposing the company to financial ruin. Unlike my membership in a union or NRA, I and many of my fellow stockholders did not buy stock in this Wall Street company because I and its executives have the same ideological views.

Liberal Justice Stevens said the majority had committed a grave error in treating corporate speech the same as that of human beings. He added that lawmakers might want to consider requiring corporations to disclose how they intended to spend shareholders' money or to put such spending to a shareholder vote. Stockholders have many rights, one of which should certainly be how the company's executives want to spend company money on influencing campaigns. Britain requires shareholders to vote on corporate political contributions, thus ensuring that shareholders' funds are used for political spending only if that is how the shareholders want their money spent. Congress could protect shareholders by giving them the power, under statute, to authorize political spending by corporations.

Unlike the Democrats and Republicans who are constantly at each other's throats, it would be a rare congressman who says that the lobbyists are a negative force in the American political system (other than during an election campaign). Democrats and Republicans allow the lobbyists to do most of their thinking for them; therefore, the lobbyists are shaping American policy and profoundly influencing the course of American government.

In 1968, there were 62 lobbyists in Washington; today there are 34,000, outnumbering members of Congress and their staffers two to one. Between 1998 and 2004, lobbyists spent a total of $13 billion to influence legislation. Individual firms, corporations, and national organizations spent an average of $5.5 million per day in 2004, lobbying Congress and federal agencies.[18] By the 2008 election year, they were spending approximately $3.2 billion per year or $8.9 million per day for influence.[19]

For congressmen, what is there not to like about lobbyists? It's an unofficial party without a single platform that represents as many causes as there are clients willing to pay for its loyalty. The real beauty of the lobbyist party is that most of them are willing to share their exorbitant fees with Democrats and Republicans without bias toward party affiliation. In recent years, approximately 43 percent of the eligible congressional members who departed government and half of all eligible departing senators have found very comfortable positions as lobbyists, as have many high-level congressional staffers.[20] Perhaps some of these retirees find that they can write or influence more legislation as lobbyists than as members of Congress.

There are numerous examples of outrageous tax legislation passed at the insistence of lobbyists. A great example is the American Jobs Creation Act of 2004, dubbed the "No Lobbyist Left Behind Act" by Senator John McCain. Initially, it was to be a simple adjustment to a foreign tax subsidy, but it resulted in $140 billion in tax concessions. By the time the lobbyists were finished with the legislation, there were tax breaks for professional golfers, racetrack owners, and cruise lines and a "manufacturers" designation break given to Starbucks for the coffee-grinding part of its business.[21]

NPR commentator Connie Rice dubbed the act the "Corporate Looting and Piracy Act" and identified her top ten outrages. With a title of "American Jobs Creation Act," one of Ms. Rice's top ten outrages was a provision of the act that she calls "The Texas Tax Cheats Repatriation Act: Instead of being indicted for tax evasion, a special group of big Houston corporations that dropped American citizenship to hide their profits in overseas tax havens will be forgiven and allowed to take advantage of the one-year tax holiday and one-seventh of the former tax rate." She goes on to state that "the same House Republicans who are the handmaidens to this corporate looting cut out $2 billion in tax credits to subsidize salaries of military reservists called to active duty!"[22]

What Americans must understand is that the lobbyist party practices Don Corleone–style politics. If you're laying out $13 billion in campaign contributions, the use of corporate jets, extravagant gifts, and lucrative speaking engagements to members of Congress, you expect something in return. In the 1972 movie classic *The Godfather*, Don Corleone is asked by a man if he would have his daughter's and his family's honor avenged. The Godfather agrees and says, "Someday, and that day may never come, I will call upon you to do a service for me." Nothing is done in Washington for anyone without the expectation of reciprocity—and that day always comes.

It's not just big corporations that have lobbyists. Unions, farmers, the elderly, lawyers, accountants, teachers, and bankers, among others, all feeling compelled to have lobbyists. Each group has its own agenda. While these individual agendas may be of benefit for a particular group, they may not always be good for the nation as a whole.

As money needed for campaigns has risen, members of Congress and presidents have focused less on what is best for the American people and have become increasingly interested in issues lobbyists bring to their attention. Most in Congress say that without the money, which allows them to get elected, voters would not benefit from their insight and wisdom. In most cases their insight and wisdom is focused on raising money for their campaigns. Wouldn't it be great if they could use those same skills to raise money to reduce our national debt?

At one time, most lobbyists represented voters and made sure Congress and the president understood the issues of the American public they represented, but now every special-interest group has the right to express its concerns and push its agenda with our political leaders. Today, however, it is no longer about how many voters a lobbyist represents but rather how much money that lobbyist will spend to influence a vote. If we could stop the $8.9 million lobbyists spend on Congress and federal officials each day, the number of lobbyists would likely drop to 1968 levels, and the voters would be better represented. Even if the only campaign funds that could be used were from federal or state treasuries, the cost to the American people would be dramatically less than the current method that too often promotes the desires of special-interest groups at the expense of the American public.

PAY TO PLAY

The American people pay the salaries of our elected officials, but it is the special-interest groups and their money who often decide who is hired and who is fired. In his book *Rome Wasn't Burnt in a Day*, Joe Scarborough, MSNBC commentator and former member of Congress (1994–2001), describes what congressional rookies are taught upon entering Congress. He states that they start with a lesson on the importance of party loyalty. Both freshmen congressmen and senators learn very quickly that new members who play ball with the party leadership will be rewarded. They will be assigned to the best committees, and powerful leaders and chairmen will be put on their fund-raising committees. Arms will be twisted in the lobbying community to provide financial assistance. For the best-behaved, the Speaker of the House or the majority leader will travel to their home districts to help raise a few hundred thousand dollars. Scarborough goes on to state, "If the carrot fails to entice, the stick is quickly pulled from the party leader's back pocket to beat the wayward member over the head. And if a member dares to speak out against his party leader's latest stupid bill or embarrassing statement, the offending member is quickly reminded that the party neither forgives nor forgets— ever."[23] This may not always be the case, but it often is.

In the 2008 election, according to the Center for Responsive Politics (CRP), winners of House of Representative seats raised an average of $1,100,000 to get elected, and senators averaged $6,500,000 (see figure 1, on page 50). Of the top hundred individual contributors, all but five were associated with major corporations, professional services (e.g., law and accounting), entertainment companies, foundations, or large private educational institutions. Individual contributions for this group during the 2008 election cycle ranged from $201,350 to $348,268. Buying influence is not expensive when you consider what it can get you.

In 93 percent of House of Representatives races and 94 percent of Senate races in 2008, the candidate who spent the most money ended up winning.[24] The CRP estimated the total cost of the 2008 elections for Congress and the White House at $5.3 billion, making it the most expensive United States election ever. Is it reasonable to expect that the elected politicians owe their campaign contributors for helping them win?

HOUSE		SENATE	
Average Amount Winner Spent	Most Expensive Race	Average Amount Winner Spent	Most Expensive Race
$1,100,000	$11,527,027 New York	$6,500,000	$43,050,976 Minnesota

FIGURE 1: The Price of Admission: House & Senate Election Cycle 2008

Source: Center for Responsive Politics

In his 2007 book *The Audacity of Hope*, then-Senator Barack Obama wrote candidly about the costs of running a campaign in terms of dollars and their potential for redirecting a candidate's purpose. Like Mark Green, Obama also wrote that without money, a candidate is pretty much guaranteed to lose. He indicated that he could not assume that the money chase didn't alter him in some ways, and that as a consequence he became more like the wealthy donors he met. He believed that in one fashion or another, he suspected this was true for every senator. Obama went on to state, "The longer you are a senator, the narrower the scope of your interactions. . . . The path of least resistance—of fund-raisers organized by the special interests, the corporate PACs, and the top lobbying shops—starts to look awfully tempting, and if the opinions of these insiders don't quite jibe with those you once held, you learn to rationalize the changes as a matter of realism, of compromise, of learning the ropes."[25]

As a senator, Obama made it clear in his book that lobbyists don't explicitly demand a quid pro quo when helping elected officials. They are given more access, more information, and they have more face time than the average voter. With this, he states by way of example, they are able to promote obscure provisions in the tax code that could save their clients billions of dollars. So we may rightfully ask: Who is lobbying on behalf of America's future, for our children and their children's futures?

Clearly, in order to be elected, President Barack Obama took considerable sums from contributors with whom his opinions did not quite jibe. How much will he compromise his beliefs to repay these contributors on whom he and his party must depend for future elections? Can we do anything to create a better method for our political leaders to get elected other than selling themselves?

Lobbying can't be completely extinguished as many would like. We Americans have the constitutional right to petition the government for redress of grievances. I don't believe there are many Americans who would argue against this most essential right. The issue many of us find most difficult to understand is how we, as a nation, have allowed a minority of wealthy individuals, corporations, and governments to influence our nation's political leadership through campaign contributions. What we find most offensive is that so many politicians set themselves up to be influenced, often to the detriment of their constituents and the nation as a whole.

In his book *Selling Out: How Big Corporate Money Buys Elections, Rams Through Legislation, and Betrays Our Democracy,* Mark Green offers four solutions to reforming our electoral democracy by elevating the voters over donors. His solutions include campaign spending limits, public financing of campaigns, a restructured enforcement agency, and free broadcast time and mailings.[26]

As will be shown, our current system has caused the American people and their economic future great harm. Perhaps someday we can go back to electing candidates who are the best at representing the people rather than those who are the best at raising money. The vast majority of lobbyists and their clients are doing what they are allowed to do under United States law. Ultimately, it's our political leaders who should be looking at the big picture. They have the power and responsibility to say no when the American economy and its people will be hurt. Congress has the power to change the laws and the way in which business is conducted in Washington. Thus far, Congress has chosen to maintain the status quo.

LEADERSHIP VACUUM

As Americans, we are desperate to have political leaders once again whom we can respect and even admire. A 2006 poll by the *New York Times*/CBS News found that the majority of those polled said that "members of Congress were too tied to special interests and that they didn't understand the needs and problems of average Americans."[27] In 2008, President George W. Bush's approval ratings ranged from 20 percent to 39 percent—and Congress from 12 percent to 33 percent—depending on the poll and the time it was taken. By the end of 2009, Obama's approval ratings dropped from a high of 76 percent at the beginning of his term to between 47 percent to 57 percent, and the Democrat-controlled Congress ranged from 21 percent to 30 percent. Poll results like these clearly reflect an erosion of trust in our government.

America is desperate for a hero, but not a sports hero or a movie star or a rock star. We need a political hero with a clear vision for the nation, a leader who will put the good of the nation as a whole above all party politics and special interests, a leader who will get us back on a path of economic and political strength and international respect.

In a nation more than of three hundred million people, it is difficult to believe that in our recent history Americans haven't been able to elect a president who can rise to hero status. It's been a long time since we have had a president who was widely respected, much less revered. Is it that the pool of politicians from which we must pick is so bad, or is it that the sound-bite system we use to elect them is so poor? Or does the system, driven by lobbyists who feed gridlock, obviate the possibility of an effective hero? Time will tell if President Obama proves to be a hero.

Here, at the dawn of the twenty-first century, for the first time in our history as a nation, we are not in a position, in the words of Theodore Roosevelt, "to carry on the task that our forefathers have entrusted to our hands; and let us resolve that we shall leave to our children and our children's children, an even mightier heritage than we received in our time." When our elected officials can only see as far as the next election or the next fund-raiser, and when the will of one's political party takes precedence over what is best for the future of the nation, how can a politician make decisions that are best for America's children and their children?

The United States does not have to continue to experience a diminishing of its economic superpower status, nor does the American middle class need to experience a diminishing of their standard of living. We are still a superpower. Prior to the recession, our economy was still growing, averaging annually 3 percent over the prior twenty years—higher than Germany, France, and Japan. Productivity growth has been over 2.5 percent for a decade, which has been higher than European productivity gains. We are still the world leader in technology, innovation, and spending on research and development. In spite of rapid gains in education in India and China, the United States still ranks first in quality of research institutions. US firms still lead the world in terms of profits and productivity. However, like the British in 1900, we as a nation do not realize how fast the world is catching up, nor do we realize how this will affect us economically and how it will ultimately make us vulnerable to external forces. We as Americans are also to blame for the state of the nation.

If America is to be governed for the people, then voters must be better informed and willing to exercise their right to vote. In the middle of the cold war (1964), only 38 percent of Americans knew that the Soviet Union was not a member of NATO.[28] We may want to believe that things have changed in this day of the "Information Revolution," but they have not. A report prepared by the Cato Institute in 2004 found that barely a majority of Americans know which party controls the Senate at any time, and 70 percent can't name either of their own state's senators. Only 51 percent knew that defense spending is one of the two largest expenditure areas in the federal budget. Sadly, only 40 percent could approximate the number of troops killed in Iraq at the time of the survey.[29] John F. Kennedy said, "The ignorance of one voter in democracy impairs the security of all."[30]

Political scientist Curtis Gans of American University estimated that between 60.7 percent and 61.2 percent of eligible voters voted in 2008, compared to 60.6 percent in 2004.[31] Most developed democracies have much higher turnouts for critical elections, like Germany (80.6 percent), Sweden (83.6 percent), France (84 percent), and Italy (92.5 percent).[32] We need only look at polls examining approval rates for Congress or former president Bush to see how little we Americans think of our leaders.

Caricatures and criticism of politicians, while a national pastime, is in the end generally unproductive. While we may not want to admit it, politicians most often behave much like the majority of Americans do—doing whatever they can to seek personal gain. Of course, since we select these individual as our leaders, we hold them to a higher standard. We want to assume that what they tell us in their campaigns is true, and that they will hold the public's interest above all special interests and certainly above their personal interest. When this does not happen, we may not be surprised, but we are always disappointed. We place our political leaders in an untenable position, one in which they must sell out in order to get elected, and then we feel betrayed when we realize that they have sold us out. As long as these leaders must gain special-interest funding and political party support in order to get elected or reelected, we will continue to be disappointed and betrayed.

Because of the manner in which our system has developed, we as a nation have lost our leadership and our way. The great American philosopher Yogi Berra could have been talking about the United States in his response to someone who told him they thought they were lost. He said, "Yeah, but we're making great time!"[33]

CHAPTER 3

EAST IS THE NEW WEST
The Shift in the Balance of Power

The test of a first-rate intelligence is the ability to hold two opposed ideas in the mind at the same time, and still retain the ability to function. One should, for example, be able to see that things are hopeless and yet be determined to make them otherwise.

—F. Scott Fitzgerald
1896–1940

EMERGING SUPERPOWERS

Who will be the world's next superpower? As noted earlier, there appears to be no question that the balance of power is shifting to the east as China and India evolve. Just as the nineteenth century was dominated by the British and the twentieth century by the United States, so the twenty-first century will belong to China and India. During most of the latter half of the twentieth century, these nations were in a state of self-induced exile from the rest of the world. By the beginning of the twenty-first century, they progressed in an extraordinary manner. Driven initially by a substantially lower-cost labor force of a combined population of nearly 2.5 billion people, China and India became forces of economic growth with few rivals. With the world's largest emerging markets representing one-third of the world's population, the question is not whether they will lead the world but rather which one will emerge as the ultimate leader. While India has experienced phenomenal growth, it is likely to lag behind China. Certainly, China is the top contender to take the United States' position as the world's number-one economic superpower. Since it would be impossible to discuss the current or future status of the US economy without understanding our competition and its impact on our economic status, we need to take a closer look at China and India.

Contrary to what some may believe, globalization did not bring China and India into the world economy; rather, they were two critical keystones that helped create the twenty-first-century global economy. Prior to the emergence of China and India, in the last minutes of the twentieth century the world economy was focused on the United States, Western Europe, and, to a lesser extent, Russia. China's and India's emergence turned the world's attention to the east and a more global perspective.

Americans are beginning to realize that they no longer have an automatic right to the world's best jobs and the highest standard of living. Contrary to the beliefs of many, I would disagree that the greatest financial challenge we have faced as a nation since the Great Depression of the 1930s was the 2008 financial collapse. The financial collapse received a great deal of attention from the press and our political leaders because it was sudden, with immediate adverse impacts. I believe the bigger challenge will come from competition with China and India. Their impact on our economy and standard of living will be more severe and has the potential to last decades. The most difficult part of this problem has been the fact that it is occurring at a slow, consistent pace, so it is not as evident as a sudden recession.

The role the United States will play as a twenty-first-century superpower is certainly questionable when you examine the current state of our economy. To be a superpower, a nation needs more than a strong military; it requires a strong, solidly based growth economy. We need only look at the fall of the Soviet Union to see what happens when military might is not supported by a strong economic system.

The emergence of China and India as economic keystones to the world economy translates into a far different future for Americans—one that challenges US dominance economically and, possibly, militarily as well. Goldman Sachs predicts that China's economy will overtake the United States' economy in 2027, and it will be nearly twice as large by 2050 (though millions of Chinese will still be poorer than Americans).[1] The Economist Intelligence Unit estimates China will pass the United States by 2030. China's economy is expected to continue growing well after 2030 because its economy will still be considered small in terms of gross domestic product per capita. At the end of

2009, China's real GDP growth rate was estimated at 8.4 percent, and the United States' GDP was estimated at 2.4 percent.[2]

By the mid 2020s, Shanghai and the five fastest-growing of China's twenty-two provinces will have the same standard of living as the United States in terms of GDP (gross domestic product). In total, these five provinces and Shanghai will represent a population 27 percent larger than the United States.[3] According to the Organisation for Economic Co-operation and Development, in 2007 India became the world's third-largest economy, behind the United States and China when measured in terms of real prices and purchasing power.[4] By 2050, China and India will likely account for one-half of the world's output.

Myth Number 10: Productivity in China is simply not as good as in America. Beijing has already proven its ability to manage its economy, tripling the per capita income of its workers in a single generation, propelling three hundred million of its population out of poverty, and attracting tens of billions of dollars annually in foreign investment. China's growth in productivity in terms of the use of labor and capital has been increasing at the fastest rate in the world since 1995. A study by the Organisation for Economic Co-operation and Development in 2006 found that return on equity in China was similar to that of the United States and Europe.[5]

India is also quickly emerging by putting into place the necessary infrastructure to support its growth, reduce bureaucracy, and shift from a service-outsourcing specialist into a broad-based manufacturer. As early as 2005, the *New York Times* reported that in information technology (IT), India was already perceived as a global leader. Growth in this sector was so strong that wages in some areas were rising by 25 percent per year, making the supply of qualified graduates from the country's best schools barely able to meet the demand.[6]

It's also significant that the economic strengths of these two nations complement each other. Today, China is one of a few nations building heavy manufacturing and electronics plants; as a result, it is securing its role as a dominant force in mass manufacturing. India is the world's rising power in software design, high-skilled services, and precision industries. Many multinationals now have their products built in China, with software and circuitry designed in India.[7] The importance of technical and managerial skills in both China and India are increasingly of more consequence than their cheap labor.

Myth Number 11: Many of the jobs sent offshore to China and India will come back to the United States. This myth is based in part on wishful thinking but mostly on reports that there is a shortage of qualified workers and that the cost of labor is rising, making these countries less attractive. Certainly, it is getting more difficult to find skilled factory workers, educated executives, and technical workers in China and India. Also, due to competition for these workers, they are getting more expensive. However, the terms "more difficult" and "more expensive" are relative. With nearly 2.5 billion people in these countries combined, the Chinese and Indian labor markets are certainly deeper than anywhere else in the world. Though long-term labor availability is diminishing and costs are rising, both are still substantially better than in the United States, Japan, or Western Europe. For example, wages in coastal China are growing two to three times faster than in any other low-wage country. To counter this, companies need only move farther inland to take advantage of a vast untapped low-wage workforce. It will be many decades before the cost of labor in these countries begins to approach that of the more advanced industrialized nations.

Americans must not misunderstand the real strength China has today. Most of the attention given to China focuses on its tremendous market potential and its exporting power. However, if we are to understand the real competitive nature of China, we must look also at its intellectual and economic power. It is these strengths, which are growing more rapidly than in any other country, that make China a world-class competitor.

Is China the new America? In many economic respects, it is like America on steroids. For two centuries, keys to American prosperity and power were the extraordinary physical scale of our land, our natural resources, and the drive and determination of our population and government. Modern-day China has similar advantages, and it has been able to develop at a speed unrivaled in history. It is achieving in just three decades what it took the United States over two hundred years to accomplish. While China's economy is less than a third the size of America's at market exchange rates, and its GDP per head is one-fourteenth that of America, its economic growth rate far outpaces that of the United States.

There still remains a huge gap in innovation and defense budgets, however. America's defense budget is six times that of China, but here again China's growth rate is rapid enough to have many military analysts concerned. In terms of human rights, China can't compare to the United States, as will be discussed. Certainly, one of the scariest things about China today is the fact that it owns approximately $900 billion of American debt—enough to give it the power of life or death over the US economy.

SHIFTING TECHNOLOGICAL SUPREMACY

Myth Number 12: India and China could never surpass the United States in our ability to innovate. Has the United States lost its lead in innovation? The best answer is: not yet. According to RAND Corporation National Defense Research Institute's *United States Competitiveness in Science and Technology* (2008), of the total funds spent on research and development in the world, 40 percent are spent by the United States. The United States still has thirty of the world's forty leading universities and 70 percent of the world's Nobel laureates.[8] Within the Organization of Economic Co-operation and Development (OECD), we produce 38 percent of new patented technologies and employee 37 percent of the researchers.[9] While China and India are growing at a faster rate in terms of science and technology than the United States, we still maintain a considerable lead. However, here in the United States, 41 percent of the science and engineering PhDs performing research are non-US citizens. (As will be explained in chapter 5, this will become a growing problem for the United States.)

There is no doubt the gap is narrowing, and it is difficult to say when we will lose the lead. Certainly, we have the ability but, it would appear, not the will to stay in the lead. Since the end of the cold war, growth in federal spending on research and development dropped to

2.5 percent per year for the period 1994–2004 from an average of 3.5 percent since 1953. After four years of real decline in spending on basic and applied research from 2004 to 2008, the 2009 spending and the 2010 budget proposal represented a real-dollar improvement in federal research investments across the spectrum of the sciences and engineering. Obama's 2010 budget included $147.6 billion for research and development, an increase of $555 million (or 0.4 percent) above the 2009 budget.[10]

Federal spending on research and development (R&D) accounts for approximately 30 percent of all USs R&D expenditures.[11] Two questions need to be addressed: (1) Of this federal spending, how much is being outsourced offshore by research organizations receiving federal research grants? and (2) Of the other approximately 70 percent of the privately funded US R&D expenditures, how much of this research is actually being performed here in the United States? In the past few years, US R&D spending in China and India has increased substantially.

In 2006, China spent more on R&D than Japan did and became the world's second-highest investor in R&D after the United States. The OECD estimated that China spent just over $136 billion on R&D, more than Japan's forecast of $130 billion. China now ranks second worldwide with 926,000 researchers, just behind the United States (more than 1.3 million).[12]

According to the Chinese National Bureau of Economic Research, China will produce more PhDs per year than the United States by year end, 2010. William R. Broady, past president of Johns Hopkins University, told a congressional panel, "There is a good chance that United States competitiveness in virtually all important high-tech areas will fall behind that of China."[13]

Long-term, India's niche will likely become manufactured goods that require smaller runs of products with high levels of engineering or research content. China is now the world's largest exporter of technology products. Much of this production is on behalf of foreign firms, including many in the United States. The list of high-tech firms with operations in India reads like a who's who of the high-tech industry, including Cisco, Dell, Hewlett-Packard, IBM, Sun, and Oracle.[14] Bangalore, India, as early as 2004, had 150,000 information technology engineers, which is twenty thousand more than are employed in the Silicon Valley.[15]

The United States faces a crisis in engineering, which is the nucleus of many vital industries. This crisis jeopardizes our economic future. Pacific Rim nations are graduating great numbers of engineers and threatening to seize the mantle of industrial innovation that was pivotal to making the US economy globally dominant. *Engineering Trends* did an exhaustive study and determined that the United States ranked sixteenth in the number of doctoral graduates and twenty-fifth in engineering undergraduates per million citizens. While India was not included in the study, China ranked thirtieth in undergraduate degrees and thirty-fourth in doctoral degrees.[16]

"Our ability to innovate in this country is diminishing. If you look at the number of patents, they are shifting now to other places. Scientific papers that are published, citations—we are clearly losing ground in terms of the competitive stance we've had," said Don Giddens, the dean of the College of Engineering at the Georgia Institute of Technology.[17]

Medicine is already outsourcing many aspects of healthcare and administrative functions to India. A growing number of medical services are being outsourced to India via the Internet, such as teleradiology and other clinical services, including aspects of oncology, orthopedics, molecular imaging, and disease management. Clerical services, such as medical billing and transcription, are readily offshored.

Medical tourism agencies have developed in India and are sending medical tourists from the United States to hospitals all over India. The cost of the comprehensive treatment packages offered are typically a fraction of that found in the United States, even with travel expenses taken into account. To compare prices, a hip replacement, for example, costs about $44,000 in the United States and about $9,000 in India. Bypass surgery, which can cost more than $130,000 in the United States, can be performed for $10,000 in India. A liver transplant, expected to cost $350,000 in the United States, can be had for as little as $55,000 in India. No official statistics are available on how many Americans have participated in medical tourism, but estimates run as high as 150,000 annually in recent years.[18]

Forrester Research predicts that by 2011, 10 percent of associates hired by large law firms will work overseas. In the financial services industry, JP Morgan Stanley and Goldman Sachs have operations in India, where research is turned out by financial analysts while Wall Street sleeps. These are not just low-level back office workers; these employees are working on some of the most sophisticated transactions in the world.[19] These are exactly the types of jobs that US workers thought would always remain in this country. Today, the threat for the potential loss of a US job to a foreign worker is increasing at a more rapid rate than the potential loss to a worker in another state.

As *BusinessWeek* reported as early as 2005, "American business isn't just shifting research work because Indian and Chinese brains are young, cheap, and plentiful. In many cases, these engineers combine the skills-mastery of the latest software tools, a knack for complex mathematical algorithms and fluency of new multimedia technologies that often surpass those of their American counterparts."[20] It's not just the American press that is singing the praises of India and China; it's also American business leaders. It's these executives who now question America's future right to these high-tech jobs.

American Executives Support Offshoring

Cisco Systems. Daniel Scheinman, Senior VP: "Companies come to India for the costs, they stay for the quality, and they invest for the innovation."[21]

Philips Semiconductors. Leon Husson, Executive VP: "We will see China in a few years going from being a follower to a leader in defining consumer electronics trends."[22]

There are simply no high-tech skills or professions that workers in other countries like China or India cannot learn just as fast and master just as well as US workers. Given the declining state of education at all levels in the United States (see chapter 5), countries that put a serious emphasis on education have a distinct advantage over the United States. Even US high-tech workers who are attempting to stay ahead of the curve by learning new skills and obtaining advanced degrees are finding that such efforts do not protect them from offshoring. Many high-tech workers believe that if you sit in front of a computer screen, your job is in jeopardy.

Today, corporate America, especially the nation's largest corporations, so depends on the global marketplace that the demands of production costs and markets have taken precedence over concerns of keeping jobs in the United States. If these companies are to survive, they must tie their future to the global market.

KEEPING OUR ENTREPRENEURIAL SPIRIT

Myth Number 13: When it comes to entrepreneurial spirit, no country will ever surpass the United States. Start-ups in the United States' Silicon Valley still have one major advantage over Indian start-ups, and that is access to venture capital. India remains a capital-starved country. Companies with one foot in each country are at a distinct advantage. A growing number of these corporations are returning to India with US-acquired funding to start new businesses or to expand R&D labs for Silicon Valley companies, such as Cisco Systems, Intel, Oracle, and Microsoft. Charles E. Phillips Jr., president of Oracle, has said, "We're convinced that a good portion of the next generation of software companies will emerge from India."[23]

Keeping these entrepreneurs in the United States is essential if we are to maintain a critical role in the development of technology for the twenty-first century. In the United States, our entire economy has grown as a result of the American entrepreneurial spirit. This growth was encouraged by a government focused on providing the proper environment for that spirit to flourish.

For over two hundred years, we have attracted the best and brightest from around the world; no other country has ever provided the opportunities available in the United States. The question we must ask is: Can we continue to maintain the environment necessary to hold our position as the world leader that most encourages an entrepreneurial spirit?

With a combined population of over 2.5 billion, China and India have millions of hungry, aggressive, creative entrepreneurs eager to prove themselves. With economic national growth rates as high as 8 to 10 percent, the opportunity and time to achieve their goals is now, in the twenty-first century. With governments that have finally, after decades, gotten their acts together to create business-friendly environments to encourage the entrepreneurial spirit, the results are not surprising. How can America hope to compete when our governments, both federal and many states, continue to create roadblocks to entrepreneurs?

As a nation, our greatest economic strength has been our entrepreneurial spirit. It is our entrepreneurs who have been responsible for the innovations upon which this nation has been built. We need to encourage innovation and the capitalist spirit. Today, far too many bills coming out of Washington are developed by special interests and their lobbyists. These bills are being designed to favor existing big business— businesses that can afford K Street lobbyists. Often these bills favor incumbent corporations and stifle innovation or direct resources away from small businesses and entrepreneurs that are struggling to keep afloat. Entrepreneurs, working at their dining room tables or in small offices and factories, are often not aware of nor do they have any chance of influencing this legislation. Until we change the rules in Washington that help finance congressional campaigns that favor only the incumbent financed by large corporations, we will not be in a position to promote entrepreneurial innovation.

DIFFICULTIES TO OVERCOME

Keeping pace with the rest of the world will, without question, be increasingly difficult. To do so in the twenty-first century will take not only an entrepreneurial spirit but also the ability to innovate here in the United States. Microsoft's research and development lab in Beijing is becoming a world leader in innovation in computer graphics and language simulation. In spite of achievements like this, and the fact that China's thirty-five software colleges graduate approximately two hundred thousand software engineers per year, the country still lags in innovation.[24] Many multinational companies continue to be skeptical about making heavy investments in China, due to its lack of intellectual property protection laws and enforcement. The Chinese government has placed heavy emphasis on and invested in the development of its own high-tech industries.

Most foreign companies outsourcing to China are amazed at how quickly the Chinese factories can become proficient at producing products so inexpensively. In some cases, nonetheless, under pressure by customers or management to cut costs further, cost cutting may affect the quality of a product and/or worker safety, and may ignore environmental concerns. Not all Chinese factories practice these types of product manipulation; however, even the best and largest Chinese factories will outsource parts of production to smaller companies that may cut corners to boost profits.

In some areas, the Chinese efforts to protect intellectual property are virtually nonexistent. For example, the Chinese government restricts the inflow of foreign films. Allegedly, this is to protect the public's morals. While the Internet is heavily censored (see chapter 6) in all other respects, Western entertainment is readily accessible. If you are a Western entertainment company and your products can't be sold in China, how can you claim in a Chinese court that you have been harmed? The Chinese Web sites pirating Western entertainment are very profitable, depending on advertising revenue, which in 2008 was $1.7 billion.

China's patent office leads the world in applications, with over eight hundred thousand being filed in 2008. Until 1985, the Communist Party did not allow patents, so the concept of intellectual property is relatively new to China. China has been accused of patent infringement. Interestingly, America, in its early industrial development, was often accused of patent infringement.

US concerns with China, whether regarding currency or addressing World Trade Organization complaints or their unsafe consumer products, will be addressed seriously only when the Chinese deem it necessary. The United States can complain all it wants, and the assurances will continue to flow, solely to placate and put us off. China's attitude reminds me of an old bit done by comedian Lily Tomlin (*Saturday Night Live*, 1976). Seated at a telephone switchboard as Ernestine the telephone operator, she would put some calls through and others she would just disconnect. If anybody complained she would say, "We don't care. We don't have to. We're the phone company."

Chinese car makers had been known to build cars that showed a remarkable similarity to cars made by General Motors, Toyota, and Volkswagen. Recently, they have shifted to buying designs and manufacturing with sophisticated robotics. Having the ability to produce cars at prices well below any other car maker, with the possible exception of India, China gives its competitors reasons to be concerned.

The Chinese government is taking action to support this fledgling industry. It provides direct investment and guaranteed loans to buy the latest robotic equipment, and government universities are assisting in the development of new engines. Future legislation may force competitors who want to sell in China to conduct more research in China with their Chinese partners, thus ensuring access to their partners' latest technology and design concepts. The Chinese government has even considered a law that would mandate Chinese cars to have a 50 percent market share in the country.[25] In contrast, in the United States, we tend to give financial support to our automobile companies when they are on the verge of bankruptcy (rather than when they are on the way up).

Would we consider mandating that United States' automakers be guaranteed a 50 percent market share to protect our automobile industry and American jobs? This is highly unlikely, since most Chinese-produced cars initially will be American brands. The US auto industry recognizes that it will be able to produce vehicles in China for less and therefore achieve higher profit margins. The US auto lobby would likely resist any effort to limit imports of vehicles from China.

Most of the cars produced in China are still manufactured by foreign companies. Initially, the United States and other auto producers were invited into China. The Chinese needed our know-how, technology, and designs, which helped China's own producers gain in sophistication and production capacity. Do US and other foreign auto makers expect China to allow them to retain market share? China will do what other countries do: increasingly protect the fledgling industry and its huge home market—a market that United States' auto manufacturers have become reliant on.

In the past, Chinese threats of trade retaliation have generally been enough to cause our government to back down. When we complain that the Chinese yuan's exchange rate is a subsidy to Chinese exporters, they quickly point out that many American companies producing goods in China are also profiting. They also note that, up to the 2008 financial market collapse, US consumers had been buying the exported goods as fast as they could make them. American companies are profiting from Chinese low-cost labor, and the problem is that the American middle and lower classes are not seeing any of these profits come to them in the form of jobs with good wages. They are being supplied with low-cost merchandise, which they are finding increasingly difficult to afford without going into debt (see chapter 16).

BUILDING A NEW CHINA? DO NOT RESTRAIN YOUR EXPECTATIONS

During the 1980s and 1990s, encouraged by the US presidents of the period, China was integrating into a world economic system dominated by the United States. In a sense, we were their mentor. Today, much has changed; we are no longer seen as a nation to be modeled after; we are paid little attention, other than to be chastised for interfering in China's economy or internal affairs (e.g., human rights, environment, Iran, Tibet, and North Korea). China did not need the United States to become a capitalist nation. However, it did at one time need the United States to become a *wealthy* capitalist nation.

Today, China recognizes that the idealism that the world held for America is deteriorating, and that of China is growing. They need only hold up their recovery from the worldwide recession in comparison to that of the United States as an example of their economic and managerial power. China demands respect and has grown extremely confident in its international position. As Fareed Zakaria stated in the February 15, 2010, issue of *Newsweek*, "If American politicians cannot muster up the courage to make the United States economy competitive again, and Beijing perceives that it is dealing with a superpower in inexorable decline, relations between China and America will change fundamentally. Of course, if that happens, America will have plenty else to worry about as well."[26]

There has been a great deal more written and said about the fragility of the Chinese economy than that of India. It would, however, be a serious misjudgment to assume that China will not overcome these problems. Certainly, after our own financial market collapse in 2008, we should be cautious with our criticism. If we consider that the government in Beijing represents a nation of 1.3 billion people (one-fifth of the world's population), all living in one sovereign state, what they have accomplished is nothing short of a Herculean feat. If we combined the European Union, Russia, Japan, Mexico, Brazil, and the United States, they would have roughly the same size population. The combined gross domestic product for all these nations, including China, is $47.26 trillion. China's GDP represents over 18 percent of the total, exceeded only by the European Union and the United States (approximately 30 percent each).[27] While China's GDP ($8.7 trillion) is substantially less than that of the United States ($14.2 trillion), its contribution to global growth continues to exceed that of the United States. What Beijing has accomplished in a couple of decades is truly a renaissance.

China's successful navigation of the Great Recession, which started in 2007, was a surprise to many, especially those who find it hard to believe that an authoritarian government with the largest population in the world could be accommodated and prosper in a global economic system under such strain. In 2008, the pessimists said China would not be able to withstand a collapse of American spending and its impact on imports from China. China simply decoupled from the United States and became more dependent on its own huge market and other international markets it had been developing. Chinese car sales increased by 53 percent in 2009, while industrial profits rose by a staggering 70 percent in the first ten months of the year. Exports were not cut but rose 18 percent, while imports rose 56 percent.[28] Of course, these figures run counter to China's long-standing argument that it must hold the value of the yuan down to support its suffering industries.

In his book *China Road: A Journey into the Future of a Rising Power*, Rob Gifford states that everything in China is big, including its government cycles, which are measured in centuries, not years or even decades. China's history has been one of a succession of dynasties. As Gifford contends: "In some ways, China is the same as it has always been. It is still the same kind of imperial, one-party government that the First Emperor from two thousand years ago would recognize. And that means there are no effective checks and balances, and there is terrible corruption, as there always has been."[29]

Still maintaining a one-party system of government, China's political leaders may be attempting to be more responsive to the people, but this effort is lagging behind their economic and social advances. The argument is often made that the one-party system has allowed Beijing to control and direct economic growth in a manner in which democratic societies cannot. At present, as long as growth and prosperity continue, most Chinese are willing to accept the status quo. And those who disagree are really not tolerated. Nonetheless, the Chinese people see the economic miracle that is unfolding, and they see opportunities they would never have imagined twenty years ago. The Communist Party's strength and acceptance by the people is now coming from this economic growth, which brings hope for the future.

China is a nation torn between capitalism and socialism. To believe that China is a nation of 1.3 billion hard-driving, aspiring capitalists is as absurd as believing that it will slip back into Maoism. It is just as ridiculous to believe that China will become a democracy in the foreseeable future (see chapter 13). China is in the midst of a new "cultural revolution" of the capitalist variety, not the Maoist variety. Yes, when we look at the face of China we see many blemishes, but if we look past these we will see a depth of strength and determination that cannot be denied and will carry the nation over many hurdles—a force to be reckoned with.

CHAPTER 4

TO THE VICTOR GO THE SPOILS

*The United States of America has not the option of
whether it will or will not play a great part. All that it can
decide is whether it will play the part well or badly.*

—Theodore Roosevelt
US president, 1901–1909

HOT WAR VS. ECONOMIC WAR

Myth Number 14: The only way China will ever be able to influence America's destiny is through military power, and it is not even close to that. China bashers have emerged all across the American political spectrum. On the left, the unions think that China's harsh labor conditions are a form of unfair competition that destroys American jobs. On the right, defense hawks feel threatened by China's accelerating military buildup, not to mention its record of supplying arms to pariahs, such as North Korea. America's trade deficit and the loss of jobs to China have compounded the problem.

China exports six times as much to America as it imports, with a rapidly widening gap. Chinese textile imports rose by 97 percent in the six months after quotas were lifted in January 2005. Taking our jobs and telling us we should be happy about it also tends to upset many Americans. An editorial in the official *China Daily* newspaper declared that America's textile industry, instead of seeking protectionist measures, should instead embrace "restructuring," which the article went on to explain meant the migration of textile manufacturing to countries such as China.[1]

American defense planners also view China's rise with great concern. They see a Leninist government system with a rapidly modernizing army larger than China's defensive needs require. An annual Pentagon review noted that "China does not now face a direct threat from another nation. Yet it continues to invest heavily in its military, particularly in programs designed to improve power projection." The review added that current trends in military modernization could pose "a credible threat to other modern militaries operating in the region." The preparations made by the People's Liberation Army (PLA) include an expanded force of ballistic missiles (long-range and short-range), cruise missiles, submarines, advanced aircraft, and other modern systems, against the background of a policy toward Taiwan that espouses "peaceful reunification."[2]

Chinese authorities become quite upset if anyone even suggests that its buildup could be interpreted as threatening. When the Obama administration issued a national intelligence strategy that briefly mentioned China's "increasing natural-resource-focused diplomacy and military modernization among the factors making it a complex global challenge," the Chinese boldly protested, calling on America to abandon its "cold-war mentality and prejudices."[3] The term "soft power" was used by a Chinese leader for the first time in 2007. China is working very hard to convince the rest of the world that its rise should not be feared but embraced. China may not have the military power at this time to threaten America, but it does have the economic power to wreak havoc on our economy. Most troubling is the fact that the United States has indirectly been a principal financier of China's military buildup through our outsourcing, offshoring of jobs, and trade policies (see chapter 12).

In 2005, the congressionally mandated report *United States Congressional–China Economic and Security Review Commission Annual Report to Congress* concluded that "on balance, the trends in the United States–China relationship have negative implications for the long-term economic and security interests of the United States. To prevent or reduce the negative impact of these trends, the United States needs to establish and implement policies and provide course correction." Some of the key findings of the commission were relative to trade and included the following: (1) a rapidly rising United States trade deficit with China; (2) undervalued Chinese currency; (3) Chinese government subsidies to companies (particularly to companies favoring export-oriented production); (4) weak intellectual property rights protection; (5) repressive labor practices; and (6) violation of critical commitments it made in order to enter the World Trade Organization. The commission also states, "China's continued recalcitrance is causing material injury to United States companies, workers, and communities. It is also contributing to a highly skewed bilateral economic relationship marked by a soaring United States trade deficit and a weakening competitive position for many United States firms."[4] As of today, Congress has either ignored its mandated report or has been totally ineffectual in any attempt to make course corrections.

United States Congressional–China Economic and Security Review Commission

United States Defense Industrial Base

Relative to China's technology development and its implications for the United States defense industrial base, the commission states: "The increasing reliance of the United States military on the private sector for certain technology developments, coupled with the movement offshore of much of the private sector's industrial and technology production, and some of its design work and research and development (R&D), activities in which China increasingly is engaging, raises the prospect of future United States dependence on China for certain items critical to the United States defense industry as well as to continued United States economic leadership. . . . Between 1998 and 2004, the United States moved from equilibrium in trade with China of items with the highest R&D and engineering content to a deficit in advanced technology products (ATP) of $36 billion."[5]

The cold war lasted from the mid 1940s to 1991. While there was a great deal of posturing and the advent of wars with Korea and Vietnam, the United States and the Soviet Union never came to direct blows. Eventually, the Soviets were defeated, not by military force but by American economic power.

We need not fear a war with China. In time, if current trends continue, China will dominate the United States, not militarily, but economically. Some might say China is already in a position in which it can make considerable demands on the United States, and it has more influence on our trade policy than is healthy for the United States (see chapter 12). By mid-twenty-first century, will the United States be like the Soviet Union was in the latter quarter of the twentieth century, unable to sustain its superpower status financially?

With patience, time, and a good strategy, China will be able to achieve dominance without military force. This is exactly what we did to the Soviets. In the twenty-first century, superpower status will come from economic, not military, power. Without economic strength, we will be unable to sustain our military strength, much as the Soviets found they could no longer do by 1991. We saw what economic power could do in the twentieth century, why don't we see it now?

The *United States Congressional–China Economic and Security Review Commission* report indicates that the combination of science and technology is the centerpiece of China's strategy to build national power. The commission also cautions: "While the United States defense industrial base is not dependent on Chinese imports at the present time, the Chinese government's coordinated strategy of utilizing incentives and subsidies to spur development of domestic capacity in dual-use technology industries is weakening the health of key United States commercial sectors on which the United States defense establishment relies."[6] The Chinese have stated that their fast-paced advancement in technology is evident by their trade surplus with the United States in advanced technology products.[7]

China has not been pleased with restrictions placed on it by the US government on high-technology exports that could possibly be used for military purposes. Chinese companies would moreover like to have a free hand in buying high-tech American companies. Chinese nationalism is a growing and potentially complicating factor in our relationship. Generally, the Chinese are suspicious of America and resent our political and military power, which they believe the United States uses to restrict their rise to power.

There are those who believe the Chinese threat of an economic war is overstated. In his book *The World Is Flat: A Brief History of the Twenty-first Century*, Thomas L. Friedman discusses his Dell Theory of Conflict Prevention. Under this theory, he explains that with the advent of just-in-time global supply chains in the flat world, there has developed a restraint on geopolitical adventurism. "The Dell Theory stipulates: No two countries that are both part of a major global supply chain, like Dell's, will ever fight a war against each other as long as they are both part of the same global supply chain. Because people embedded in major global supply chains don't want to fight old-time wars anymore.

They want to make just-in-time deliveries of goods and services and enjoy the rising standards of living that come with that."[8]

If we talk of economic warfare, however, we must recognize that it is waged on a different kind of battlefield, one on which lives are not lost and infrastructure destroyed, but one on which one nation may find itself with a worsening standard of living as well as political and social instability. In the twenty-first century, we will see economic super-powers capable of wielding an economic club powerful enough to make demands, both political and economic, on whomever they wish. This is a position that during the twentieth century was often attributed to the United States by other nations. This power, whether employed by the United States, China, or India, is applied to gain even more economic power. Why destroy another country's infrastructure and other resources when you can keep them intact and use them to your economic advantage?

Winning an economic war is not about winning a decisive battle or series of battles but achieving victory by positioning your country to win small skirmishes, while keeping your eye on the main objective of economic dominance. Victory goes to the country that has the strongest economy and can withstand and counter internal as well as external forces that might weaken its economy. An economic war is similar to a hot war, in that the country with the greatest resources, especially human resources, technological ability, and resolve, will win. The winner will also be the country with the most allies. In an economic war, we are not talking about allies with a similar political or social philosophy but rather those that provide markets and international supply chains. (International supply chains are the interconnected businesses involved in the management, movement storage, and work-in-progress inventory from point of origin of raw materials to finished goods at the point of consumption.)

If you are China, and you have what is to become the world's largest market, and your supply chain tentacles stretch across to more businesses in more countries than any other nation, you become a major economic force. Disruption, or even the threat of disruption, of these supply chains in the twenty-first-century global economy can be very hard on a nation's economy, its businesses, and its workers.

INDIA: OUR OTHER COMPETITOR

If China is our major competition, where does India, our other competitor, stand? Like China, India is a nuclear military power. It is also like China in terms of military personnel, with an army larger than that of the United States. With the eleventh-largest military budget in the world, India is buying or building sophisticated military equipment. But unlike China, India does not appear to have any designs on being a global military superpower.

It will take many years before India is able to catch up to China when it comes to building its national infrastructure of roads, power plants, airports, and water and sewerage facilities. Unlike China's growth, which is very organized due to a strong central government that decides where new highways, airports, and industrial parks are to be built, India's growth is not as well organized.[9] For India, this lack of organization is causing growing problems. If India cannot build its infrastructure at a more rapid pace, it will not have a chance to rival China in mass manufacturing. Indian companies have grown incredibly fast, posting annual gains as high as 15 percent, 20 percent, and even 25 percent.

Today, India's strength in manufacturing is in small-batch, high-value products that require higher levels of engineering than those of China. Many Indians are concerned that if the Chinese government continues to push software development and intellectual property rights protection, most of the design work conducted in India will be shifted to or near production sites in China. In technology, India does have a big head start over China. Pharmaceutical companies, investment banks, and other American and European companies are opening R&D centers in India. A college-educated Indian earns approximately one-fifth of a comparably educated American. While India's companies tend to be better organized and use their capital more efficiently than Chinese companies, the Chinese government is better organized and makes better use of its capital than the Indian government.

India has had a democratic government for over sixty years. Indians, especially young Indians, relate very well to the United States. Use of a common language and having many relatives in the United States has helped create this bond. Like the United States, Indian culture encourages the individual, an essential factor in a society and economy that thrives on an entrepreneurial spirit.

India is steadily becoming more intertwined in the global economy. Its foreign assets and liabilities add up to over 60 percent of its GDP. In the 1990s that ratio was only 49 percent. India's companies are acquiring foreign firms. In the first quarter of 2009, India's stock of direct foreign investment abroad was worth over $67 billion, or twice what it was two years earlier.[10]

When it comes to business, however, we can expect a level of ruthlessness from both India and China to match that of America in the twentieth century. Like America, India is driven not by a central government but by powerful business interests. China's destiny, on the other hand, is still crafted by a strong central government, which sees China as both an economic and military superpower.

A MARRIAGE MADE IN HEAVEN?

Myth Number 15: The Chinese and United States governments recognize that they have stakes in each other's continued prosperity, and therefore they will never do anything to harm each other's economies. To some, it would appear that the United States and China have a marriage made in heaven. The recession, like many catastrophic events in a relationship, has sent the marriage into a tailspin. The Chinese have weathered the world recession much better than the United States has. Over the years, China expanded its exports far beyond the United States and therefore was not as seriously affected as many originally thought when over-leveraged Americans slowed their consumption of Chinese goods. If we ask why the Chinese have done so well compared with the United States, it is because they have a highly coordinated strategic approach to controlling and growing their economy. There are many flaws with their economic and social systems as well as their record on human rights, but the one thing they do not suffer from is a lack of a winning economic strategic plan (see chapter 18). (Contrary to what some may believe, a country need not be communist or fascist to have a highly coordinated, strategically planned economy.)

Accounting for one-third of the world economy, China, like the United States, is a critical force driving the world's economic engine. China responded to the 2008 worldwide financial market collapse with its own economic stimulus package of $586 billion to be spent over a two-year period. Coming off of a long period of double-digit growth, the government was able to maintain a recessionary growth rate of at least 8 percent to avoid high unemployment. Of course, if the frugal Chinese citizens dipped into their large savings, domestic consumption would have been increased, and the impact of a reduction in exports would have been lessened.[11]

Unlike the United States, there was no housing bubble to burst in China. Average home price increases slowed but still remained lower than the rate of growth in income, unlike in the United States, where incomes were not rising and housing prices dropped rapidly. In the United States, 100 percent home financing became common, which resulted in overbuilding. Everyone was allowed into the housing market, whether they could afford a house or not. In China, buyers were required to put down 20 to 30 percent, much as Americans did when the housing market was stronger and banks were working with their own money. Banks in China therefore had a comfortable buffer when the market slowed and prices fell. Also, unlike in the United States, Chinese banks took a much more conservative approach to lending to real estate developers, which accounted for less than 10 percent of their loans.

By mid-2009, investment in China had risen 35 percent, car sales had increased 48 percent, and home purchases had jumped 80 percent, with a stiff increase in prices. Twenty percent of lending went into the stock market during the first part of 2009. All this occurred with funds from Chinese banks, which tend to be very conservative in their lending practices. This hardly sounds like an economy suffering greatly due to a downturn in US imports of Chinese goods.

China's economic dependence on the United States as a customer for its exports is greatly exaggerated. China's economic slowdown began earlier in 2007, before exports started to slow, when its real estate market and construction industry began to slow. Only 6 percent of China's workforce is in its export-oriented sectors.[12] China's domestic demand is a much larger driver of its growth than its exports to America. Even if net exports from China dropped to zero, its growth in GDP would still be in the high single digits due to its strong domestic demand. In fact, domestic demand is a much greater driver of China's economy than it is for the United States.[13]

It's not only China that has relied on importers other than the United States. The reliance of emerging countries on the United States is generally often exaggerated. Most of the growth in exports from emerging economies has been to other developing countries.[14]

Losing the United States as a customer would not have a devastating impact on China's economy. In 2007, the Middle East accounted for 40 percent of China's export growth and the United States only 10 percent. While exports account for 40 percent of China's GDP, much of the exports are made up of raw materials and parts that were imported into China and further processed by Chinese workers, thus adding value. Exports account only for approximately 18 percent of domestic value added and less than 10 percent of jobs.[15] A more significant driver of China's economy than exports is investment that accounts for 40 percent of China's GDP. Most of this investment (over 50 percent) is in infrastructure and real estate. Only 14 percent of investment is dependent on exports.[16]

By the time of the financial market collapse in the United States, Chinese consumers were in a much more comfortable position than the United States. In China, household debt amounted to approximately 13 percent of GDP, as opposed to the United States, where it was a whopping 100 percent. Chinese consumers were not facing bankruptcy due to slight rises in interest rates or inflation—they had something in the bank. Unlike the United States, the Chinese were paying a very low (5 percent) tax on income earned in savings accounts, thereby encouraging savings. In the United States, we are encouraged to spend all that we earn and are yet to earn.

China was in a much better position to pull itself out of any economic downturn than the United States. China simply shifted more of its production to supplying its own vast consumer markets. With ample financial reserves (the best of any major economy), China can use its own cash to grease its economy. The United States, in debt up to its eyeballs, must borrow the money from countries like China, adding more to the risk of future economic problems.

For years, China has supported our economy by buying our treasuries, thereby helping to finance our current-account deficit at low rates. This, in turn, has allowed us to maintain low interest rates. These low interest rates allowed Americans to get themselves into trouble with over-leveraged real estate and credit card debt. At one time, the China/America marriage appeared to be phenomenally successful, as both economies soared between 1998 and 2007. In reality, we have had a marriage that was relatively one-sided. In most divorces, one side often comes out in better financial shape, and in this case China is the clear winner.

YUAN VS. US DOLLAR

Since before the commencement of the recession, the Chinese have been lecturing the United States on how poorly we have handled our economy. Their biggest concern is with the treasuries they bought. Falling prices for United States bonds and/or a fall in the purchasing power of the dollar will not bode well for their investment in United States treasury bills. This encouraged China to go on a buying binge of foreign assets using US dollars.

China, India, France, and Russia have all called for an end to the dollar as the dominant currency in the international monetary system. In 2009, the dollar accounted for 65 percent of the world's foreign-exchange reserves, followed by the euro at 26 percent. Three-quarters of these reserves are held by emerging economies, with China holding one-third of such reserves. As the US printing presses are running at warp speed, China rightly fears inflation in the United States and the resulting depreciation of its huge reserve holdings of dollars. Continued devaluation of the dollar relative to other currencies, including the Chinese yuan, could result in an improvement of the US foreign trade position relative to China, however.

China rebounded relatively quickly from the recession, yet its currency has fallen in value since the beginning of the recession. Pegged to the United States dollar, the yuan slid down as the value of the dollar declined with the recession. Contrary to the trend, the Japanese yen climbed against the United States dollar. By holding the value of the yuan down, China encourages foreign capital inflows and the growth of its exports. If pressured to raise the yuan's value, domestic spending would be boosted by increasing the purchasing power of the Chinese, which would help rebalance the international trade playing field. But this has not been a top Chinese objective. Still, keeping the value of the yuan low creates a problem internally, in that the Chinese consumer is reluctant to spend, thereby hurting the growth of their own market.

With the onset of the US bailout programs, China has begun to diversify its holdings of foreign securities. If the Chinese attempted to dump their dollars, it would cause a plunge in the dollar's value, which would hurt their reserves. Anti–United States hard liners in China are known as "economic nationalists," and they are not happy that their government has nearly $1 trillion in Chinese foreign reserves invested in United States securities. The economic nationalists are demanding that Beijing stop buying US T-bills and invest the money in China to build the military, infrastructure, and social services.[17]

DECOUPLING CHINA AND THE UNITED STATES

The United States is rapidly losing research and development and production, and it is struggling to hang onto its status as the number-one market. America's importance as an engine of global growth is exaggerated. Between 2000 and 2007, its share of world imports dropped from 19 percent to 14 percent. The increase in consumer spending (in actual dollars) in China and India now add more to global GDP growth than does consumer spending in the United States.[18]

In June 2009, the BRICs (Brazil, Russia, India, and China) held a summit. These emerging markets were already showing a more rapid economic recovery than leading Western nations. This quicker recovery of the BRICs may be indicative of a shift in international economic power toward the East or of another trend referred to as "decoupling" by Ayhan Kose of the International Monetary Fund, Christopher Otrok of the University of Virginia, and Eswar Prasad of Cornell University. Their research indicated that from 1985 to 2005, there was some convergence of business cycle fluctuations among industrialized countries and emerging market economies due to trade and financial integration. They also found that while business cycles in Europe and the United States were converging, business cycles of emerging countries like China and India were as well. At the same time, they found a decoupling between the industrial countries and the emerging markets.[19]

China and India would therefore be expected to be affected in a different way than the Western nations by a recession, and to undergo recovery at a different pace. Asia's decoupling from the United States is reflected in the fact that the region's downturn was only partially caused by the US recession. A decrease in domestic Asian demand was more responsible for Asia's recession than was a decrease in exports to America. Higher food and energy prices and a tighter monetary policy intended to slow inflation contributed significantly to the Asian slowdown.

The state of codependence between the United States and China will continue to wane if current trends continue. How will this affect the United States, our economy, and our society? To the victor in an economic war go the spoils, that is, the right to make the rules and the right to demand that its country, its businesses, and its people receive the most benefits and that no one should complain about it. This right could extend beyond economic rights to human rights and how the environment will be dealt with.

Imported Chinese food, drugs, toothpaste, seafood, pet food, and other products have been under intense scrutiny because some have been found to contain deadly substances. When Mattel, the world's largest toy maker, recalled millions of Chinese-made toys for safety reasons in the summer of 2007, the Chinese government was outraged and claimed that many of the toys were recalled due to Mattel's design problems. Design problems may have caused some of the recall issues, but others were due to the fact that some of Mattel's vendors in China or their subcontractors violated Mattel's rules by using lead paint or tiny magnets that could be dislodged and swallowed.

The pressure from the Chinese for a full apology was intense.

Mattel sent one of its top executives to China to make a public apology to China's product safety chief, Li Changjang.[20] Why such a public apology? Li upbraided Mattel for its lack of safety controls and reminded Mattel executives, "A large part of your annual profit . . . comes from your factories in China." Some China experts believed it was an effort to prevent China from imposing additional taxes or regulations on Mattel. Mattel understands how China works, having established a presence in China over twenty-five years ago, and the company is now producing 65 percent of its products there.[21] China's power over US companies comes in many forms. In 2005, Microsoft agreed to ban the word "democracy" from parts of its MSN Web site in China.[22]

In shaping public opinion by controlling the media, China has restrictions that are among the most severe in the world. They are not only strict; they are enforced with a heavy hand. When it comes to product safety, China operates largely in a lawless environment with hardly any effective regulation and little recourse to law. According to Susan Aaronson of George Washington University, the Chinese do not have a culture of compliance and cut corners on safety and quality when squeezed on price.[23] Corruption, counterfeiting, and blackmail are not uncommon. It is also not uncommon for corporate executives in America and Europe to turn a blind eye to these practices. When these executives pressure Chinese suppliers to cut costs, we see the predictable consequences in the end products.[24]

As Ted Fishman aptly points out in *China, Inc.*, in China, foreign "executives and their corporate communication staffs turn into another breed. Anxious to please the Chinese government, they seem as informal agents for the Ministry of Propaganda, tying their corporate message points to China's official line." Fishman quotes a German journalist who spent time in China, "It's amazing how it works on you. Even as a reporter I find myself getting sucked into the message. The thing is that as soon as I step out of the country, I can better see things for what they are. You have to give the Chinese credit. They are really good at the mindshare game."

Because American and other foreign executives are expected to toe the party line of providing the Chinese government's version of reality, Fishman explains, important economic security and trade issues are never discussed as they should be by political leaders around the world. Essentially, if you want to do business in China, the government expects you to behave in ways that serve the party's best interests.[25] If a foreign company complains about currency values, theft of intellectual property, environmental degradation, labor rights, religious freedom, trade barriers, business rigging in favor of Chinese companies, or lack of product safety controls, it can expect to pay the price for such talk.

The China–United States marriage is not one made in heaven. We became dependent on their purchase of our treasuries to finance our spending on products they made. We lost our best jobs and economic independence to this system, which was pushed by special-interest lobbyists and supported by our political leaders desperate for the financial support provided by the lobbyists. Should the marriage be saved? Can it be saved? It should and it can if Congress and the administration would only admit that they have allowed themselves to be manipulated by both China and special interests here in the United States. This is not a situation that was created by the Obama administration but by past administrations that have passed the baton on to subsequent administrations. Until our political leaders learn to "just say no" and develop a national strategy to address this reconciliation, our marriage will continue to harm America. This strategy will likely result in some short-term pain in the United States, but for the long-term, we must stop our free fall or we, our children, and our children's children will continue to pay the price in terms of a deterioration of the American dream.

CHAPTER 5

TWENTIETH-CENTURY EDUCATION DOES NOT PRODUCE TWENTY-FIRST-CENTURY JOBS

All who have meditated on the art of governing mankind have been convinced that the fate of empires depends on the education of youth.

—Aristotle
384–322 BCE

IMPORTANCE OF EDUCATION TO ECONOMIC DEVELOPMENT

I doubt anyone would argue against the fact that for the United States to remain an economic superpower, it will have to be a leader in the twenty-first-century world of high technology. China and India recognize this most basic and obvious fact, and both countries have devoted a great deal of effort to position themselves to compete for technological leadership. In my experience, corporations place a very high value on quality education when looking for a location—whether a manufacturing operation or a research facility. With high labor costs, US manufacturing survival relies on the most sophisticated, efficient, and highly automated operations possible. It is the only way we have any chance of competing with low-labor-cost nations like China, India, Mexico, or Brazil. If American factories are to survive, they will require highly trained workers capable of running computer-controlled machines.

Poor education and its impact on job growth are not confined to big-city schools—these issues are a national problem. I have spent over thirty-five years visiting communities and schools across the country. I am constantly amazed at how often communities spend huge sums of money on administration costs and/or athletic programs, while ignoring the academic performance of their schools.

Several years ago, I was representing a major corporation that was searching for a site for a new manufacturing plant that would employ approximately three hundred well-paid workers. We were looking for a Midwestern blue-collar town. There were numerous communities in the Midwest. The officials of one of the states under consideration suggested a particular town they wanted us to include in our analysis. Since this was to be a highly automated plant, we needed a well-educated and trainable workforce. Upon examining the educational achievement levels for the community's high school, we found it lacking; in fact, it was relatively poor. The state officials continued to insist we at least look at the community, even though we wanted to drop it from further consideration. Discussing the state's recommendation with our client, the president of the company agreed to visit the community.

Generally, on a first tour, a community may be given only a couple of hours to make its case. Prior to the tour, we informed the community that the company was concerned about the high school's achievement scores and general quality of its K–12 education. When we met the mayor and his team, they took us on a whirlwind tour of the community, and we stopped at the high school. The school was very old and looked to be in poor condition.

The mayor did not take us into the school or introduce us to the principal, teachers, school board members, or anyone else who could satisfy my clients' concerns about the school's academics. We went around to the rear of the school, where there stood a brand-new football stadium. Yes, a stadium. This was not a football field with some bleachers. The mayor took most of his allotted two hours to show off his new stadium and discuss the school's outstanding football history. The closest he came to talking about academics was to tell us that each year several of the players would receive football scholarships. I asked what percentage of graduates was accepted into the state university, what percentage went on to college, and what the high school's science and math programs were like. I also asked what they paid their teachers, what was the size of their classes, and what type of computer training they provided. I could not get the mayor on track. He had none of these answers, but he had all the school football statistics on the tip of his tongue. As we left the community, my client asked, "Is this mayor, or for that matter the entire town, ignorant or just stupid? Don't they see what they're doing to their kids?"

Sure, a few kids with athletic ability went on to college, but the rest paid a very large price for these few, as did the community as a whole. I wish I could say this community was an anomaly, and that I see great strides being made in American education as I travel around the nation, but I can't and I don't. Don't misinterpret me here—we need athletic programs and our students certainly need the exercise. The issue is one of allocation of resources and the return on those assets. Focusing huge amounts of assets on a few students is not providing a student body with an efficient or effective athletic program. Misallocation of resources is responsible for many of the problems with American education, whether we are talking about athletic programs or bloated big-city administration systems.

As a nation, we are failing our society's and our children's educational and economic future. If we step beyond manufacturing into management, and more significantly into research and development, then education geared to the twenty-first century becomes even more critical. Education is the cornerstone of the future of the United States' ability to compete for jobs. I have seen many communities, states, and even countries bypassed as potential locations for corporate operations due to poor educational achievement.

Myth Number 16: If we don't have enough high-tech people, we can always attract them from overseas. According to the National Bureau of Economic Research, in 1970 the United States was the king of higher education. Approximately 30 percent of the world's college students were enrolled in the United States, and the United States granted half of all doctorates in science and engineering. It is statistics like these that made the United States the world's technological leader. Within a thirty-year period, we saw a substantial decrease in the percentage of US student enrollment in these fields, a gap that was quickly filled by foreign students. According to a National Science Foundation study, in 2005 (the latest available at the time of writing), the foreign student population in the United States earned approximately 34.7 percent of the doctorate degrees in the sciences and approximately 63.1 percent of the doctorate degrees in engineering.[1]

China is now expected to overtake the United States in producing

PhDs in science and engineering in 2010.[2] A Duke University study found that for bachelor's degrees in engineering, computer science, and information technology in 2004, the United States produced 137,437, India 112,000, and China 351,537.[3] The question that is often asked is whether the colleges and universities in India and China are comparable to those in the United States. There is no simple answer. Each country has its leaders that are generally considered of the highest quality. At the same time, each country has lesser-quality institutions. The real test of India's and China's educational quality is proven by the fact that so many major international companies have moved or outsourced their research and development operations to these countries. We have educational institutions in the United States that in a matter of days will grant an online PhD based solely on life experience. All you need to do is submit your life experience or, if lacking life experience, a thesis on a topic of your choice. Within fifteen days of charging your credit card a total of less than $1,000, you will receive your degree from a "university."

Numerous business and trade organizations have asked Congress to reform the H-1B visa program. They argue that foreign nationals that have received master's degrees and PhDs should be exempt from the requirements of the program's annual cap. After 9/11, the number of H-1B visas, which allow highly qualified foreign workers to remain in the United States for up to six years, was reduced from 195,000 to 65,000 per year due to security concerns. Attracting these individuals as students, and keeping them here after graduation, is essential to the future economic strength of our nation.

Suppose you were a Nobel laureate with numerous highly advanced technology patents to your credit and you wished to come to the United States to live and work. You would think Uncle Sam would buy your ticket and give you a luxury apartment until you found a job and got settled. But let's say Uncle Sam was not your biological uncle and you had no relatives in the United States. You would have to fall in line behind thousands of uneducated and untrained laborers who had a relative here.

How does the United States select doctors and scientists who will develop the drugs and medical technology that may provide a means for early detection or a cure for cancer, diabetes, or the hundreds of other maladies plaguing the world? How do we select the engineers and scientific leaders who will develop the products and technology we desperately need to remain a leader in the twenty-first-century global economy? Since not enough Americans are interested and capable, it would be logical for us to open our arms to the scientific and technological leaders of the world. But guess again!

Each year on April Fools' Day, 65,000 highly educated foreigners with corporate sponsors receive H-1B visas. This leaves hundreds of thousands of other very highly educated individuals with US sponsors sitting offshore. You would think that we are too smart to leave all this talent offshore for India, China, or the EU to gobble up. By a stroke of political genius, the candidates that don't make the first round of selection can enter their name in a lottery, from which 55,000 are issued visas.[4] We use "Power Ball" technology to pick a potential Albert Einstein, Enrico Fermi, Jonas Salk, Ludwig Mies van der Rohe, or Igor Ivanovich Sikorsky (all immigrants).

Is it any wonder that many of these people are saying it's not worth the effort, and the companies that sponsor them are saying it's easier to employ this talent offshore? The problem is that offshore they must compete for this talent with foreign competitors, and if this talent decides to start its own companies, these entrepreneurs do so offshore. If scientific and technology jobs cannot be filled with qualified US citizens, then there should be no limits placed on the number of immigrants, as long as legitimate sponsors are willing to guarantee employment.

Today's young Chinese college graduates living in Beijing know that a $15,000 to $20,000 income in China will buy a better lifestyle than a $45,000 to $60,000 income in the United States. Indian college graduates, like Chinese grads, see no advantage to moving to a strange land away from friends and family. Why move from their home, which they see as a place with a rapidly expanding economy and opportunity, to a country where the economy is perceived to be in decline and the people hostile?

THE R&D BLACK HOLE

Why would bright Indian students come to the United States, when India has developed universities that rival the best that the United States has to offer? India now has the high-tech, twenty-first-century companies and jobs necessary to support these universities and hire their graduates. Half of IBM's 190,000 engineers and technical experts are located offshore, 30,000 of whom are in India. General Electric has a similar pattern in manufacturing and in high technology, claiming that if the company requires a deep technical pool of talent, GE can find it in China and India.[5] Bill Gates has said, "The only thing that limits us in India is the speed at which we can recruit."[6] China and India recognize that to be an economic force in the twenty-first century, technology will be the key. Both have a vision and are willing to make the necessary effort to achieve their goals. The United States appears to have neither the vision nor the will to stay competitive.

We are constantly told that new industries will be developed that will generate new jobs. In the twenty-first century, new industries are synonymous with new technology. Due to pressure to increase return on assets (see chapter 7), we are cutting back on research personnel and facilities. Supporting large, expensive research operations in the United States simply does not help your return on assets. Wall Street analysts don't give extra points for products being developed today that may be a huge commercial success in five or more years. Much of the great technology that fostered industrial growth and jobs in the United States came out of corporate laboratories like Bell Labs, RCA Labs, and Xerox's Palo Alto Research Center. Many companies such as DuPont, Microsoft, IBM, Cisco, and Hewlett-Packard have research facilities, some here in the United States but increasingly offshore. Why shouldn't they go offshore when costs are so much lower, governments more encouraging, and the scientific minds more available? Professor Willy C. Shih of Harvard Business School notes that in 2000, we had a $29 billion trade surplus in high-tech products, which turned into a $54 billion trade deficit by 2007.[7]

If we are to create new industries and jobs in the United States, we need a new network of US-based labs financed both publicly and privately. If Congress were to take the $20 billion plus it spends each year on pork barrel projects or the $20 billion plus it spends on agricultural subsidies to wealthy agricultural interests, we could finance serious research in the nation that would develop new industries and new high-paying jobs. We need federal funding for meaningful university research that will develop commercially viable products. We also need political commitment and a tax system that encourages scientific development. This could be accomplished through the use of government tax incentives for corporations to develop new technologies and produce the resulting products here in the United States.

America has been developing new industries and shipping them to Asia for decades. This started in the 1980s with televisions and cars and has progressed to computer chips, cell phones, and computers. Unless the United States can resurrect its manufacturing base, any breakthroughs from US research will quickly slide into the offshore black hole. An excellent case is illustrated by the development of the solar cell. Federally funded labs in the United States developed many of the breakthroughs in solar cell technology, yet it has been the Japanese and the Chinese who have capitalized on this technology and now dominate this $30-billion-a-year industry. The United States manufactures just 5 percent of the world's solar cells.

If the federal government would allow companies investing in research and development and high-tech manufacturing to write down the entire amount in the first year rather than over time, we would see an increase in US research and development and manufacturing. Real estate tax abatements, free or low-cost land, job training assistance, readily available and low-cost utilities, and quick issuing of permits are some of the incentives that aggressive states and communities have used to attract and keep industry (see chapters 8 and 10). These incentives should be more uniform nationwide and therefore need to be part of a federal program. With development of these technologies and a more pro-business federal approach, the venture capital will be waiting to turn them into viable commercial products and new jobs for Americans.

US Competitiveness in Science and Technology

The Task Force on the Future of American Innovation in a report stated: "The United States still leads the world in research and discovery, but our advantage is rapidly eroding, and our global competitors may soon overtake us."[8]

The National Science Board warned of a "troubling decline" in the number of US students studying science and engineering, in spite of the number of jobs growing in these fields. "These trends threaten the economic welfare and security of our country."[9]

John E. Jankowski of the National Science Foundation, said, "Science excellence is no longer the domain of the United States."[10]

Denis Simon, dean of management and technology at Rensselaer Polytechnic Institute, said "We are in a new world, and it's increasingly going to be dominated by countries other than the United States."[11]

Bill Gates, founder of Microsoft, has said, "Training the work force of tomorrow with the high school of today is like trying to teach kids about today's computers on a 50-year-old mainframe."[12]

America can still boast of having seventeen of the world's twenty top universities. These universities employ 70 percent of the world's Nobel laureates. Nevertheless, the public is hardly aware of the fact that the United States is being rivaled and surpassed by foreign researchers in many basic scientific fields. The implications for the future of jobs, national security, and the economic, cultural, and intellectual viability of the nation are not very positive. Without a continuous flow of highly educated individuals from our universities and a financial environment that encourages new technology development, we stand little chance of maintaining our role as a technological leader in the twenty-first century. If we lose that position, the trickle-down effect throughout our economy will be devastating.

THE K–UNDERGRADUATE DISASTER

Myth Number 17: If we can't attract enough talented people from abroad to fulfill our high-tech needs, we will just train more Americans to take the jobs. Most troubling for the United States is that despite restrictions on experienced foreign scientists and engineers and foreign graduate students, American students are not being trained to fill the gaps. In spite of the poor results that American K–12 students achieve on international tests, we have made little if any progress in raising these scores and changing the way our schools perform.

One major problem is that we have ignored our higher educational system's inability or lack of effort to train K–12 teachers to teach math and science more effectively. Nationwide, over half of those teaching physical science classes (chemistry, physics, earth or space science) did not have a major in any of the physical sciences. Over 30 percent of public school math teachers did not major or minor in math while in college.[13] The real problem is that our own US students are simply too poorly prepared in science and math to succeed in those areas. Our universities have not been interested in bringing up students to match their foreign peers, and, frankly, US students have not been interested in engineering, science, or math careers.

Myth Number 18: Our children don't score well when compared with other countries because our education system stresses creativity, not rote learning. When Thomas L. Friedman asked Bill Gates about the American advantage of creativity over rote learning in Japan and China, he was utterly dismissive. Gates believes that anybody who doesn't believe Japan and China can compete with Americans in terms of innovation is sadly mistaken. "I have never met the guy who doesn't know how to multiply who created software. . . . Who has the most creative video games in the world? Japan! I never met these 'rote people.' . . . Some of my best software developers are Japanese. You need to understand things in order to invent beyond them."[14] Todd G. Buchholz, in his book *Bringing the Jobs Home*, states that when American schools lost their edge because school quality began to crumble, teachers and administrators turned from enhancing skills to enhancing self-esteem to avoid admitting the problem. He continues, "It has worked beautifully. Now our kids have high self-esteem but low test scores. American schools have not made our kids dumb. They've made them delusional."[15]

It is not just our schools that make our kids delusional—it is also their parents. A Harris Interactive poll explains in part why US students rank sixteenth out of thirty countries in science. When 1,304 US adults were asked to name the most influential role models for America's youth, 50 percent picked an entertainer or an athlete.[16] According to the American Society of Engineering Education, scientists and engineers make up less than 5 percent of our population but create up to 50 percent of our GNP. Less than 6 percent of our high school students plan to major in engineering, down 36 percent from the mid-1990s. At the beginning of the decade, 56 percent of all Chinese undergraduate degrees were in the hard sciences.

Myth Number 19: Even if the American education system has fallen somewhat behind, it is rapidly catching up: our children won't be left behind. Science test scores for mid-decade provided by the National Assessment of Education Progress showed that fourth graders from 1995 to 2005 had a slight improvement, eighth graders had no improvement, and there was a decline for twelfth graders.

There are many things wrong with education in the United States, and one of them is that unions continue to protect incompetent and lazy teachers. In New York over a four-year period, only two teachers out of eighty thousand were fired for incompetence, according to a 2006 ABC *20/20* report titled "Stupid in America."[17]

We can't expect the good teachers to compensate for the weak teachers. In teaching, we give our children to an individual for an entire term or semester. For many children, the damage done may not be rectified by the child's next teacher. Overly protective unions must assume their share of the guilt for the state of the American educational system, and politicians should stop dancing around the issue. Teachers' unions can be very harmful if the power they wield is abused. At the same time, without teachers' unions, our underpaid teachers would be paid even less, class sizes would be larger, and classroom conditions would be worse.

Parents should also be held accountable. To pack your child up and send him or her to school and expect a miracle to happen on its own is an absurd idea. Without support and encouragement at home, even the brightest child will not thrive at school. Too many parents believe a public school is a depository into which they place their children each day to be educated, disciplined, taught civil behavior and good hygiene, given psychological counseling, and trained to be a professional athlete. Schools are for educating children; the rest is our responsibility as parents. There are enough good students performing well in poor schools to show that good parenting can make the difference.

STAYING COMPETITIVE IN THE TWENTY-FIRST CENTURY

In the twenty-first century, the brass ring will go to technology workers who are innovative. The individuals or teams that develop computer programs and chips to solve new problems are the computer scientists who will be of the greatest value and who will receive the highest pay. It will be these innovators, and not the technicians, who are in greatest demand. These high-technology innovators will be the rainmakers of the high-technology economy of the twenty-first century, yet the US educational system is still trapped in a system training students for twentieth-century low-tech jobs.

If we look at the US population of more than 300 million, India's 1.1 billion people, and China's 1.3 billion, it becomes easy to see how India and China have the greatest potential to become dominant in the high-technology environment of the twenty-first century. What India and China lacked throughout much of the twentieth century was a high-quality educational system for the masses. This is quickly changing.

If we also assume that among every one million people, regardless of their location in the world, approximately an equal percentage are creative and have the potential to be entrepreneurs, then you can see why India and China will climb the success ladder rapidly during the twenty-first century. Consider that creativity and entrepreneurship are dormant in many people and require education and opportunity to develop. Throughout most of the twentieth century, China and India were asleep, and as they awoke, the United States fell asleep.

Myth Number 20: Our college students understand the competition they will face in the global economy of the twenty-first century and are working to acquire the skills they need to meet the challenge. The average American student is growing up in a wealthy country with many opportunities. Many of these kids feel a sense of entitlement—things will be even better for them than for their parents. But most of these kids and many of their parents are clueless, given the forces in the world that are altering their expectations.

While the number of universities is growing rapidly in both India and China, they do not come close to filling the needs of the millions of students seeking entry. The students who pass the rigorous entry exams and who are fortunate enough to make it into the best schools come from a huge, inexhaustible pool of bright students hungry for success. China is obsessed with education. A typical middle school student attends school from 7:30 a.m. to noon, breaks for lunch and returns from 2:00 to 5:00, breaks for dinner and comes back at 7:00, then goes home at 8:30. Ted C. Fishman, in his book *China, Inc.*, aptly describes university conditions and students: "Crammed six to a room, with no private space to speak of and perhaps just a single large table for all to sit at and a flickering fluorescent lamp overhead, China's university students rarely fail to display the diligence that delivered to them the treasure of higher education."[18] The competition to get into and stay in school is so intense that little time is left for social activities common in American schools.

For many Americans, entry into a college or university is as much, if not more, a social adventure as an educational endeavor. While the American college student is joining a fraternity or sorority, partying, and pondering where to go for spring break, the Chinese college student, as noted, is living in a small room with five other students studying. The Chinese student's biggest worry is that if his grades are not high enough, he will immediately be replaced by any one of a hundred students clamoring to take his place. The only part of his social life that he is concerned with is the disgrace he will bring upon himself and his family if he fails.

In the twenty-first-century global economy, an American fourth grader, upon graduation from college, will not simply be competing with his peers in the United States for jobs but with graduates in China, India, and other nations. In China today, a fourth grader is putting in approximately three hours more per day in the classroom than the American student. According to Tom Loveless, director of the Brown Center on Education Policy at the Brookings Institution, the popular belief that the amount of homework American students do is rising and becoming onerous is simply not true. The typical American high school student spends less than one hour per day on homework. Of twenty nations, the United States tied for next-to-last place. Students in France, Italy, Russia, and South America spend twice as much time on homework than do American students.[19]

In twenty years, the American student, as Todd G. Buchholz says, will be educated to enhance his or her self-esteem. Of course, he will learn other things of great importance as well. Mr. Buchholz may be overstating, but there is some validity to what he says. But the Chinese student will be educated to master the skills necessary for the high-technology twenty-first-century economy. Of these students, given the Chinese's emphasis on math and science, which do you think will be best prepared to handle these jobs? Which will be offered the best jobs? Which will be most successful? Which will have the best chance of rising to become twenty-first-century leaders?

If our American fourth grader, upon graduation from college, is fortunate enough to land a job with a twenty-first-century blue chip multinational company (well established and financially sound), there is a good chance that the job will not be located in the United States with a US company. The odds are likely to be better that she will find a job with an emerging market company in Brazil, South Korea, China, India, or South Africa. The list of the blue-chip companies in twenty years will read differently than it does today, with fewer American companies and more new names, many from emerging markets.

For foreign students who receive an advanced degree in a field critical to the US economy, the government, in addition to giving them a green card, should make partial, if not full, payments on their student loans for as long as they remain in the United States. American students who receive such advanced degrees in critical fields should also have their student loan payments made. Any student, foreign or American, who receives an undergraduate degree or advanced degree in math, science, and other priority disciplines, and then becomes a certified teacher, should receive the same benefit as long as he remains a full-time teacher. This should apply for K–12 teachers as well as those at the university level. Most school districts pay all starting teachers the same wage. Why shouldn't teachers with skills in areas in which we need to stay internationally competitive receive salaries competitive with industry? If we fail to do this, we will not attract the number of teachers needed in critical fields, such as math and science.

Many of us recognize that education improves our earning power and improves our ability to maintain a healthy lifestyle, thereby decreasing taxpayer cost of medical care and likely decreasing crime and its cost to society. Then why is it that so many education referendums are defeated nationwide? Virtually all states, with the exceptions of Michigan and California, are financing education primarily through local property taxes. Many Americans are already faced with high property taxes. With an aging population and many seniors finding it increasingly difficult to afford homes that they have often spent decades paying off, it is hard to gather support for increased property taxes. One solution frequently discussed is to replace that portion of the property tax devoted to education (typically the lion's share) with an increase in income tax and or sales tax. "Replacement" is the key word often missed by political leaders. Such a tax would fall more heavily on younger Americans still earning an income and those who are more likely to have children in school. By taking school finance out of the local taxing district, we may even be able to provide a fairer distribution of funds for school districts. Why should a child receive less of an education because he is in a less affluent community?

Tuition for higher education has risen 439 percent since the early 1980s, according to the National Center for Public Policy and Higher Education. Family incomes haven't even come close to this rate of increase. For 2009, the average private college tuition ran about $25,000 according to the College Board, while public universities have an average price tag of about $6,500 a year for in-state tuition. Two-thirds of graduates from four-year programs have debt averaging about $20,000 on graduation day.[20]

So, where else is the money to come from? If our political leaders can finance an unpopular war with hundreds of billions of dollars and provide hundreds of billions more for a financial market bailout, why is it so hard to find the funds to pay our teachers and educate our children? Would it not be more productive to put this money into education?

Does money solve all of our educational problems? Take the nation's capital, where spending per pupil is 50 percent higher than the national average. It spite of this spending, the educational achievement in Washington, DC, schools is horrible. If Washington, DC, was a state and it was compared to all states' test scores, it would rank last.[21] As long as teachers are sheltered by their unions from being dismissed, no amount of increased spending will help improve educational levels. Like many school systems, teachers in DC schools are paid based on seniority. Such systems tend to attract the lazy and mediocre, and if they are not lazy and mediocre to start, it encourages many to become so.

The Bush administration's method for improving education was to implement the No Child Left Behind program. The *Chicago Tribune* reported on November 1, 2009, that Park Forest's Rich East High School in the Chicago area had reported a 37 percent increase in two years for its juniors' test scores. So impressed, the school was asked to host a seminar to help other schools. The only problem, as reported by the *Tribune*, was that 40 percent of the school's juniors did not take the test. This other group just happened to be the school's lowest achievers. By ratcheting up the credit hours needed to qualify as a junior, this school and others used a loophole for defining sophomores to keep them from taking the test. The *Tribune* found 20 percent of Illinois sophomores were held back and did not officially advance to junior level. These students then took the tests as seniors, but their scores were not used for the federal No Child Left Behind accountability requirements. If students' achievement levels are substandard, the No Child Left Behind program requires schools to provide free tutoring, or in the worst case, to close.[22]

A 2009 poll for the *Economist* conducted by YouGov found that nearly three-quarters of Americans believe that the problems facing education are as grave as those facing healthcare. In addition, they found that 61 percent believed that George W. Bush's No Child Left Behind law has either had no positive effect or has actually hurt education.

On February 17, 2009, President Obama signed into law the American Recovery and Reinvestment Act of 2009 (ARRA), legislation designed to stimulate the economy, support job creation, and invest in critical sectors, including education. Of the $100 billion in Obama's stimulus for education, most has gone to shore up budgets or to prevent layoffs. The ARRA is supposed to support investments in innovative strategies that are most likely to lead to long-term gains in school and school system effectiveness. Approximately $10 billion will be available to improve the system, with the largest amount ($4.35 billion) for the Race to the Top program. This competitive grant program is designed to encourage and reward states that are creating the conditions for educational innovation and reform, including significant improvement in student achievement, increasing high school graduation rates, and ensuring student preparation for college and careers. Race to the Top is supposed to:

1. adopt standards and assessments that will prepare students to succeed in college and the global economy;
2. build data systems that measure student growth and success, and inform teachers and principals relative to how to improve instruction;
3. recruit, develop, reward, and retain effective teachers and principals; and
4. turn around our lowest-achieving schools.

Race to the Top will reward states that have demonstrated success in raising student achievement and have the best plans to accelerate their reforms in the future. The Race to the Top Fund will reserve up to $350 million to help states create assessments aligned to common sets of standards. The remaining $4 billion will be awarded in a national competition. Implementing the Obama program will likely be where the program runs into problems, just as No Child Left Behind did. The Obama program takes a carrot approach rather than the stick, as was the case with No Child Left Behind, and it has the potential to result in significant improvements. The biggest problems will derive from those initiatives that may require concessions from the teachers' unions and in keeping the testing process above reproach.

Will the Obama administration have the guts to follow through with the programs that will work, or will the administration mimic past presidents and dance around the problems? The bottom line for most politicians is how much political capital they want to spend on a problem that has solutions that won't be recognized as successful until years into the future. Do you want to take actions that will alienate unions and other special interests and will cost financial support and votes now, when the results of your efforts will not be recognized until long after the next election?

As a nation, we are so focused on the economic problems triggered by the 2008 financial market collapse that we have lost sight of a more subtle threat that will also have a devastating effect on our way of life. If current trends continue, and economies like China's and India's surpass ours during the first half of this century, what legacy will we Americans leave for our children and our children's children? Will we simply say we didn't see it coming, or we didn't have the will to do what needed to be done? Most important: how do we impress on our young people the importance of education, that high school and college are not an eight-year social event? How do we convince them that more than ever before in our history, they will be competing for jobs with the brightest in the world?

CHAPTER 6

OUTSOURCING NATIONAL SECURITY

Our liberty depends on the Freedom of the Press, and that
cannot be limited without being lost.

—Thomas Jefferson
US president, 1801–1809

OUTSOURCING THE MILITARY AND CIA

If Americans could say, "Yes, the cost of government is very high, but we are receiving in return a better, more secure standard of living," we might be more accepting of the high price we pay. But the standard of living is not getting better for the vast majority of Americans, nor do Americans really feel protected from future terrorist attacks. An August 2009 CBS News poll found that only 25 percent of those surveyed thought that government policies have made the nation safer from terrorism. After sacrificing thousands of American lives and spending hundreds of billions of dollars on wars in Iraq and Afghanistan and on homeland security, to have a majority of the American people feel no safer is not a ringing endorsement of our government.

During the George W. Bush administration, we saw an unparalleled amount of government outsourcing, all in the name of cutting costs and improving efficiency. The Bush administration's vision was a government run, wherever possible, by select friendly contractors. According to Naomi Klein of the *Los Angeles Times*, contractors treat the government "as an ATM, withdrawing massive contracts to perform core functions like securing borders and interrogating prisoners, and making deposits in the form of campaign contributions."[1] For the period fiscal years 2001 to 2010, Congress appropriated $1.08 trillion. With a full ATM, average monthly obligations for contracts and pay as of July 2009 were about $10.9 billion. Assuming troop withdrawals, Congressional Budget Office funding projections for Iraq, Afghanistan, and the Global War on Terror could total $1.3 trillion to $1.8 trillion for fiscal years 2001 to 2019. In its role as an ATM, the government's war on terrorism has become a huge new economy—one based on continued disaster, instability, and fear.[2]

Not all outsourcing has negative repercussions on the American people, and not all outsourcing results in jobs being offshored. Two best-selling books released in 2007 made some frightening statements relative to how we are domestically outsourcing critical aspects of our government. In his book *Blackwater: The Rise of the World's Most Powerful Mercenary Army*, Jeremy Scahill writes about Blackwater USA, the powerful mercenary force or, as they prefer, "private military contractor," that the Bush administration hired to operate in both the United States and international war zones. With the exodus of the Bush administration, Blackwater USA began a period of transition, starting with a name change to Xe.

Blackwater USA provided security personnel for governments, corporations, and wealthy individuals on a global scale. It has a 7,000-acre training base in North Carolina and a military force of 25,000.[3] With payments of approximately $1.3 billion from 2000 to 2008 by the federal government, this heavily armed force served in New Orleans after Hurricane Katrina and in Iraq and Afghanistan.[4]

The CIA, our own agency, is scrutinized in another book, *Legacy of Ashes: The History of the CIA*, by Tim Weiner. Weiner chronicles the disastrous sixty-year history of America's top covert operations agency. The agency never had much luck placing agents in the Soviet Union or China during the cold war; it did not foresee the Soviet detonation of the atomic bomb in 1949, the invasion of South Korea in 1950, the uprisings in Eastern Europe in the 1950s, the installations of missiles in Cuba in 1962, the Arab-Israeli war in 1973, the Iranian revolution or invasion of Afghanistan in 1979, the end of the cold war in 1991, or Iraq's invasion of Kuwait in 1990. It underestimated Fidel Castro in the disastrous US-sponsored Bay of Pigs invasion, and it incorrectly determined that Iraq had weapons of mass destruction in 2002 and 2003. Unfortunately, this is not the complete list of errors and outright blunders Weiner credits to the CIA. After September 11, 2001, Weiner stated that the outsourcing of the agency went out of control. According to Weiner, "Great chunks of the clandestine service became wholly dependent on contractors who looked like they were in the CIA's chain of command, but who worked for their corporate masters."[5]

Like the military, the CIA developed two workforces. As with the military, one workforce is paid substantially better and answers to masters not elected by the people. Both the CIA and military private workforces depend heavily on recruiting the best, most highly trained personnel from their government-sponsored counterparts. Could there be two more vital organizations to the nation's international security than our military and the CIA? The Office of the Director of National Intelligence (ODNI), in May 2007, stated that 70 percent of the intelligence budget went to contractors.[6]

According to Weiner, corporate clones of the CIA have sprung up all over the suburbs of Washington and beyond. During the Bush administration, it is estimated that it became a $50-billion-a-year business, or about the size of the entire American intelligence budget.[7] President Bush spent millions of public dollars building a parallel private army. Much of this income stream was based on high-value, no-bid contracts. Scahill estimated these contracts at more than half a billion dollars.[8] Businesses employ outsourcing to decrease personnel and overhead, and in general to cut costs and improve efficiency. In this period of unparalleled government outsourcing, if we consider the national debt (figure 4, on page 182) and the growth in government employment (figure 2, on page 138), it would appear that something is amiss. Somehow, when the federal government outsources, cost and employment continue to rise rapidly.

Even if we discount the cost of outsourcing our security services, should we be concerned about disseminating our nation's secrets to hundreds of consultants? In this information age, how secure are the nation's outsourcing partners? In recent years, the United States government and its growing numbers of defense contractors have been the victims of a rapidly increasing rash of cyber attacks. Attacks on military networks and on private contractors have been rising. General William T. Lord, commander of the Air Force Cyber Command, has said, "You don't need an Army or Navy, or an Air Force. . . . You can be a peer force for the price of the P.C. on my desk."[9] General James Cartwright, vice chairman of the Joint Chiefs of Staff, contended in 2007 that China was carrying out widespread "reconnaissance" of US networks.[10]

Military and intelligence community experts agree that the People's

Republic of China is the United States' biggest cyber menace. China disputes the spying allegations made against it, claiming that its military position is purely defensive. On July 4, 2009, there were attacks on South Korean and American government Web sites simultaneously, overwhelming computers with fake requests sent from infected computers. In the United States, the targets were the Treasury, the Department of Transportation, and the Secret Service. In this case, North Korea was blamed by many. A good cyber spy has the potential to steal considerably more military and technology secrets than a human spy.

Allen Peller, of the security research organization SANS Institute, said hackers are breaking into military and government computers by exploiting the side doors of private contractor networks that are connected.[11] National Intelligence director Mike McConnell told Congress, "If someone has the ability to enter information systems they can destroy data. And the destroyed data could be something like money supply, electric power distribution, transportation sequencing, and that sort of thing. . . . The federal government is not well-protected and the private sector is not well-protected."[12]

It's not just hacking from outside that scares security experts; it's also the fact that many government contractors do not vet employees in the same way that the government does. These same contractors are also accused of hiding employees breaches in security by quietly firing the employee and allowing them to go to another government contractor.[13]

A 2006 Chinese military white paper claims that they are aggressively improving their information warfare capabilities, with the goal of being "capable of winning informationized wars" by the mid-twenty-first century. Can we expect full disclosure from our outsourcing partners if their computers are hacked, or will they conceal such incursions for fear of losing lucrative government contracts?

When private businesses control critical elements of our national security with private armies and intelligence-gathering organizations, we must ask at what point profit from them comes before the American people. This is not to imply that the outsourced consultants are not patriotic Americans. It should not be surprising, however, that corporate motivations are different than those of government. A corporation's first responsibility, like government, is to stay in business, and that is accomplished by making a profit. Governments also must stay in business, but their profit is not viewed in terms of dollars, but rather in the security and well-being of their citizens.

There is a world of difference between a mercenary army and the United States military. We have the undisputed finest military force in the world. This military is controlled by the president and Congress of the United States. But a mercenary force is not subject to the checks and balances of our federal government, both conservative and liberal, nor is it subject to the structure of the United States military chain of command and the Uniform Code of Military Justice. How will the American people's safety be ensured if special interests or foreign governments can rent a US-based intelligence service or army? What human rights guarantees will they follow? What happens if a vendor decides that it makes good business sense to offshore aspects of an intelligence-gathering contract or decides it is cheaper and more profitable to hire all foreign mercenaries to beef up its military force?

An important aspect of this outsourcing is the message it sends not only to the American public, but to our intelligence service and our military. Perhaps the CIA has not had a stellar record, but outsourcing its functions is not the answer to the problem.

As a nation that wants to have a strong all-volunteer military, we are engaging in counterproductive practices. How do you encourage young military personnel who are considering having a family and staying in the military when they see their peers with families forced to use food stamps? They see that we have the money to pay mercenaries considerably more than they earn, but we do not pay our own soldiers enough to feed their families. Some members of Congress have argued that a reduction in the tax rate for the military would open the door for all government employees to demand the same. It would appear that we have no difficulty recruiting bureaucrats and paying them more than private sector workers (see chapter 8), but we seem to have considerable difficulty recruiting people who are asked to put their lives in danger for their country.

While we have not done a very good job of taking care of our troops' families, we have done a disgraceful job taking care of our wounded service members. In February 2007, the *Washington Post* broke a story about the conditions in which our wounded troops were being treated at the nation's leading military hospital—Walter Reed, in Washington, DC. After five and a half years of treating wounded troops involved in combat in Iraq and Afghanistan, the hospital was severely overtaxed, and our wounded were receiving less than the care a grateful nation should have provided.[14] As is customary, it took the press to motivate congressional and executive action to rectify the problem. Most despicable was that some members of Congress admitted to having been informed of the problem as early as 2004, but they did not hold hearings for fear that it would embarrass the army.[15]

Perhaps our military personnel need a powerful Washington lobbyist devoted solely to improving the standard of living for enlisted personnel and their families. Unfortunately, they do not earn enough to pay for such a lobbyist and must depend on our political leaders and the American public to support their cause. Thus far, our response has been to hire mercenaries.

The fact that we outsource any part of our military or our intelligence service is a testament to the mismanagement of our government, and at worst a result of political corruption. It's not just military and security, but, as we've seen, Congress has opted to outsource much of its legislative function to special-interest lobbyists. These lobbyists not only use legislators to introduce bills but also draft them and push other legislators to vote for their bills.

THE FREE AMERICAN PRESS OF INDIA

Myth Number 21: If there is one thing we can count on, it's that the American press will always be there to protect us. Are we Americans in the process of witnessing the erosion of our primary source of information—information vital to our democracy? During the American Revolution, our leaders identified a free press as a critical element of liberty. The First Amendment of the United States Constitution restricts Congress from abridging the freedom of the press, along with freedom of speech. Thomas Jefferson recognized that a free press was essential to the education and national security of the American people. In his second inaugural address, he made it clear that a government that could not withstand the criticism of the press did not deserve to remain in power. Jefferson said, "No experiment can be more interesting than that we are now trying, and which we trust will end in establishing the fact, that man may be governed by reason and truth. Our first object should therefore be, to leave open to him all avenues of the truth."

But even industries that aren't dependent on global competition and markets, such as news organizations, are offshoring American jobs. "Whether you're at a desk in Pasadena or a desk in Mumbai, you're still a phone call or e-mail away from an interview," said James Macpherson, the editor of PasadenaNow.com, when asked if he could outsource local political reporting to India. Macpherson said he hired two well-trained Indian reporters for a total of $20,800.[16]

Reuters, one of the world's largest news agencies, started offshoring in 2004, hiring six Indian reporters to cover United States financial markets; by the beginning of 2007, Reuters had fifteen hundred employees in India, including their IT database. Reuters claims its Indian journalists are as well trained, if not better trained, than US journalists. In 2004, David Schlesinger, Reuters global managing editor based in New York, said, "Technically, it isn't outsourcing, which involves handing off work to another company."[17] I love it when members of the press start talking like politicians.

Most reporters rank right up there with teachers, social workers, police, firefighters, and our military when you consider how little they are paid compared to the value they add to our society. The median salary for newspaper reporters nationwide is about $43,000.[18] Obviously, they are not in it for the money.

However, if you can hire a reporter for about $58,000 per year in New York, or two reporters in India for $20,800, with training comparable to that of the New York reporter, it's not hard to believe we will see a shift in how news is covered in the United States. Reuters admits costs are 60 percent less in Bangalore than in its New York, British, or Singapore centers.[19] Other wire services and newspapers have been beating a path to Bangalore. The World Association of Newspapers says the trend in offshoring is gathering strength.

Why couldn't Indian journalists, in addition to reporting on financial markets, also cover transportation, real estate, or labor, or critique our politics, books, television shows, and movies? How will this influence how Americans think? Will our culture change? In ten years, will we be watching a television show in which movie critics in Mumbai, India, give two thumbs up to *Pirates of the Caribbean VII*?

There are significant advantages to keeping journalists based within the United States. For example, after a June 4, 2006, NBC News *Dateline* broadcast titled "Inside the World of Counterfeit Drugs," the FDA announced new rules to require prescription medicine to be tracked every time it changes hands from the factory to the pharmacy. Pharmaceuticals, including Viagra, birth control pills, and even Tamiflu, have been flowing into the United States from counterfeiters in China and other offshore locations. Sold in major chain drugstores, these fake drugs are almost impossible to detect. Smuggled into the United States, they are bought and sold by a series of drug wholesalers before being sold to legitimate pharmacies. The journalist at NBC News found that Chinese counterfeiters, Russian organized crime, and Mexican and Colombian drug cartels were behind this extremely lucrative business.[20] By late 2008, the US Food and Drug Administration had seized eleven lots of the blood-thinning drug heparin, which has been linked to chemical contamination from faulty processing in China. Also at about the same time, 1.6 million cribs made in China, Indonesia, and Taiwan were recalled after two babies died.

The *Chicago Tribune* reported that after thirty years of federal regulations, the government is still unable to stop the flood of children's toys entering the United States with lead in them. The federal watchdog charged with ensuring these toys are stopped is overwhelmed, understaffed, and often ineffective.[21]

If our news was coming from journalists located offshore, would we have the same protection that the American press has provided us for over two centuries? Would reporters in India and China have uncovered and reported the counterfeit drug problem or exposed the Chinese-made children's toys painted with a lead-based paint, the tainted pet food, the toxic toothpaste, and the faulty tires? Would they pursue these issues with the same dogged efforts? Would their government allow them to break the news if it were companies in their country exporting the fake drugs or dangerous toys?

Reporters without Borders (RWB) annually ranks countries in terms of freedom of the press. The United States is far from perfect, ranking 27 in 2009, while India, a likely source for future reporters, was ranked 105 of 175 countries.[22] In India, the constitution provides for "The right to freedom of speech and expression" without any mention of the press. This freedom is subject to restriction for reasons of "sovereignty and integrity of India, the security of the state, friendly relations with foreign states, public order, preserving decency, preserving morality . . ." India has used its Official Secrets Act and Prevention of Terrorism Act to limit press freedom.[23]

Democracy is held back by censorship of the press, as is evidenced by the suppression of the press in China. The Constitution of the People's Republic of China, chapter II, article 35, states: "Citizens of the People's Republic of China enjoy freedom of speech, of the press, of assembly, of association, of procession and of demonstration."[24] While the Chinese people may have a constitutional right to a free press, in practice the Communist Party oversees all reporting to ensure it is favorable to its regime. The way the party regulates the press, while not giving the appearance of violating the Constitution, is by narrowly defining the harm done under its Protection of State Secrets law. This law allows the government to designate as spying anything the government deems a secret. The penalty for spying can carry a death sentence.[25] The party decides what the press can report and how it is to be presented. The media must toe the official propaganda line.

Access to e-mail and the World Wide Web has allowed politically disenfranchised groups to communicate more freely. The Chinese government continues to regulate anything other than e-commerce on the Internet. Assisted by US companies, China has developed what is commonly referred to as the "Great Chinese firewall." This state-managed Internet-filtering system has been very effective in insulating the Chinese people from any news or protests that the government deems to be harmful to the government.[26] In January 2010, Google announced that it would stop censoring its China-based search engine. Alleged attacks by hackers in China on its Gmail service and increased restriction on free speech on the Internet were reasons given by the company that may cause them to pull out of China, Google said. A primary goal of the hackers was to gain access to Chinese human rights activists' Gmail.[27]

Americans hold as sacred a free, unbiased press dedicated to protecting the American people. People around the world envy the American press, its ability to report on everything—its ability to investigate and expose political and corporate corruption. Perhaps in twenty years, all news about the United States will be gathered and reported by journalists offshore, including television commentary and reporting. In twenty years, who will be safeguarding our interests if we continue to offshore journalism jobs? Will we be able to even call it the American press? In twenty years, will our votes for president be based on political commentary produced by an Indian national writing or broadcasting from Mumbai, India?

Myth Number 22: In many countries of the world the press is censored by political leaders, big business, and the press itself. We are fortunate, as this will never happen in the United States. As long as gathering and reporting news remains big business, whether you receive your news via the Web or a newspaper, publishers will be looking to cut costs, stay competitive, and keep advertisers happy. In her book *Into the Buzzsaw: Leading Journalists Expose the Myth of a Free Press*, editor Kristina Borjession explains the journalist predicament. The "buzzsaw" is what is happening today at major news organizations where stories are killed that may have an adverse impact on ratings or upset advertisers or investors. Borjession relates eighteen firsthand accounts from prominent reporters and television producers from some of the nation's largest news organizations who have had to challenge their organizations in order to get important stories out. These reporters regularly run the risk of destroying their careers if they buck corporate or government powers. Investigative reporting requires time, money, and some risk components that few news organizations are willing to consider, preferring to focus on profitability. We are often fed news that doesn't matter and are being short-changed relative to our rights under the First Amendment's assurance of a "free press." Contrary to what many may want to believe, there is a pervasive censorship in America today often imposed by the media itself.

Television and newspapers have dramatically cut their foreign correspondent staffs, making Americans more ignorant of international trends. Between 2002 and 2006, the number of foreign-based newspaper correspondents was reduced from 188 to 141 (excluding the *Wall Street Journal*, Asian and European editions). Only eight US papers—the *Wall Street Journal*, the *New York Times*, the *Washington Post*, the *Los Angeles Times*, the *Chicago Tribune*, the *Christian Science Monitor*, *USA Today*, and *McClatchy* newspapers—still have foreign correspondents. Approximately 80 percent of the public obtains most of its foreign and national news from TV, but TV's coverage of the world has become increasingly selective and superficial. American TV networks each maintained about fifteen foreign bureaus during the 1980s. By 2007, they had six or fewer. Africa, India, and South America, home to more than two billion people, as of 2007 had no network bureaus.[28]

In a speech at Columbia University in February 2007, one of the nation's most respected former TV news anchors, Walter Cronkite, warned that media companies, under pressure to generate increasing profits, are threatening our nation's values and freedom by leaving people less informed. In today's world, "the need for high-quality reporting is greater than ever," he said. "It's not just the journalist's job at risk here. It's American democracy."[29] If the global recession has done nothing else, it has shown how intertwined our economy has become with the global economy. Our knowledge of the world is not a luxury—it is a necessity for every American.

The blending of the nation's media groups occurs as the number of groups controlling newspapers, magazines, radio, television, books, and movies dropped to six within the last twenty-five years. We must also be concerned not just about where news is being produced, but also about who is hiring journalists, distributing the news, and influencing how to spin that news. With only six major corporations battling over market share and profits, it's not much of a stretch to believe news media executives will rationalize that with a 60 percent reduction in costs, reporting US news from offshore makes a lot more sense and won't compromise quality.

In the twentieth century, there was a great deal of competition between newspapers. Their goal was to be the first to dig up and expose political corruption and incompetence. Democrat or Republican, no politician was safe. Newspaper reporters have, since the inception of the nation, been one of America's first lines of defense, just as the framers of the Constitution planned. Being an investigative journalist was what reporters aspired to, and those who were good were respected by the public and their papers.

While investigative reporters and war correspondents remain at the high end of the news pyramid, there are too many reporters and editors satisfied to take the stories given them by the political spin masters and use them, in many cases, virtually verbatim. The best example, and one of the lowest points in American journalism, was how the press dealt with the Bush administration's justification for going to war with Iraq. For fear of being deemed un-American, the press never really questioned or investigated what the administration's spin-meisters were telling them. There were certainly those in the administration and at the CIA and Pentagon who knew or suspected there was no evidence of weapons of mass destruction, as the United Nations investigators said.

Stephen Colbert, comedian and satirist, described the process of reporting well, saying: "Here's how it works: the president makes decisions. He's the decider. The press secretary announces those decisions, and you people of the press type those decisions down. Make, announce, type. Just put 'em through a spell check and go home." Publishers do not give their editors, and editors do not give their reporters, the time and resources to pursue the truth. Is it any wonder newspapers are losing readership?

Myth Number 23: It will not be a problem when the newspaper industry finally collapses. We will still be just as well informed through the Internet. The recession and resulting slump in advertising, along with more advertisers using the Internet, are devastating the newspapers. Broadcast television news has also been struggling. Democracies cannot function well without news. Our press has often been the first line of defense from corrupt and incompetent politicians. The press has served as the police and, in some cases, as judge and jury for corrupt politicians when the judicial system failed. While powerful and corrupt politicians have been able to manipulate the nation's legal system, they have feared the press above all.

According to the Pew Center surveys, young people are about as well (or as badly) informed today as they were ten years ago. Younger Americans have become more dependent on the Internet for their news. Most of these sites depend on the more traditional news media as their primary source of information. Yahoo! and Google News, for example, are collectors of news from a multitude of sources such as Reuters and the Associated Press. This news can simply be a headline with a link to a newspaper or television Web site where the full story may be available. Inexpensive to operate, these sources are making money by providing advertising space on the pages readers view, much as newspapers do. But the appropriation of free news content from such bastions of journalistic integrity as the *New York Times* is threatening the very economic viability of newspapers. How can they sustain worldwide investigative reporters if their efforts are repeated by numerous sites on the Web? They will need to charge.

The most important question is where and how we will acquire our news if more newspapers fade into the sunset and budgets for television news continue to be cut. With so few sites staffed with reporters seeking original sources, will we be able to rely on the multitude of Internet news sites to gather news? What will happen to these Internet sources as major newspaper newsrooms continue to shrink? Newspaper revenues went from $48.7 billion in 2000 to $34.7 billion in 2008.

Can we rely on the vast assortment of Internet sources not to manipulate the news, thereby making it less reliable? Some of these online sources have their own agendas and operate without any standards, and some are simply the ranting of extremists, both from the left and the right. Many of the mainline news sources have been accused of left or right leaning; however, in most cases they at least attempt to be unbiased in reporting the news, unlike many of the extremist online sites.

A YouGov poll by the *Economist* magazine found that 26 percent of Republicans believe Obama is likely foreign-born. Other claims that he is a closet Nazi or an antichrist are certainly just as absurd, yet the Web is loaded with such claims that appeal to those who are desperate to believe. Considering the vetting process that a presidential candidate is put through by his own party, to say nothing of the opposition's investigation, the absurdity of these accusations is mind-boggling. This kind of absurdity is not limited to the right wing alone. A 2007 Rasmussen Reports poll found that among those not affiliated with either party, 18 percent of Americans believed that President Bush knew of the September 11 attacks in advance. A 2006 Scripps Howard/Ohio University poll found that 12 percent of Americans believed that it was likely that the Pentagon was not struck by an airliner captured by terrorists but instead was hit by a cruise missile fired by the US military. (This would have certainly ranked as the ultimate act of disgruntled employees.) The Internet is loaded with such nonsense.

Greek orator Demosthenes said, "A man is his own easiest dupe, for what he wishes to be true he generally believes to be true." Too many television and radio talk-show hosts encourage their followers to bring up the absurd, and then they act as if these are reasonable issues that people are supposed to believe, which is nothing short of irresponsible shock journalism. It should be no surprise that the Southern Poverty Law Center has found an increase in the number of "Patriot" militia organizations.

We desperately need a free, unbiased, and informed press. Such a press corps is as important to maintaining our freedom as a strong military. The loss of either threatens this nation's future. Successful democracies are dependent on being kept informed. Thomas Jefferson said, "Were it left to me to decide whether we should have a government without newspapers, or newspapers without a government, I should not hesitate a moment to prefer the latter."

CHAPTER 7

DRIVING AMERICAN COMPANIES OFFSHORE
It's More Than Cheap Labor

We contend that for a nation to try and tax itself into prosperity is like a man standing in a bucket and trying to lift himself up by the handle.

—Sir Winston Churchill
1874–1965

RETURNS ON ASSETS—CORE COMPETENCE DEATH SPIRAL

Myth Number 24: If it weren't for the cheap labor, companies wouldn't outsource offshore. There are many forces at play that are responsible for American companies moving offshore. In their book *The Innovator's Solution, Creating and Sustaining Successful Growth*, professors Clayton M. Christensen and Michael E. Raynor describe the powerful pressure investors apply to companies to increase returns on assets (ROA). Companies that assemble component parts to produce products that they sell—such as cars, televisions, cell phones, or computers—often find that they can outsource the production of component parts to another company that can produce the component for less than they can. This not only cuts the cost of the product but also reduces the assets or capital needed to produce that component. In addition, this action has the favorable effect of increasing a company's return on assets or capital employed, thus making the company more attractive to investors.

Christensen and Raynor use an example of a personal computer company under pressure to improve its ROA. The fictitious computer company, TCC, finds that Components Corporation can perform some assembly tasks cheaper, so they outsource to them. Eventually, Components Corporation approaches TCC and suggests that they outsource the entire assembly function, as this is not TCC's core competency. Of course, they can do it for less and improve TCC's ROA by eliminating all of TCC's capital intensive manufacturing.

TCC's revenues remain the same, but return on assets improves, as does its stock price. Components Corporation, through the growth of its manufacturing, improves its profitability due to its efficient use of its manufacturing assets. In time, TCC asks Components Corporation to handle inbound parts and outbound logistics to customers, as this is not really TCC's core competence. Again, TCC's revenues are unaffected, but it disposes of more assets and profits, and stock prices improve.

Finally, Components Corporation suggests that, since they are performing all manufacturing and have all the relationships with the parts vendors who do much of the design work, they should just take over all design and development. Although revenues will not improve, this will further improve ROA, profits, and stock price. After all, TCC's core competency is customer relations, and its real strength is its brand. In time, Components Corporation or an affiliate can produce a new brand with comparable quality at a lower cost.[1]

What Christensen and Raynor have described, without specifically stating it, is to a large extent what we are witnessing relative to offshoring. Customers and brand loyalty can shift quite rapidly, if a new brand can produce a better or even a comparable product for less cost. It's happened in the United States with cars, electronics, and many other consumer products. Today, many American companies, including those that sell toys, tools, and clothing, are nothing more than a brand and a marketing arm for products that are designed and made offshore.

To outsource to other companies within the United States is not as risky as outsourcing to China, for example. With a powerful central government that is striving to gain economic power, the Chinese can bring together all component part manufacturers to create a new brand more readily than would likely happen in the United States. Not only do they have the ability to create the brand, but they also have the financial ability to capture a market, driving out competition by selling at cost or below cost.

American companies using ROA as justification simply cannot divest themselves of components of their businesses that they do not consider core competencies fast enough. These companies do not grasp that the activities being offshored aren't core competencies of the foreign companies, yet the foreign companies accept the business and develop the competency. As Christensen and Raynor state, "Whether or not something is a core competence is not the determining factor of who can skate to where the money will be."[2] US companies and the American people are skating on rapidly thinning ice. While many companies create their own death spiral, federal and state governments also play a significant role in pushing them out onto the thin ice.

Myth Number 25: Labor costs may be lower in other countries, but the United States is still the most profitable place in the world to run a company.

In addition to the pursuit of improved ROA, there are four other principal factors driving the offshore trend. First, an increasing share of work can be digitized or conducted by telephone in places like Bangalore, India, making these locations functionally as close as the office next door. Second, wages in low-cost developing nations are on average 20 percent of US wages. Third, many low-wage, low-cost nations, such as China and India, have developed the infrastructure, educational systems, skilled workforce, and business climate to make themselves attractive to multinational corporations. Fourth, while other nations are making themselves more attractive places to do business, the United States federal and most state governments have either stood still and allowed others to pass them by or, in the worst case, made themselves unattractive places to operate a business.

Neither the Clinton, Bush, nor Obama (as of the time of writing) administration has insisted on a level international playing field. Also, both political parties have been unwilling to provide the international policy support that would be necessary to make companies with operations in the United States more competitive internationally. The recession has become a very convenient excuse for job loss. The fact is that the nation was well on its way to losing jobs critical to our economic growth and prosperity well before the beginning of the recession.

The differential in wages is a primary, but not the only reason US and Western European corporations choose to move their operations to Asia, Latin America, or central and eastern Europe. Yes, some of the governments of these foreign countries have issues with political and economic instability and corruption. In spite of these problems, relocation or offshoring may make better economic sense for some US companies than dealing with governments that tax and regulate virtually all aspects of business. This is especially the case if there is a wide differential in wages and a greater market growth potential offshore.

US TAX CODE—DESIGNED TO BE AVOIDED

The hurdles placed before US businesses take many forms, including the United States corporate tax codes, with all of its marvelous loopholes that favor offshoring. In 1940, individuals and corporations shared the federal tax burden equally. In recent years, corporations account for less than 15 percent of federal income tax revenue, while individuals pay over 85 percent.[3] A 2008 United States Government Accountability Office (GAO) study found that 66.7 percent of American corporations avoided paying taxes between 1998 and 2005.

In January 2009, the GAO released a study that showed of the one hundred largest public United States companies, eighty-three do business in tax-haven hotspots like the Cayman Islands, Bermuda, and the British Virgin Islands. The United States Treasury estimates that it loses $100 billion a year in tax revenue as a result of companies shipping their income offshore. Members of Congress admit that the Internal Revenue Service is outgunned in trying to track down who is crossing the line.[4]

As soon as one year after the start of the Iraq war, a GAO study found that fifty-nine of the nation's one hundred largest publicly traded federal contractors had set up subsidiaries in offshore tax havens. Of the companies studied, they had a total of 464-tax haven subsidiaries, many with no more than a postal box to allow corporations to move profits to the tax haven, thereby avoiding paying taxes in the United States. Senator Byron Dorgan (D-ND) has said, "Some of the biggest corporations in the United States are setting up mechanisms to avoid paying United States taxes, even as they earn millions in contracts paid for by United States taxpayers."[5] The IRS, along with some members of Congress, have attempted with little success to patch the holes in our tax code. With $70 billion per year in offshore tax-avoidance possibilities, there are armies of accountants and tax attorneys eagerly seeking new and more creative methods to poke holes in the IRS dike.

Myth Number 26: The best way to raise needed federal and state tax revenue is to increase taxes on corporations. Ronald Reagan recognized that high marginal tax rates discourage economic growth, savings, and investment, and promote tax avoidance. The Reagan Economic Recovery Tax Act (ERTA) of 1981 provided a 25 percent across-the-board cut in personal marginal tax rates. A marginal tax rate is the highest tax bracket relative to your taxable income. In a graduated taxing system like that of the United States, the marginal tax rate increases as the income rises, and the highest income bracket would have the highest marginal tax rate. By reducing marginal tax rates and improving economic incentives, ERTA increased the flow of resources into production, boosting economic growth. The reduction of high marginal tax rates reduced taxpayers' reliance on tax shelters and tax avoidance, and exposed more income to taxation. The net effect was a marked shift in the tax burden toward the top.

Reagan's Tax Reform Act of 1986 further reduced taxes. The base of the corporate income tax was expanded by eliminating many tax shelters, and the top rate was cut from 46 percent to 34 percent, the largest cut since the tax was started in 1909. The tax shelter industry suffered large but temporary losses. By 1990, the tax code was again riddled with new abusive tax shelters.

Congress should be using the tax codes to encourage companies to do business in the United States rather than providing reasons for them to move offshore. Loopholes do not benefit the American people or our economy and must be eliminated and countered by providing companies significant but targeted tax concessions for the following: (1) new investment in domestic plants and equipment; (2) increases in employment; (3) job training; (4) R&D in the United States; and (5) employee medical benefits. All such benefits would help the American people by providing jobs and would boost United States economic growth.

According to the nonpartisan Tax Foundation, the average combined federal and state corporate tax rate in the United States is 39.3 percent, second among Organisation for Economic Co-operation and

Development (OECD) countries to Japan's combined rate of 39.5 percent. In addition to federal corporate taxes, many states add a state corporate income tax. The national state average is 6.6 percent, but some states are higher, like Iowa, which has the highest corporate tax rate of 12 percent, followed by Pennsylvania's 9.99 percent rate and Minnesota's 9.8 percent rate. Add these rates to the federal rate, and you have rates far in excess of all other OECD countries.[6]

The Tax Foundation points out that when compared with other OECD countries:

- Twenty-four US states have a combined corporate tax rate higher than top-ranked Japan.
- Thirty-two states have a combined corporate tax rate higher than third-ranked Germany.
- Forty-six states have a combined corporate tax rate higher than fourth-ranked Canada.
- All fifty states have a combined corporate tax rate higher than fifth-ranked France.

Even those three states that don't impose a state corporate income tax (Nevada, South Dakota, and Wyoming) still have a higher corporate tax rate than fifth-ranked France and twenty-four other OECD countries because of the 35 percent federal corporate rate. While the burden of state-level taxes is lessened because they can be deducted from federal taxes, they add a second layer of taxes and complexity for multi-state and international businesses.[7] Most states have been intransigent relative to their corporate tax structures as well.

A study of income tax rates in eighty-five countries by the World Bank and Harvard University found a strong effect of corporate tax rates on foreign direct investment (FDI), as well as entrepreneurship. For example, the average rate of FDI as a share of GDP is 3.36 percent. Increase the statutory corporate tax rate by 10 percent, and you can be expected to reduce FDI by nearly two percentage points.[8]

According to the Tax Foundation, many of the countries with the highest corporate taxes, such as the United States, Germany, and France, have lower-than-average corporate collections as a percentage of total collections. Of the thirteen countries with the highest tax rates, nine experience below-average collections.[9] Cutting all US tax loopholes would expand the tax base enough to cut the corporate rate to 27 percent, according to the United States Treasury Department.[10] The key to improving America's business tax competitiveness is lowering the overall business tax burden in the United States, both state and federal. Without this, the United States will continue to fall behind in the global economic battle to keep and grow employment. High corporate tax rates kill business expansion and job growth by diverting resources that could be reinvested.

When taking office, President Ronald Reagan slashed income tax rates and abolished numerous tax shelters and cut the number of tax brackets. These actions pulled the nation out of a deep slump, and we experienced one of our greatest economic boom periods. Federal revenues doubled, and the wealth of the nation increased by $17 trillion, exceeding the national debt by ten times.[11] Under President Bill Clinton, only one modest tax cut bill became law. Budget tightening, due in large part to a reduction of military spending in the immediate post–cold war era and an economic boom, resulted in the first balanced budget since 1969, and therefore Clinton was under no pressure to cut taxes.

Tax cutting was a key policy of the George W. Bush administration. However, during the Bush administration, only one corporate tax bill was signed into law, in October 2004. While there were some important simplifications in the treatment of foreign income by multinationals, the federal corporate rate was not cut, except for certain favored industries. Another shortcoming of the Bush tax cuts was that they weren't permanent. For Bush it was hard to make tax cuts permanent when the federal deficit was rising nonstop. Even most of those Republicans and Democrats who were more fiscally conservative went along, taking advantage of the pork-barrel pig-out that was a major part of the spending.[12]

In May 2009, President Obama revealed his plans to reform the tax code relative to taxing foreign earnings of American companies. He said he would tighten rules on taxation of offshore earnings and the use of tax havens. The rules would make it harder for multinationals to shift income to foreign subsidiaries in low-tax countries and to claim deductions on taxes paid offshore.

Under strong multinational corporate pressure, the Obama administration backed off of its effort to garner the $160 billion estimated to have come from taxing multinationals' overseas profits. Many US multinationals pay far less than the statutory rate of 35 percent, with some paying in the high teens.[13] While the proposed improvements are needed, it has been argued that the changes would make American companies less competitive and induce companies to move their headquarters offshore. Frankly, if they are not paying taxes in the United States, and their employees are offshore, the loss may not even be noticed. A simpler and better approach would be to cut the tax dodges but also lower corporate tax rates substantially, as has been previously suggested.

During Barack Obama's campaign, he pledged to close these offshore business tax loopholes. Obama has stated that his tax plan would deliver broad-based tax relief to middle-class families and cut taxes for small businesses and companies that create jobs, while restoring fairness to our tax code. He has also indicated that his plan to lower the rate on corporate taxes was possible if the many loopholes in the tax code were closed. He recognized that the tax rate "on the books" was high in the United States and stated that, "in practice, depending on who it is—what kind of accountant you can hire—they're not so high. That's an area we can work on." For businesses, the tax cuts would include breaks for small employers and a "new jobs credit." At the time of writing, President Obama has not signed any bill that would reduce corporate taxes.

Eliminating the tax loopholes would certainly help the nation generate much-needed revenue. This must be done in conjunction with a lowering of the corporate tax rate to 25 percent or 26 percent, which would stimulate job growth. Contrary to what some politicians may believe, this is not a zero-sum game. It is important to note that in terms of jobs, the tax reduction would stimulate US long-term job growth for those companies whose labor forces, current and future, are primarily here in the United States. This, in turn, would stimulate economic growth and tax revenue, which would have the potential (barring increased spending) to reduce the deficit. If profits generated in the United States were treated with preference (lower rate), we would likely have more multinationals looking at the United States as a place in which to locate new operations and expand existing facilities, and thus increase jobs.

How can we expect to keep our existing employers, much less attract new employers or expect companies to choose the United States for expansion of existing facilities, when we tax them more than any other nation besides Japan? Other nations understand this most basic economic concept and have taken the necessary steps to be more competitive.

Closing all the loopholes alone would not stop offshoring, though it would likely have a dampening effect. Our current corporate tax code, with all of its loopholes, punishes not only the individual American taxpayer but also companies that remain in the United States and cannot afford legions of accountants, tax attorneys, and lobbyists. These companies and the American public must make up for the lost taxes of those companies that are going untaxed as a result of the offshore loopholes. Making the United States a better, more friendly place to conduct business will not come from a single, silver-bullet solution but from a combination of many factors. Simply eliminating existing offshore loopholes, without a commensurate decrease in corporate tax rates and the implementation of other pro-business actions to encourage domestic growth, would be counterproductive. Thus far, Congress has not been able to muster the votes needed to stand up to the lobbyists who fight to preserve the loopholes. Without a corresponding reduction in the tax rate, lobbyists and their clients have little choice if they are to be competitive in the global market of the twenty-first century.

In addition to corporate tax rates, capital gains taxes stifle economic growth and with it job growth. A capital gain is the difference between what you paid for an investment and what you received when you sold that investment, which is then taxed. Capital is essential to fuel the investment necessary to maintain and grow a healthy economy. When the reward for risking capital is not great enough, capital is not invested. A major part of evaluating the risk/reward scenario for an investment is the tax repercussions of the investment. Capital gains taxes lower the return on an investment and increase the cost to acquire capital. They also slow the movement of capital through what is called a "lock-in," when investors hold off selling an asset to avoid paying the tax. Wealth that is locked in is not working for the nation where, it is needed most. Economists estimate that trillions of dollars in equity are locked into assets because investors refuse to pay a high tax on their profits.[14] To help the flow of capital, in 2003 the long-term capital gains rate was reduced to 15 percent and to 5 percent for individuals in the lowest two income tax brackets. These rates were passed with a sunset provision and are effective through 2010, after which they will revert to 20 percent.

A further and permanent capital gains tax reduction or elimination would lower the cost of capital and stimulate investment, help promote economic growth, benefit taxpayers across the income spectrum, and mitigate the unfair effects of taxing inflation-generated gains. The effects would reverberate throughout the entire economy by slowing the downward spiral of wages and living standards and would stimulate job growth. Importantly, the United States' ability to compete globally would be enhanced.[15] IRS data show that, historically, tax revenue paid on capital gains have tended to increase after a reduction in the capital gains tax rate. Conversely, when the tax rate was increased in 1987, revenue began declining.

Those who attempt to reduce the capital gains tax rate face opponents who portray it as a windfall for the rich. Affluent investors would benefit from a capital gains tax reduction, but so would individuals across the income spectrum. During recent decades, the stock market has seen a surge of middle-income investors as corporate pensions have been eliminated or cut. Considering that at least 50 percent of American households own stock directly or through some form of retirement account, capital gains affect most Americans.

Capital gains taxation adversely affects job growth through its impact on entrepreneurial activity and business creation and expansion. Entrepreneurs are directly affected by their ability to raise capital to finance projects. Capital gains taxes dampen potential returns on venture capital, thus restricting the amount of venture capital. Some argue that most venture capital comes from tax-exempt sources, such as pension funds and foreign investors. At the earliest and most critical stages of most business ventures, private individuals invest more funds than any single source.[16] Formal venture capital becomes more important during later stages of development. A study by Coopers & Lybrand concluded: "Creating new jobs—especially in young technology companies—requires risk capital. . . . The risk capital invested in technology companies is provided primarily by investors subject to capital gains taxation. [Furthermore,] risk capital investors seek capital gains, not dividends."[17]

While broad tax reform is needed to address the deficiencies of the existing tax code, reducing or eliminating the capital gains tax rate would be a very effective and quick way to enact an immediate and efficient way to improve the economy for a wide range of Americans and create meaningful jobs. A capital gains tax reduction would benefit the government as well as taxpayers in all income brackets. The permanent elimination of the capital gains tax would have these benefits plus the benefit of reducing the tremendous cost of compliance (e.g., cost of IRS for collection, accountants, and attorneys) by the government and taxpayer. The Office of Management and Budget has estimated that the cost of all tax compliance for the nation is over $200 billion per year.

CHOKING ON RED TAPE AND LITIGATION

Taxes aren't the only problem inhibiting US economic development; regulation is another complex issue. Regulation can be an effective tool that benefits the public as well as industry. Too little regulation, and we experience a situation like the meltdown of the housing market and subsequent collapse of the financial industry in 2007 and 2008. Overregulate, and we strangle industry and kill job growth.

We tend to overregulate some industries and underregulate others. Generally, smaller industries with the least political clout and funds tend not to hire experts and lobbyists to help circumvent regulations, and therefore tend to be stifled. Those industries that can afford to influence Congress and regulators, and have the funds to circumvent regulations, are the least troubled by regulation.

It is one thing for an industry to be under a regulatory agency, and another for that agency to actually understand and control the industry.

There are five federal regulatory agencies for the banking industry, plus fifty state banking regulatory agencies, and a myriad of other federal and state consumer protection agencies. Add to these federal regulators for the securities and derivatives industries and one for government-sponsored mortgage agencies. On top of all this, add US congressional oversight of the Federal Reserve. With all this federal and state regulation and regulators, there should have been ample protection for the public. At the state level alone, there were thousands of state-regulated loan brokers and finance companies responsible for a large share of the toxic mortgages and other overly aggressive loan practices that contributed to creating and bursting the housing bubble. I have no idea how much these layers of regulators have cost the nation over the years they were supposed to be protecting the public, but whatever it was, it was too much.

In spite of the number of federal and state agencies, they all failed to foresee the industry's collapse, or if they did see it, they were ineffective in preventing it. It would appear that we do not need more regulatory agencies but rather better regulations and regulators. Crisis generally fosters a demand for more government control. This is problematic if government, as we've seen, is in large part responsible for the crisis. The financial panic of 1907 resulted in the creation of the Federal Reserve. The Great Depression resulted in the creation of the Securities and Exchange Commission, the Federal Deposit Insurance Corporation, the Federal National Mortgage Association, Social Security, and unemployment insurance.

Even the most adamant free-market advocates must admit that the system often needs controls placed on it. The problem is that each element of the system believes it can regulate itself. In recent years, thanks to a constant whittling away of existing regulation and absent or fragmented oversight, the system went out of control. There is no question that the financial industry, like the environment and healthcare industries, needs close monitoring and control. The fly in the ointment comes when Congress is left to structure the legislation. Each special-interest group, *through its lobbyists*, can destroy the best-intentioned legislation. With all new legislation comes a new pool of favors to be given out by Congress to lobbyists and, as is the custom in Washington, the reciprocating of favors to be garnered.

Our effort to regulate the financial industry has been an utter failure. On the other hand, we have performed so thoroughly with other industries that we are strangling growth and job creation. Dealing with the Occupational Safety and Health Administration (OSHA), the Internal Revenue Service (IRS), the Equal Employment Opportunity Commission (EEOC), the Environmental Protection Agency (EPA), and predatory tort laws has played a role in driving employers offshore. At the local level, permitting-review and permitting-approval periods that should take days or weeks can in many states take months or sometimes years. Exceptionally high permitting fees, tap-on fees, and development fees, together with the world's highest litigation rate, do not make for a pro-business environment.

US-based companies are among the most highly regulated in the world, with regulations imposed at the federal, state, and local levels, often with duplication. Over the years, these regulations have been enforced by ever-growing federal and state bureaucracies, with companies being forced to hire armies of accountants, lawyers, safety engineers, environmental engineers, benefit analysts, compensation analysts, and a wide range of other experts to interpret and implement the requirements. For even a small business, just trying to determine what to pay in federal, state, and local taxes can be a Herculean feat. The United States Constitution that has served this nation well for over two hundred years contains five thousand words; the Holy Bible has fewer than eight hundred thousand words. The United States tax code is nine million words.[18] It is perhaps one of the most confusing documents ever written. We have endless court cases over how to interpret it. It is so confusing for small businesses that they do not take advantage of their lawful deductions. The federal Office of Advocacy issued a 2005 report that estimated the cost of federal regulations on employers at $1.1 trillion. The annual average cost of federal regulation was $5,282 per employee for firms with five hundred or more workers, and a staggering $7,647 per employee for firms with fewer than twenty workers.[19]

Since the 1930s, various administrations have attempted to address this issue with little success. In addition to the federal agencies, regulations, and paperwork, there are numerous layers added at the state and local levels. Are all of these regulations bad? Government regulation has its benefits: protecting the environment, making consumers more confident in the quality and safety of our products and services, and making investors more confident in the integrity of our stock market. The issue is that they are unnecessarily complex and difficult and costly for both government and business to administer. We need only look at the growth of government employment (figure 2, on page 138), relative to all other employment, to understand how out of control government and all its laws and regulations have gotten.

Can corporations be trusted to self-regulate? No more than we can expect all Americans not to cheat on their taxes. Most executives manage with a high moral standard and a strong sense of fairness. This cannot be said for all executives, as has been illustrated in the press in recent years. The housing market and the Wall Street financial industry collapse of 2008 are graphic illustrations of industries unable to regulate themselves. But then the same can be said about many of those who are making the laws and creating and growing federal agencies. The reality is that small businesses that represent a critical and essential part of the nation's workforce and economy cannot afford to pay $7,647 per employee to comply with government requirements. Most of these small companies must make one of two choices: either follow the letter of the law and go into bankruptcy, or say "screw it" and perform in a safe and ethical manner that they can afford while providing their employees with a reasonable income. If our political leaders believe anything else is happening, they are indeed in a dreamland.

I have seen large and small companies drop their planned expansion programs because of the months, and sometimes years, it may take to apply for and receive federal and/or state permits. I have negotiated with many state and local governments relative to cutting the time periods for reviewing environmental and construction permits. When necessary, clients have selected states and communities that understood the importance of time. The issue for many companies is not whether they would qualify for an environmental or other permit, if applied for, but rather the time and effort necessary to acquire it.

Would we be better off spending more money on the enforcement of laws that are broken and eliminating much of the paperwork and bureaucracy? The bottom line is that between our tax policy and our regulatory policy that regulates with such an inept and overwhelming system, we have cost this nation millions of needed jobs and vital economic growth (see chapter 8). Add to this the cost of being the most litigious society in the world, and you can see why companies are running away from America.

If we're not strangling our companies with regulations, we're beating them to death in our courts. The cost of litigation is staggering in terms of individual and class-action lawsuits. No other nation in the world comes even close to the United States when it comes to the amount of litigation or the amounts paid on verdicts.

Litigation in the United States

- The United States spends $250 billion per year in litigation costs, or $838 for every man, woman, and child.
- US litigation costs are equal to 2.7 percent of our gross domestic product.
- Asbestos litigation has resulted in awards of $200 billion to $265 billion, causing seventy companies to go bankrupt and sixty thousand jobs to be lost.
- The National Academy of Sciences reported that the United States has spent more on liability lawsuits than on research and development.

Because juries have been eager to listen to class-action attorneys when it comes to awarding punitive damages and because many companies choose to avoid negative publicity, nine out of ten actions are settled out of court. Whether people have truly been injured, our courts and legal system have allowed for the absurd. In Texas (the asbestos litigation capital), nine doctors claimed in an asbestos-related case that they had diagnosed nine thousand plaintiffs, stating that all nine thousand had asbestos-related illnesses. In many of the courtroom settlements, the majority of the money goes to attorneys and for litigation costs, not to the injured parties, who may receive only 42 percent of the award.[20]

According to the nonpartisan Center for Responsive Politics, during the 2008 election cycle, the number two ranked industry after retired in terms of political contributions was lawyers/law firms, with over $90 million contributed. Obviously, with $250 billion in annual litigation, their dollars were well spent.[21]

Is it any wonder that corporations want to leave the United States? Why stay here when less litigious employees are eager to work in other countries? A class-action lawsuit, whether successful or not, can have a devastating effect on a corporation's survival, its shareholders, and its employees. As long as tort lawyers continue to disproportionately benefit, compared to the awards to their clients, the system of abuse will continue.

Great care must be given to a full understanding and reaction to the issue of tort reform. Like many problems, we can't respond with a knee-jerk action. Tort reformers do not discriminate between attorneys who file frivolous class-action suits and the individual who has been the victim of medical malpractice or a serious accident due to automaker negligence. These tort reform movements and their proposed legislation must be examined with care to ensure that judicial remedies for legitimate victims of accidents, medical malpractice, and product liability are not diminished or lost. At the same time, we must ensure that we don't have a system that wrecks the economy by driving small companies out of business, or driving doctors out of their practices due to frivolous lawsuits or high-cost insurance requirements. Many corporations ask only that the tort reform movement bring some semblance of fairness to the legal system.

CHAPTER 8

THE GREAT AMERICAN JOB PURGE
We're Making Little Effort to Stop It

*Politics is supposed to be the second oldest profession. I
have come to realize that it bears a very close resemblance
to the first.*

—Ronald Reagan
US president, 1981–1989

OFFSHORING OUR WORKFORCE

**Myth Number 27: Offshoring high-paying US jobs will lead to new jobs
by allowing US companies to relocate capital to new US opportunities.**
Surveys of CFOs by *CFO Magazine* in 2004 and 2008 illustrate how corporate America views offshoring. Few CFOs accept the argument of
some economists, or their own lobbyists, that offshoring will lead to new
jobs in the United States. In 2004, only 11 percent of the CFOs surveyed
thought offshoring would lead to a net increase in US jobs, 61 percent
thought it would create a net job loss, and the remaining 28 percent were
unsure or would not comment.[1]

2004 *CFO Magazine* Survey

- Sixty-four percent of those already outsourcing plan to use more
  overseas workers in the next two years.
- Forty-seven percent of survey respondents say most of the jobs
  that moved overseas paid $50,000 or more before being outsourced.
- Negative publicity ranked last on the list of potential outsourcing
  risks.

As Kate O'Sullivan of *CFO Magazine* stated in 2008, "For many
companies, the question is not whether to offshore but which functions
to outsource and when." She went on to say that in 2008, the executives
they surveyed were even less fearful of public backlash than in 2004,

when negative publicity for offshoring ranked last in terms of risks. Growth in offshoring does not appear to be slowed by the fact that 13 percent of those surveyed claimed they failed to achieve any savings when offshoring.[2]

2008 *CFO Magazine* Survey

- Thirty-six percent of all companies surveyed use offshore out-sourcing—double the percentage in 2004.
- Forty-nine percent of companies surveyed with annual revenues of more than $1 billion use offshore outsourcing.
- Fifty-five percent of companies currently offshoring will increase offshore levels over the next two years.
- Of companies currently offshoring, they plan to send the following job functions overseas:

57%	Information Technology	13%	Research and Development
31%	Manufacturing	7%	Human Resources
31%	Financing and Accounting	1%	Legal
17%	Customer Relations/Call Centers		

If only 11 percent of CFOs surveyed believe offshoring will lead to a net increase in US jobs, why have lobbyists for offshoring and free trade told us that offshoring and free trade will stimulate the economy and create more jobs in the United States? (See chapters 12–14.) Their theory is undermined by a simple fact: between the end of the 2001 recession and beginning of the recession (December 2007), we experienced a period of intense offshoring. Corporate profits recovered, but job growth in the critical area of manufacturing decreased, and high-tech and other professions showed little improvement in growth (figure 2).

When offshoring does create new jobs, by its own logic these new jobs will be created overseas, not in the United States. Profits from off-shoring are reinvested offshore, where costs are lowest and where ample talent is located. If I had to bet on whether the lobbyists and their beltway economists or the CFOs are correct, I would put my money on the people actually doing the hiring, rather than the economists' theories or the lobbyists' rationalizations.

The US economy was the greatest job-generating machine in the world. It is now taking longer and longer for the nation's employment to recover from recessions. In the 1970s and 1980s, it took less than twelve months for jobs to bounce back from recession. By the 1991 recession, it took twenty-three months for recovery and thirty-nine months after the dot-com bust of 2001. Simply to keep the unemployment rate from rising, we need 150,000 net new jobs per month.

The United States Department of Labor collects information on workers who were displaced from their jobs after working for their employers for three or more years. If we look at a prerecessionary period from January 2003 through December 2005, of the 3.8 million workers who lost their jobs, 28 percent held manufacturing jobs.[3] The Bureau of Labor Statistics' ten-year projections for job growth indicated that of the ten areas of greatest projected growth, eight are low-paying service jobs, such as retail sales, customer service, food preparation and servers, office clerks, home care aids, nursing aids and orderlies, and janitors.[4]

When I talk about this subject at conferences, parents often ask me what field their college-age children should consider for careers. This is a very tough question, especially when the parents emphasize that their children have no interest in science or math. Some parents are more blunt, like the father who asked, "How do I and my son know that after four years of school and nearly $150,000 in tuition, fees, and living expenses, he won't lose his job to offshoring?"

Myth Number 28: If Americans lose their jobs to offshoring, the government needs only to provide a safety net to protect their healthcare and pension while retraining them for a new, more secure job. High-skilled and technology jobs don't exist in the numbers necessary to accommodate the millions of Americans who have lost their manufacturing jobs. Additionally, many Americans would find it very difficult to qualify for such jobs. According to the United States Education Department, one in seven US adults would not be able to read this paragraph.

How are these Americans to be trained to operate sophisticated manufacturing equipment? The United States government, while spending billions of dollars to shore up its banks and other industries, has the distinction of spending less on training its citizens than almost any other country in the Organisation for Economic Co-operation and Development (thirty high-income, developed countries).[5] Obviously, those who believe we can simply retrain Americans for high-tech jobs need to get out of their offices and closer to the American people.

There are some political leaders at the state level who are working hard to help their unemployed workers. Michigan, one of the hardest hit states in the nation due to its long-term dependency on the automotive industry, has a two-prong approach to building employment. First, it has in place some of the best economic development programs among the Great Lakes states, which as a region tends to be weak. Michigan's programs are designed to encourage the attraction of new employers and the growth of existing companies. Second, Michigan has developed the No Worker Left Behind program that provides Michigan workers with up to $10,000 for two years of training in a high-growth-sector industry. Finding these jobs may not be easy. However, if a trained workforce can be developed for specific promising Michigan industries, it will help to maintain the state's vitality and attract other similar companies. Community colleges within the state have played off of this leadership and are designing training programs around these industries. While there are a very small handful of governors in hard-hit manufacturing states that are making the effort, it amazes me how many simply talk a good talk but take little or no constructive action (see chapter 9).

What many governors say publicly and how they actually run their administrations is most often miles apart. My company specializes in international corporate site selection. We had a project in a state with a governor who talked about having a great economic development program. He gave dramatic speeches about preserving existing jobs and creating new jobs. In his words, his entire administration had made this a top priority.

We were representing a company with a research and development facility located in a major metropolitan area of this governor's state.

This Rust Belt state had lost a large number of jobs in recent years. The company needed to expand its 280-employee operation by approximately 100 scientists and engineers, and this could not be accommodated in its current facility. The company was deciding whether it should offshore all or part of the operation or go to another location in the same metropolitan area. We estimated that, with some assistance from the state, our client didn't need to move offshore. Because this was a retention rather than an attraction (new jobs to state) project, the governor's economic development department was less than enthusiastic. This is common in many states, as retention projects do not play as well to the press as does attracting new jobs.

The CEO and CFO planned to fly in and tour their old facility. They asked if we would join them and bring the state economic development department representatives to discuss the possibility of remaining in the same area. A call was placed immediately to the two state economic development officials assigned to the project. They asked if the CEO and CFO could come to their office. We indicated they did not have time to drive downtown from their suburban facility and then back to the airport, where their plane would be waiting to take them to an appointment in another city. The state officials insisted the meeting be held in their office, admitting that they did not want to drive out to the suburbs for a 3:00 p.m. meeting, as they would get caught in rush-hour traffic coming back. They refused to make the effort. I called the secretary of commerce for the state and left a message about the problem. He didn't call back until after the meeting date, and then he provided a half-hearted apology and assurance that his people would meet with the executives the next time they were in town.

When we explained the situation to our client, the CFO said, "It's clear they're not interested." The CEO said simply, "We don't have time for this. Focus on the other locations." Within twelve months, the operation began to be phased out. Most amazing was that no one from the state ever called to find out what was happening. Keep in mind that the governor of this state was often very vocal in proclaiming publicly that preserving existing jobs and creating new jobs was a top priority. You have to wonder how he staffed his departments that had less priority.

Based on the type of jobs lost, there were at least ten governors I could have called who would have been more than willing to attend such a meeting. If these governors could not make a meeting on such short notice, they would have sent the lieutenant governor or secretary of commerce. In the end, there were 280 families worried about making their mortgage payment, school tuition, and car payments, very likely due to two bureaucrats who did not want to drive in rush-hour traffic, and a governor with an administration that did not really care.

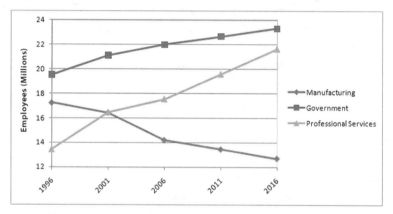

FIGURE 2: United States Employment Select Categories—1996–2016

Source: United States Department of Labor, Bureau of Labor Statistics

Figure 2 provides US Department of Labor projections for the period 2006–2016. In 1950, manufacturing accounted for 33.7 percent of all nonfarm jobs; by 2006 this had dropped to 9.4 percent. The number is projected to drop further, to 7.6 percent, by 2016. While increased productivity accounts for some of these losses, my experience tells me the majority can be attributed to offshoring of jobs.

We must stop thinking of manufacturing as a relic of the industrial revolution. Manufacturing has certainly brought many benefits to America. For many immigrants, it was their stepping-stone to the American Dream. It affects all aspects of an economy. It pays well, especially for the millions of Americans with a high school or less education, as well as those more educated. This industry employs a broad range of skills and has a huge multiplier effect on job growth of all other sectors of an economy. It is an essential element of any broad-based stable economy and is vital to the development of a balance of trade and in paying down the national debt.

Myth Number 29: We may be losing blue-collar manufacturing jobs to offshoring, but we are compensating for this with white-collar service jobs. From 1996 to 2006, professional and business service employment grew by approximately four million jobs, or 11.6 percent of total employment. For the period 2006 to 2016, this category is expected to grow by another four million jobs, accounting for 13 percent of total employment. Considering this is the segment of the labor force that is to take us into the high-technology twenty-first century, it is hardly encouraging that this category will account for an increase of only 1.4 percent over ten years. This category accounts for professionals, scientific and technical services, as well as corporate management.

In order to have a projected increase for professional and business service jobs between 2006 and 2016 of approximately four million jobs, we would have to see a substantial change in the areas of immigration, education, engineering, and scientific development. I frankly don't see this happening and therefore question the projections. Like the loss of blue-collar jobs, white-collar losses have a ripple effect on many segments of the economy. As an example, in terms of commercial real estate, white-collar job losses in the United States to offshoring equate to a fifty-four-million-square-foot negative impact on the nation's office market per year, with a loss of approximately $1.2 billion in rent per year. Pollina Corporate Real Estate estimates that white-collar losses in the United States alone equate to closing a third of downtown Chicago's office space every year, and that approximately eighty-five hundred manufacturing plants close each year in the United States due to offshoring.

GOVERNMENT, UNIONS, AND CARS

Where is job growth occurring? During the period 1996 to 2016, government employment is projected to grow by 3.8 million or over 19 percent (figure 2, on page 138), reaching an all-time high. Government, at all levels, continues to grow no matter what party is in power. Perhaps this is the job growth our political leaders are referring to when they speak of the future of employment growth in the United States. From the beginning of the recession until the beginning of 2010, federal ranks of bureaucrats increased by 9.8 percent, while the private sector shed 7.3 million jobs.

Do we need a government growing more rapidly than other critical components of our workforce, especially considering the size of our national debt? In 2000, all government spending was less than 7 percent of the nation's economic output. By 2010, it will exceed 41 percent.[6] Government leaders must believe that the services of a blotted government are needed. Look at the stellar job five federal regulatory agencies for the banking industry, fifty state banking regulatory agencies, a myriad other federal and state consumer protection agencies, federal regulators for the securities and derivatives industries and for government-sponsored mortgage agencies, plus US congressional oversight of the Federal Reserve were able to achieve relative to the "unforeseen" financial market crash. I would imagine that all of this government oversight cost the American public hundreds of millions of dollars per year, yet home owners are three and a half times more likely to lose their homes to foreclosures than a generation ago, and personal and business bankruptcies continue rising rapidly.

According to prerecession federal statistics, between 1997 and 2007, the population of the United States grew 12.5 percent, while federal employment (including military) actually decreased by 2.3 percent. State and local government employment during this period shot up 15.9 percent. Government workers, state and federal combined, earn about 21 percent more than private-sector workers and are 24 percent more likely to have access to healthcare. While only 21 percent of private-sector workers still have a defined-benefit pension, 84 percent of state and local workers are eligible.[7] It is difficult to justify the rise in state and local employment, given how out of control state and local deficits are (see chapter 9).

While the number of federal employees may not be growing as fast as state and local employees, their incomes are doing exceptionally well. *USA Today* analyzed the Office of Personnel Management's salaries data for federal employees, which excludes the White House, Congress, the postal service, intelligence agencies, and uniformed military personnel. They found that the average federal worker's pay was $71,206 versus $40,331 for the private sector. During the first eighteen months of the recession, the number of federal employees earning over $100,000 increased from 14 percent to 19 percent, before overtime or bonuses. During the same period, the number of employees in the Department of Transportation earning over $170,000 went from 1 to 1,690.[8] The enlisted American soldier does not fare as well as other federal workers, earning approximately $17,364 (private) to $85,152 (sergeant-major at thirty-eight-plus years of service). Of course, if in a combat zone, the soldier receives an additional $2,700 per year. How do the president and Congress justify this discrepancy between a bureaucrat sitting at a desk in Washington, DC, and a soldier fighting in the mountains of Afghanistan?

Lower global wage rates, especially in Asia, have put downward pressure on private-sector wage rates in the United States. The ability to raise wages was one of the key attractions to the union movement. But union membership in the United States has dropped from a high of 35 percent in the mid-1950s to about 7.3 percent in 2009. In the 1950s, most union members were in the manufacturing sector; today, the only area in which unionization continues to grow is in the public sector. This may explain in large part the higher wages for most government employees and low wages for the nonunion military. In 2009, public-sector workers made up over half of all union members.

Government has proven to be a great bastion for the unions. For politicians, whether they be Democrat or Republican, defying the unions can prove perilous to their career. Unlike private-sector jobs, few public-sector jobs can be offshored. The unions have found a near-perfect home in government. The problem is that state and local governments can't afford them (see chapter 9). While state and local politicians face political suicide relative to increasing taxes or service cuts, demands from their workers' unions dry out government coffers. In financially hard-pressed Philadelphia, for example, city workers account for 61 percent of expenditures. Is there a possible parallel between the impact of unions on the big three automakers and that of federal, state, and local government?

Blue-collar workers have been hit the hardest by the recession, suffering about 70 percent of all job losses. Since the Carter administration, blue-collar wages have been stagnant, for men in particular. Family incomes for men in their thirties grew during the period of 1974 to 2004 by an annual average of only 0.3 percent, due to an increase in women entering the workforce and their increase in income.[9] For most families, two incomes have become a necessity.

The blame for the loss of blue-collar jobs and income cannot be laid solely at the feet of politicians and global markets; the workers themselves and their unions must also assume some of the responsibility. An examination of the problems at GM, Ford, or Chrysler will show the role of the United Auto Workers (UAW). These companies, like many in the United States, were hampered in their attempts to improve productivity and flexibility on the factory floor by an extensive set of UAW work rules. The legacy costs (retiree, healthcare, and pensions) demanded by the UAW were one of the anchors around the neck of the American auto industry that added considerably to its inability to stay competitive.

In 2006, Ford Motor Company was paying its Michigan union workers approximately $27 per hour. If you include all benefits, the cost to Ford is closer to $52 per hour.[10] If Ford or GM buys a dashboard from a nonunion suppler in North Carolina, the wage rate drops to $15 to $25 per hour with benefits, depending on skill level. Parts made in Mexico might cost $3 to $5 per hour to produce, and in Asia the price could drop to less than $1 per hour.

President Obama is the most pro-union president since President Carter. Since taking office, Obama has signed orders discouraging contractors with federal contracts from hiring nonunion workers. Heavily unionized areas like manufacturing have suffered the most in the United States. As US manufacturers entered the global economy, they found that wage rates and union restrictions were a significant factor in inhibiting their ability to be competitive. Larger companies with the financial ability simply offshored their workforce to low-cost countries. Other unionized companies, especially small and midsize companies, that lost market share and were not able to compete went out of business due to their higher labor costs.

A Princeton University study that focused on the effect of new unionization on firms' equity value over the 1961–1999 period showed an average union effect on the equity value equivalent to a cost of at least $40,500 per unionized worker.[11] In other words, if President Obama enacts all that the unions would like him to do, union growth will show an initial increase followed by a decrease, as other companies either offshore or close their doors. Unions must become part of the solution, not the problem, as they have been throughout most of the heavily unionized Midwest and Northeast; until this occurs, we will continue to lose jobs to offshoring, and small and midsize businesses will find survival increasingly difficult.

In April 2009, Chrysler entered Chapter 11, and by June GM also filed for Chapter 11. GM employed 234,000 workers, 91,000 in the United States. The company also provided healthcare and other pension benefits to nearly 500,000 retirees. The impact of a GM reduced in size will be very significant on the entire economy and will affect some states more significantly than others. In the United States alone, GM had a network of 11,500 vendors, purchasing $50 billion in parts and services per year.[12]

Health and pension costs that helped bring the industry down are a joint creation of the car company's unions and the federal government. Did militant trade unionism backfire? Were the unions overaggressive or simply naive in believing that they would not ultimately contribute significantly to the fall of the industry and their own workers' futures? By 2007, each Detroit car carried a $1,400 monkey on its back attributable to pension and healthcare costs when compared with foreign car companies selling in the United States. Bucking the union might cause a strike and would hurt short-term financials, so it became easier to make concessions on wages and benefits and let a future management team deal with the ramifications. Had the federal government dealt with the high cost of healthcare earlier, the unions' demands might have been lessened. The United Auto Workers eventually made some concessions when the industry was on the ropes and fading fast. Union concessions were too little, too late to save GM or Chrysler from seeking financial assistance from taxpayers.

Detroit's problems cannot all be attributed to the unions; the auto industry management must share the responsibility. According to an article titled "Detroitosaurus Wrecks" in the June 6, 2009, issue of the *Economist*, "If Detroit had spent less time lobbying for government protection and more on improving its products, it might have fared better." In the 1970s when Japan began to flood the US market with smaller and better-made cars, GM did not respond by matching the challenge. Like many US companies (see the section titled "Steel Industry Tariff" in chapter 14), GM, Chrysler, and Ford sought the simple and quick solution to problems by running to their congressional friends. Rather than countering with better products, their political friends helped in the short run to keep profits up but did nothing to solve the industry's long-term problem. Congress made rules on fuel economy with loopholes for pickups and light trucks, which were exploited to produce high-margin pickups and SUVs that kept the industry relatively healthy and profitable for a while. Had the industry tackled the real problem of producing lower-margin quality cars more efficiently, they would have had a better long-term strategy.

The question is whether reducing labor cost alone would have helped GM, Ford, and Chrysler to be more competitive with their Asian rivals. As long as Toyota and Honda are perceived to lead GM in quality, reliability, and design, a gap will remain. The world also perceives Toyota as having superior processes, management style, and marketing strategy. Within a few decades, GM went from controlling the lion's share of the US market to less than a quarter of the market. Of course, as we saw in early 2010, even an industry leader like Toyota can suffer a major setback (sticking gas pedal) due to a quality or reliability issue. As with the US automotive industry, much can be done to improve this nation's management at home before we can say all of our problems are due to labor, offshoring, and foreign competition.

REVERSING THE LOSS OF JOBS

In February 2009, President Obama said, "I will do whatever it takes to help the small business that can't pay its workers," after signing the American Recovery and Reinvestment Act (ARRA). It has been apparent that banks didn't take a similar pledge. The number of small-business (five hundred employees or fewer) bankruptcies was higher in 2009 than in 2008. Considering that small businesses have traditionally created two-thirds of the nation's net new jobs over the past fifteen years, I find it difficult to understand why only $5 billion (0.5 percent) of the total $787 billion stimulus package was set aside for them. The only assumption I can make is that small businesses just do not have enough lobbying clout in Congress.

Several provisions of the ARRA bill were supposed to help small businesses. Small Business Administration (SBA) guarantees were increased to 90 percent of principal (up from 85 percent), and loan fees were waived for 2009. The act created the SBA's America's Recovery Capital (ARC) loan program, which provided small businesses up to $35,000 over six months, interest-free. If we consider the hassle associated with SBA loans for both the banks and small business, and the small amount available per business, it is not surprising that from June 2009 (funds first available) to November 2009, only $116 million of the ARC's $255 million allocation had been loaned. The program was scheduled to end September 30, 2010.[13]

The SBA's primary programs, the 7(a) and 504, yielded 35 percent fewer bank loans between September 2008 and September 2009 than the same period a year before. Many claimed that the banks were sitting on funding from federal programs in order to boost their balance sheets. At the same time, the SBA was tightening its standards for what qualifies as a reimbursable loan loss. This did not help banks to be more aggressive lenders, as they were increasingly wary of being left holding the bag. Small banks are at a disadvantage to larger lenders, since they must be pre-approved by the SBA, a process that can take months. Small banks, which were often strapped for cash, also were not given the funds for these loans by the government.[14]

The SBA should become a direct lender, provided it can process loans quickly and without an exceptional amount of red tape. The SBA does make direct loans to individuals and businesses affected by national disasters. Congress was able to provide loans for Wall Street quickly and efficiently, why not the small business on Main Street? Perhaps if this had been accomplished in fall 2008, unemployment would not have shot up to double digits by 2010.

In December 2009, one year into the recession, President Obama finally started to direct some serious attention to dropping the unemployment rate, which had hit a twenty-six-year high of 10.2 percent. The president gathered lawmakers, chief executives, and union leaders to the White House for a rather inconclusive jobs summit. At the same time, President Obama also called for a major new burst of federal spending, perhaps $150 billion or more, aiming to reduce unemployment. He proposed new spending for highway and bridge construction, for small-business tax cuts, and for retro-fitting millions of homes to make them more energy-efficient. Extending the economic stimulus programs was also discussed in order to keep unemployment insurance from expiring for millions of out-of-work Americans and to help them keep their health insurance. He proposed $250 apiece in stimulus spending for seniors and veterans and aid to state and local governments to discourage them from laying off teachers and public safety personnel. Obama's package included a new tax cut for small businesses that hire in 2010, and elimination for one year of the capital gains tax on profits from small-business investments. To further support small businesses, he proposed an elimination of fees on loans for them, coupled with federal guarantees of these loans through the end of next year. Small businesses account for two-thirds of the nation's workforce. The administration was pointing to the $200 billion in taxpayer-approved bank bailout funds being paid back faster than expected as a way to pay for his proposal. Republicans claimed that the leftover and repaid TARP money, based on the legislation, must be used exclusively for deficit reduction or additional bank bailouts. Congressional approval would be required for the new spending, and that is where the program got bogged down in Washington gridlock.

Based on the administration's and Congress's lackluster performance in combating unemployment, states and communities must make a greater effort if they ever expect to improve employment opportunities.

For example, loans need not be limited to federal programs. I have negotiated community-based loans for companies tied to job growth and investment in new plants or equipment. Such loans allow for the principal to be forgiven over time (e.g., 10 percent or 20 percent per year) based on net new jobs added and maintained. Another form of assistance is to reduce state corporate income taxes or local real estate taxes based on the number of jobs added above a base amount. Frankly, few states and communities are enlightened enough to see the value of such programs. These programs could last a specific period of time provided jobs were maintained. Enlightened political leaders recognize the impact of the multiplier effect (see chapter 13) and that employed taxpaying citizens will more than make up for any reduction in taxes or loans forgiven (see chapter 7).

In an effort to boost job growth in specific areas, the concept of Economic Development Zones was created. These zones go by many different names across the country, including Enterprise Zones (Virginia), Renaissance Zones (Michigan), Keystone Opportunity Zones (Pennsylvania), and Empowerment Zones (federal government). Essentially, if companies are located within such zones, they receive special tax and other benefits. Zones may provide low-cost or free sites, infrastructure, real estate tax abatements, corporate tax abatements or credits, or job-training assistance above and beyond that available elsewhere in the state.[15] By extending incentives to companies locating in these areas, governments can encourage higher levels of targeted growth where the need is the greatest. There is, however, tremendous variation in the types of benefits provided and the quality and types of locations of these zones. From a corporate perspective, some of these zones are in very undesirable locations, while others are in good locations.

Michigan's Renaissance Zones have virtually all state and local taxes eliminated initially, but they are gradually phased in over the life of the zone. In general, Michigan's zones are among the most straightforward and beneficial for companies. Other states base their zones on job creation grants or tax credits, which link the extension of benefits to the number of jobs created and the pay scale of those jobs. While a great idea for job development, many states and communities are allowing these zones to "sunset" without replacement or extension of term.

When I've asked why more zones are not created in a state with such a program or why some states do not have such programs, I have been told that local political leaders do not want to give up the tax revenue.

This argument makes sense only if you believe companies will move into the area without the zone. If we consider the difficulty keeping small to midsize companies profitable, these zones can make a considerable difference. When the program was first introduced in Michigan in 1996, many communities refused to take part for fear of losing tax revenue from companies moving into the zone during its fifteen-year term. I was always confused by this logic. As a location consultant, I found that communities with economic development zones often had a major advantage in attracting employers. In 1996, Michigan was having a difficult time building its job base, and by 2010 its unemployment rate had reached 15 percent. Had more communities created Renaissance Zones, the unemployment rate would likely have been lower. Today, those communities that refused to create the zones have neither the tax revenue nor the jobs.

The effort to make America more business-friendly must come from all levels of government—federal, state, and local. State governments cannot be expected to compete successfully for jobs on the world market without the federal government's assistance, which is in short supply. Many states are doing such a poor job of creating a pro-business environment that they can't even come close to competing with other states, much less compete globally.[16] The United States Congress, as well as state governments, must streamline the quagmire of regulations and paperwork imposed on businesses, as discussed in chapter 7. Michigan, for example, may have some good economic development programs, but it also suffers from bureaucratic hurdles and slowness, which can create a barrier to its ability to compete for jobs. Federal and state governments must encourage manufacturing growth by offering tax credits or other incentives to those companies willing to invest in technology and training, in order to allow low-skilled workers to produce products at reasonable costs. These tax credits for research and development and training must be made permanent, especially considering the length of time required for training and to invent and develop new commercially viable products. These benefits must be restricted to R&D conducted in the United States using US-based engineers and scientists.

Federal assistance must address plant and equipment financing, job training, and a general increase in employee productivity. Big companies have had little trouble in taking advantage of credit markets, whereas small companies have seen many doors close. Making capital available to small and midsize banks would help make money more available to small to midsize business. Large banks must have incentives to open their doors wider to these smaller businesses.

Not all programs need to be permanent. Some short-term incentives, like "cash for clunkers" or new home buyers' tax incentives, can be used to jump-start hard-pressed industries. Incentives to make homes and businesses more energy-efficient could help both the building materials and construction trades while helping make the country more energy-independent.

Where Federal Assistance Is Essential

- Cooperation between federal, state, and local governments
- Easing of the regulations
- Tax credits or other incentives for companies investing in technology
- Investment in employee training
- Tax credits for companies that hire United States–based engineers and scientists
- Tort reform
- Greater federal funding for scientific research at universities
- Financial aid to students pursuing engineering, math, and science degrees who remain in the United States after graduation
- Assistance to depressed communities for meaningful economic development assistance
- More money for training and paying K–12 teachers

An even more complex problem to solve than the loss of manufacturing jobs is the loss of engineering, programming, accounting, financial services, and other white-collar jobs. These jobs, whether IT, accounting, or financial services, are leaving for good. It is what economists call a structural rather than cyclical change. Even if the white-collar workers are reabsorbed, they are most likely going to be faced with lower wages, just as blue-collar workers have been. So far, there's no new industry being developed to absorb white-collar employees losing their jobs to global competition.

Federal and state governments must develop programs to make our workers more competitive globally and our business climate more attractive. The federal government should do the following: (1) create incentives for human-capital investment, such as job-training programs; (2) shorten the depreciation period for IT and other high-tech equipment; (3) establish better R&D tax credits; (4) increase federal support for broadband (permanent high-speed cable or wireless network) expansion; and (5) provide more federal funding for realistic scientific research. Incentives would help in this effort, such as tax credits for companies that hire US-based engineers and scientists and financial aid to college students who are pursuing engineering and science degrees and who remain in the United States after graduation. Moreover, waivers or reductions of student loan payments for those who stay in the United States or the state where they were educated would encourage students to go into critically needed fields.

To encourage students to enter needed socially beneficial careers such as teaching, social work, the military, and other low-income but critical careers, the federal government should assist in the payment of their student loans and give them income tax breaks. Lower income tax rates would boost disposable income, making these careers more attractive long-term choices. These inducements should be provided during the time that they remain in their respective fields after graduation. Students who opt to be educated in critical fields, such as math and science, should also be given priority in admissions to universities as well as access to financial aid.

The relationship between federal investments in R&D and technological innovation is critically important. The federal government spends over $20 billion per year for agricultural subsidies, while investing only $5 billion in science. The National Research Council report "Funding a Revolution: Government Support for Computing Research" provides evidence that federally supported R&D at industrial companies and educational institutions generate benefits to both workers and communities.[17] This government-sponsored R&D should emphasize basic and applied research in the physical sciences and engineering, and be geared toward generic and enabling technologies, productivity tools, and new and emerging technologies and services that are provided in the United States.

Myth Number 30: It's hopeless. There is no way American manufacturers can be competitive when labor is so cheap in China and Mexico. For many of the industries that have gone offshore to take advantage of low-cost labor, technology exists or can be developed to allow those products to be produced in the United States at competitive costs. Without government support, however, it is simpler to move US manufacturing to low-cost labor in countries like China, Vietnam, or India. Although the United States will not be able to cut labor costs enough to compete internationally in all industries, the use of highly automated plants with a highly trained workforce, both initially subsidized by government, will enable the United States to compete in many industries.

While Americans find it hard to deny themselves the latest technology, one lifeblood of our economy—manufacturing—is often hampered by antiquated plants and equipment. Cutting-edge technology is costly, and the federal government and most state governments have been unwilling to assist our companies with the investment necessary to support industries vital to our economic future.

Federal assistance to depressed communities, in the form of meaningful economic development assistance, is also vital. Much could be done to improve existing economic development programs. Too often, state and local economic development incentive programs are weak, and some are simply fluff legislation with little or no value to business. The majority of states provide considerably less assistance to companies already in their state compared with assistance promised to those considering moving in it. In the past, this lack of assistance has driven many companies to jump from one state to another. Today, these companies are increasingly being driven offshore.

Our nation's strength has come from our middle class, which, during the twentieth century, was anchored by a solid K–12 educational system and manufacturing jobs that provided good wages and benefits. This middle class has been eroded and will continue to erode as our workforce ages and is replaced by less educated immigrants (see chapter 5). Nearly 40 percent of our population growth is due to immigration. Unfortunately for these immigrants, the stepping-stone to the middle class that was provided by manufacturing jobs during most of the last century is rapidly disappearing.

Unions and many political leaders are quick to point the finger at a lack of rights for foreign workers, weak offshore environmental standards, artificially lower currencies, and other factors that they believe result in an unfair and unlevel playing field that brings about the loss of US jobs. Granted, the international playing field is not level. But if politicians were to focus on our internal problems, that would bring unwanted attention to the barriers they have erected that stifle the successful operation of American businesses when trying to compete in a global market. Members of Congress, supported by special-interest lobbyists, often argue for tariffs and other trade policies to restrict imports and overlook the important reasons jobs are going offshore—high wages, costly benefits, litigation, stifling government red tape, high taxes, and antiquated plants and equipment. In addition, a generally negative attitude and a lack of support from the federal government and most state and local governments for employers create a negative business environment.

CHAPTER 9

TAKING RESPONSIBILITY FOR ECONOMIC DEVELOPMENT

Greatness is not where we stand, but in what direction we are moving. We must sail sometimes with the wind and sometimes against it—but sail we must and not drift, nor be at anchor.

—Oliver Wendell Holmes
1809–1894

HELPING THE SMALL AND MIDSIZE COMPANIES

Myth Number 31: Federal and state governments recognize that small to midsize companies are the strength and future of the American economy and are focused on helping them. Unfortunately, the majority of small to midsize companies in America do not have powerful think tanks or lobbyists pushing special trade or tax policies to benefit them specifically, as is true for major US and multinational corporations. Like the middle class, these companies are mostly ignored by policymakers, yet they represent the backbone of the US economy and produce more jobs. For most US manufacturing companies, high-tech companies, and other businesses, the federal government and most state governments don't provide a good environment to conduct business. The big companies can do something about it—the small and midsize companies don't have the teams of international business attorneys and accountants, or the political muscle that comes from highly paid lobbyists.

Small to midsize companies simply do not have the powerful advocates and, as a consequence, many can't survive. When faced with offshore competition or attractive offshore markets, the big companies just move offshore and have their lobbyists create trade and tax policies that enhance their offshore activities.

The United States government does not appear to have a unified international vision of trade or of what is best for the nation as a whole. Without a vision, the nation's economic strength and the well-being of its populace will continue its downward spiral. This is, in large measure, the result of policies favoring special interests as opposed to the national interest. Federal and state economic policy should not be based on the dictates of lobbyists but rather on what is best for the American people as a whole.

Economists, journalists, and politicians will continue to debate the merits and impact of US trade and monetary policies, taxation, education, litigation, and unions. In the end, Americans are still losing jobs— the high-quality jobs necessary to keep food on the tables, maintain self-respect, pay taxes, and educate future generations of Americans.

MOST STATES RECEIVE FAILING GRADES

Myth Number 32: Most governors and state legislators truly understand what it takes to maintain and foster job growth and are aggressively pursuing these efforts. Current economic development trends are not promising for the United States. Federal efforts are very disappointing, as is true for far too many state governments. Our clients increasingly ask us the same question, "If we are to keep our operations in the United States, what states have the most pro-business climates?" In response, my company annually ranks all fifty states based on thirty-three factors, such as taxation, education, infrastructure, professionalism of the state economic development department, and state incentive programs. All thirty-one factors are controlled by state government.[1]

Over the years, I've seen efforts by enlightened state political leaders, only to be disappointed by other states that reverse a prior governor's or legislature's advances. I have seen new governors come into office and, within a few months, decimate excellent state programs and economic development staffs. I saw this happen in a Midwestern state where my company had assisted in the location of many corporate facilities. In this case, we had worked with an economic development person for years. She was highly experienced, exceptionally professional, and responsive, and most important, we and our clients liked and respected her. The new governor decided to replace her and several other excellent staff members with inexperienced political appointees.

Even if they proved to be as good at their jobs as she was, it would take at least eighteen months before they understood what they needed to do to be successful.

On one occasion, a young state economic development representative who was unable to answer any questions about his state's economic development programs told me he had not bothered to learn about them. He indicated that his uncle, a politician in the state, had gotten him the job, which he saw as lasting only another two years. Due to term limits, when the current governor would be replaced, he would be looking for another job.

The professionalism of state economic development departments varies greatly. Incompetence can harm a state's ability to retain and attract jobs. In some cases, the problem can be attributed directly to a lack of training and concern on the part of the economic development staff. In other cases, the staff is not provided the budget or economic development tools and training necessary for success.

Several years ago, we had a client with a manufacturing operation in a rural area of a northern state. The company employed approximately one hundred eighty well-paid workers. Under pressure from offshore competition, the company was considering closing the facility. To stay in business, the company needed to use new, highly energy-efficient equipment that would cut the company's high utility costs. As a user of a considerable amount of energy, it wanted to defray this high cost. The company was located in a severely depressed part of the state, so we expected the state economic development department to make a major effort to save the jobs. We were wrong. When we contacted the state, the representatives said there were no programs available and there was nothing they could do to help. We told them that without assistance, the jobs would be lost. They insisted they could do nothing and made no effort to assist.

After some digging, we found a legislated energy program that would provide a grant to purchase the necessary equipment, provided we could show a specified level of reduction in energy consumption and emissions. The department within the state responsible for the program was eager to make use of it. They indicated that no one had ever used the program because they thought no one had gotten the word out to the companies in the state. This should have been the responsibility of the state economic development department. Predictably, when the project was completed, the state economic development department took full credit in the press for saving the jobs.

In far too many states, economic development efforts can only be described as extremely weak and, in some cases, pathetic. Unfortunately, for many local and county governments across the nation, the lion's share of the burden in terms of expertise and funding falls on them, and not the state. While there are many excellent state and local economic development organizations, many are undertrained, underfunded, and, therefore, unable to foster solid economic development efforts.

Some states annually examine their economic development programs and those of competing states to make sure they have positioned their state to be in the most competitive position possible. Of all fifty states, five have consistently ranked among the nation's top ten probusiness states. Alphabetically they are North Carolina, South Carolina, South Dakota, Virginia, and Wyoming.[2] Unfortunately, after having testified before a number of state legislative groups, it becomes clear that far too many legislators and governors are not well educated when it comes to economic development. Few of these political leaders have a good understanding of the national and international competition at play for the employers currently in their states.

When testifying before state legislatures, I am often representing businesses and economic development groups trying to pass job-growth programs. It is most often very difficult to get political support to approve such programs. A senator in a Plains state, who was a well-known agriculture advocate, once told me that financial incentives for companies were nothing but "corporate welfare." I asked how he justified the fact that farmers in his state had been receiving federal agricultural subsidies for decades, and should that be considered "farm welfare." I also pointed out the fact that substantially more of his constituents were employed in nonagricultural jobs than in farming. He seemed not to recognize that his state was competing for jobs in a global marketplace, and that his state, like others, needed to be more competitive if it were to maintain and increase jobs.

During another situation in which I was testifying, a state senator said that he saw no reason to support the proposed legislation because he did not believe that his state had lost a major employer in many years. Having been warned that this senator often made this point, I came prepared. Looking at the state's six largest employers, I showed that indeed they were all growing, but the growth was occurring either in other, more pro-business states or, as was the case with three of the companies, virtually all of the growth was offshore. The senator and his colleagues seemed surprised to hear this.

In some states, financial incentives are often used as substitutes for the best method for attracting jobs—across-the-board cuts in corporate taxes and the elimination of unnecessary and costly regulations. Since the commencement of the recession, we have never seen so many states that previously had weak economic development programs all of a sudden "see the light." They waited for unemployment to reach staggering proportions (8 percent to 15 percent) before taking action, however.

Waiting for a recession before beginning a serious effort to attract jobs is not ideal. These programs are not inexpensive, if done correctly, but they are an investment that will reap many benefits, both for its citizens' job security and the state's financial security. Unemployed citizens do not generate taxes. Companies that move offshore do not create revenue for a state or community. For example, US companies are in competition with Chinese firms, which receive considerable assistance in the form of financing, protection from imports, and a legal system that favors Chinese-owned companies.

In general, the northern states come off poorly relative to the southeast states that tend to be the most pro-business. Of all the regions of the United States, none has needed help more and none has performed worse than the North. Some of these northern state governments understand that they need to make a major effort to improve their business environment. Still, they accomplish little, while others actually appear to be oblivious to their constituents' plight.

I have had speaking engagements in many northern communities and have spoken to many community and corporate leaders throughout this region. With the exception of some major cities of the region, most people and employers felt that they have been abandoned by their state governments. Corporate leaders are simply responding by expanding outside the region or offshore. Rural communities in particular in the northern states are most troubled; they see their best and brightest young people go off to college never to return, simply because there are no local jobs. In many areas, those who complete high school are also being forced to leave due to a lack of good jobs.

When some states do take action, they sometimes limit their efforts to popular environmentally related programs, while others go beyond that. Some plans proposed early in the recession included: Colorado, expanding by $1.4 million an incentive fund for clean energy jobs; Minnesota, creating a tax-free zone for renewable energy in an effort to create "green jobs"; and Missouri, subsidizing ethanol and biodiesel with $53 million.[3] While these programs would have been admirable in themselves, they would not have been enough. For the person who has lost his job and is concerned about putting food on the family's table, I don't believe he much cares if the job is environmentally related. During periods of rising unemployment, why put restrictions on the type of jobs generated? Programs that are most successful in generating jobs are those that are flexible and can be used by the highest number of employers. That is why these same states early in the recession showed wisdom by proposing other programs as well that would stimulate job growth and would likely have a wider appeal. Colorado proposed the creation of a $5 million fund for banks to open credit lines for small business. The state also proposed tax cuts for employers who created 250 jobs or more. Missouri proposed expanding funding for customized job training by 38 percent and expanding a corporate incentive fund by $20 million. Minnesota proposed cutting business taxes by half over the next six years and exempting small businesses from capital gains taxes.[4]

The InvestNJ Business Grant Program is a limited-term program that offers incentives under two programs. Under the Capital Investment program, eligible businesses may receive up to a 7 percent grant on qualified capital investments, and under the Job Creation program, they may be awarded a $3,000 grant per each new full-time job created and maintained in New Jersey.

Under the leadership of Governor Ted Strickland and Lieutenant

Governor Lee Fisher, Ohio on June 12, 2008, enacted the $1.57 billion Ohio Bipartisan Job Stimulus Package to create new jobs. This dynamic team began to map their strategy immediately upon entering office, recognizing that they needed to improve Ohio's business image. Industry-specific programs include $100 million for Ohio's biomedical industry and $50 million for its bioproducts industry. The Advanced Energy program will be funded with $150 million to expand manufacturing and research and development to transition to new products. This fund will retool production lines and retrain workers.

The sum of one hundred million dollars is set aside for Ohio's Logistics and Distribution Infrastructure program to expand connections to logistics and intermodal centers, improve the flow of freight, and increase access to new markets. Loans will be made available for eligible transportation, logistics, and infrastructure projects. This program has some very difficult nuances that limit its use, including being subject to Ohio's prevailing wage law that requires payment of prevailing wage rates for all project-related construction activities.[5]

Of the five states identified above, Missouri and Ohio had made serious efforts well before the onset of the recession to stimulate job growth, while Colorado, Minnesota, and New Jersey are latecomers to creating serious stimulus incentives to generate jobs. As the Chinese proverb states, "The superior doctor prevents sickness; the mediocre doctor attends to impending sickness; the inferior doctor treats actual sickness."

In 2008, California, a state that has a very weak business-friendly reputation, told twenty thousand of its teachers that they might be out of work due to budgetary concerns. In Vermont, there was concern that people whose health insurance was subsidized by the state may face higher fees or be cut from the program. Also in 2008, the governors of Maine and Massachusetts were seeking to legalize gambling in order to raise revenue, as many other states have been forced to do.[6] Vermont, Maine, and Massachusetts also do not have positive national or international reputations for being very pro-business.[7]

California's economy, the eighth-largest in the world, is at best stalled, and at worst is in a prolonged tailspin. In 2008, the Golden State was the scene of approximately two hundred fifty thousand property foreclosures, and it also led the nation with nearly four hundred fifty thousand initial unemployment claims—roughly the combined total of the next four worst states (Michigan, Ohio, Pennsylvania, and Illinois).[8] California's unemployment rate more than doubled from 5.9 percent in January 2008 to 12.5 percent in October 2009.[9] By January 2009, Governor Arnold Schwarzenegger and state officials halted more than $30 billion owed to taxpayers as tax refunds, indicating that they may have to resort to issuing IOUs. The governor and California's legislative leaders struggled with a budget deficit estimated at $42 billion through June 2010.

The state has shown little fiscal restraint over the past decade, with spending soaring 134 percent. Some may argue that California's economy is a victim of circumstances beyond its control. With the end of the cold war and the subsequent drop in federal defense spending, southern California's devastated aerospace industry led the state into its worst recession since the Great Depression. This was followed by the bursting of the dot-com bubble, followed by the bursting of the housing bubble. During the housing bubble, 50 percent of all new jobs in California were in related fields, such as real estate, mortgage brokerage, and construction.[10] After each disaster, California has done a dismal job of diversifying and restructuring its economy. With competition from Asia, Silicon Valley is not likely to experience the type of growth it once had. And Hollywood and Silicon Valley do not hold much hope to produce the number and type of jobs middle-class Californians need.

The state also has the distinction of consistently ranking as one of the most difficult places in which to conduct business, according to the *Pollina Corporate Top 10 Pro-Business States* report.[11] In 2009, the independent Tax Foundation ranked California as forty-fifth for its Corporate Tax Index, forty-ninth for its Individual Tax Index, and forty-third for its Sales Tax Index.[12] The state has, for many years, been generally considered to have made one of the nation's worst economic development efforts. Other states in the region view California as the easiest place to poach employers. California is an excellent example of a state with many assets that has burdened itself with lowering tax revenues and rapidly rising unemployment.

There are some bright economic development lights in California at the community or regional level, such as the City of Victorville Economic Development Department and the Central California Economic Development Corporation. These efforts have been carried on for decades and have had many successes, in spite of a historical lack of state support.

The federal stimulus package pumped $135 billion into state budgets, most of which will be spent by the end of 2010. Unless more federal funds are given or state economies skyrocket, total budget gaps for states through 2011 are expected to exceed $350 billion. The federal economic recovery act closed roughly 40 percent of state budget shortfalls. In 2009, twenty-five states raised taxes, realizing that the budget holes were too big to be filled by cuts alone.[13] Such tax increases will not help foster job growth and will likely perpetuate unemployment and lower tax revenues (see chapter 7).

Some states fared better than others during the recession, such as Louisiana, which has fared better than most, despite the August 2005 effects of Hurricane Katrina on New Orleans. High oil prices helped keep unemployment down and the state's finances strong, which, in turn, helped the state's budget situation. The state has a very small financial sector that helped it survive the Wall Street/banking crash. Louisiana has managed to hold its unemployment well below the national average. If the state can deal effectively with its two biggest problems—a long-standing reputation for political corruption and a weak public educational system—it is positioned to continue on a rapid ascent. The state has put into place a new workforce development program called FastStart, has done away with some taxes, including its sales tax on manufacturing equipment, and is dedicated to resisting any new taxes. Louisiana is an example of a state in which the governor and legislators "get it" and are making an effort.

Even when offering assistance to save jobs, many states still don't get it. Several states have a bizarre policy in which a company planning to relocate within the state can be disqualified from receiving any financial incentives offered by the state or another community unless the mayor of the original community gives her approval. We had a manufacturing client (who had 250 employees) with a facility it had outgrown in a Western Plains state. The client needed to double production by adding another 120 employees. The site was landlocked, so we were engaged in finding another location and negotiating state and local incentives.

The client was under some pressure to relocate to Mexico by several of its largest customers. With state and local assistance, the numbers were marginally in favor of staying in the United States. The key to staying in the United States was the ability to receive financial assistance and maintain the same labor force. Since there was no facility in town that came close to meeting the requirements, we warned the company of the state's policy requiring approval of the mayor of the town in which the old facility was located. About fifteen miles away was a facility that would be ideal. We also found existing facilities in Mexico and in an adjacent state that met their criteria. Fulfillment of new contract commitments required that they take one of these existing facilities.

The company's first choice was to move to the facility in the next town, thus maintaining virtually the entire workforce. With such a long and successful relationship with the community, the company decided to approach the mayor for his approval so it could receive the incentives offered by the state and the other community. The mayor flatly refused to approve, stating that the company would have to build a new plant in his town and its customers would have to understand. An appeal to the governor was fruitless, as this was his policy too, and he indicated that he did it to discourage companies from moving just to get tax and other state concessions. Frankly, the incentives offered by this state were nominal, and I could not imagine any company relocating solely to gain such incentives.

Through our negotiations, we were able to improve the incentive programs offered by the other state and community. The state and community in Mexico also provided an attractive financial incentive package. The company decided that if it had to move and retrain a new labor force, it would be better off moving the operation to Mexico. In the end, nearly all the 250 employees lost their jobs, and, as is customary, the company never gave the press the real reason for the relocation. I wish I could say that this example is the only one I could cite about political leaders who just don't get it, but that decidedly is not the case.

HOLDING CORPORATIONS AND POLITICIANS RESPONSIBLE

Today, corporate America, especially the nation's largest corporations, are so dependent on the global marketplace that the demands of production costs and markets have taken precedence over concerns of keeping jobs in the United States. If these companies are to survive, they must tie their future to the global market.

Myth Number 33: The federal government and major US global corporations can be counted on to safeguard our economy and American jobs. While it may sound harsh, it's not the responsibility of US corporations to safeguard the US economy or US jobs. To try to shift this responsibility from US political leadership to US corporations is simply not going to have any effect. Today, most US-based corporations are increasingly dependent on foreign customers and markets, and they are increasingly fearful of foreign competitors. To be competitive and to survive in a global market, they must continue to strive for higher productivity, lower costs, and larger international market share.

As corporate stockholders, we demand that the companies we invest in constantly increase profits. One method to accomplish this is to decrease costs. This may include chasing low-cost labor offshore or relocating to an area where taxes are lower or to where their largest markets are. It may also include the use of lobbyists to create tax loopholes or other legislation that may benefit them but that would not benefit the nation. It is the responsibility of the president and the legislature to ensure that proposed special-interest legislation does no harm to the nation as a whole. This has been and continues to be a major weak link in the American political and economic system.

Companies, whether US-based or multinational, owe their primary allegiance to their stockholders. To imply that they owe greater allegiance to their US employees is naive. If they can't compete in the international marketplace, they won't survive, and no one will be better off. Criticism should be directed at federal, state, and local political leaders who create the laws and policies that drive companies offshore.

We must stop looking at these companies as ours and expecting them to be obligated to operate in a manner that is less than ideal in order to keep jobs in the United States. Rather, we must make the United States a better, more attractive, and more profitable place to do business. Our federal government and many state governments are encouraging offshoring, if not pushing companies offshore. There are states that consistently lose employers year after year, and their legislatures' response is to raise corporate taxes on those companies that remain in order to make up for the loss of revenue due to this corporate exodus. Putting more tax pressure on corporations will not result in new job growth or stem the exodus of employers. This same pressure applied to small and midsize companies will not result in an exodus of employers but rather in their closure.

In 2000, when the Institute of Policy Studies examined the world's top hundred economies, they found more companies (fifty-one) than countries on the list. For example, individually, General Motors, Wal-Mart, Exxon Mobil, Ford Motor, and Daimler Chrysler had larger economies than Poland, Norway, Indonesia, South Africa, Saudi Arabia, Finland, Greece, and Thailand.[14] While the recession may have caused a reshuffling of rank, with some of the companies like General Motors, Ford, and Chrysler falling, the same could be said for many nations. Many of the companies, like Wal-Mart and Exxon, are still likely to rank high on the list if it were compiled today. Is it surprising, then, to expect these companies to confront the president and Congress in the same or even more aggressive manner than a foreign government? Just like foreign governments that put their constituents' best interest above all else, these corporations must place the interests of their stockholders first.

Our political leaders' assurances that free trade and offshoring are good for the nation have largely been based on research from Washington think tanks and the financial influence of powerful business lobbyists. With hundreds of millions of dollars to spend annually, multinational companies are able to control the knowledge base upon which Congress makes decisions and the financial base upon which politicians depend to get elected. These think tanks range from the conservative to the liberal. Most depend on contributions from donors, many of which are corporations, foundations, and executives. These think tanks give the impression of being impartial and objective, and many do make the effort, but their results are often biased to a varying degree. Some just provide a platform for issuing studies that support their contributors. Don't misinterpret this. The research coming from these institutions is not necessarily incorrect; it just comes with a warning label, like medications do. Also, not all Washington research institutions are partisan. Nonpartisan think tanks include the Atlantic Council of the United States, a foreign policy–oriented organization; the Institute for Collaborative Engagement, an internationally focused organization; and the RAND Corporation, a global policy organization.

Within the academic world, outside funding can corrupt the integrity of academic institutions. For most of Washington's think tanks that depend entirely on funding from either liberal or conservative contributors, there exist the same corrupting influences. The difference between think tanks and universities is that the former have no students or systems of peer review, which ensures that real academics conduct their research first and draw their conclusions afterward. This process may be seen as reversed at some policy-driven think tanks.

Lobbyists use this knowledge base to feed congressmen feel-good statements such as "Outsourcing of jobs, including high-tech jobs, will lead to new jobs in the United States by allowing companies to reallocate capital to new opportunities." The survey of CFOs by *CFO Magazine* (see chapter 8) illustrates how corporate America is really thinking, but it is not a feel-good message. Many of our federal political leaders seem to be far too influenced by special-interest groups, both domestic and foreign, to implement policies to reverse the loss of jobs.

The executives of most publicly held US corporations are not long-range planners, and the pressure from Wall Street and stockholders is for profits *now*. Concerns about the impact of actions taken today on potential profits five or ten years in the future are simply of little interest because they don't affect the price of stock today. Publicly held companies not only have more masters, but those masters, who are from all over the world, have limited interest in international borders, unless they restrict profits. These international owners have little unified world concern for one nation over another.

In this post–cold war period, corporations and governments no longer have the concerns they once had when some countries experienced trade restriction. During the cold war, there was a common enemy that threatened not only the free world's political systems but also its economic systems. Lobbyists were not pressing Congress to lower trade barriers so that their corporate clients could produce sophisticated electronic equipment in China or Eastern Europe. They certainly were not trying to convince Congress that this would be good for the American people and the economy. If we lost the cold war, it was pretty clear what impact this would have on the stockholders.

We now often seem to select our political leadership based on who can wage the most vicious thirty-second TV smear campaign, and then we allow these leaders to be controlled by the lobbyists, individuals we don't elect. Ultimately, the American people must take responsibility, for we select our political leaders. My father, a man who worked with his hands and a lifelong Democrat—back when you knew what Democrats stood for—had a relatively consistent philosophy on voting: "Never re-elect the guy who is in office." When asked why, his response was, "Democrats or Republicans, after they have been in office a year or so, they learn how to steal. If you get a new guy in the office, the taxpayers get a little break while he's learning." Now, you must understand that my father grew up on a strawberry farm in Louisiana during the Great Depression reign of the self-proclaimed "Kingfish" Huey P. Long, governor, United States senator, and presidential hopeful. My father, like many from Louisiana, admired Long's opposition to wealth and privilege and his many successes in helping the poor and middle class. He and others also recognized that Long created a political machine whose corrupt methods caused critics to view him as a demagogue and political thug. In realistically assessing Governor Long, my father said, "Most people assumed he and his boys were stealing, but at least they were doing some good things for the people; the other politicians just stole."

Perhaps the "vote them out" philosophy would still work in the twenty-first century. While it may send the right message, unfortunately, we are not even given a short reprieve when new members of Congress arrive in Washington. With few exceptions, they become indebted to special interests during the election process. What many of our political leaders are stealing is the future of our children and our grandchildren.

CHAPTER 10

OUR REPRESENTATIVES AREN'T REPRESENTING US
Federal and State Leaders Just Don't Get It

*Suppose you were an idiot, and suppose you were a
member of Congress; but I repeat myself.*

—Mark Twain
1835–1910

DISCONNECT BETWEEN GOVERNMENT AND BUSINESS

**Myth Number 34: With the poor condition of our state's economy,
our state and local governments are doing everything possible to preserve jobs.** In spite of the many obstacles to doing business in the
United States, I have yet to be involved in a corporate relocation where
the executives did not consider the repercussions of those lost jobs with
the greatest of concern. In fact, I have worked on numerous projects
where the company did not relocate, in spite of the fact that the numbers showed relocation would result in increased profits. This is especially true for small to midsize companies that are owned locally. But I
have seen many of these locally owned companies eventually find that
they can no longer compete in the global market. These companies are,
in many cases, either closed or absorbed by larger global corporations.
When there are no ties to the local community and workers, the companies then have a very high risk of relocating.

There are far too many federal, state, and local officials who feel that
these employers have a moral and financial obligation to support them,
while they have no reciprocating responsibility. President Theodore
Roosevelt understood the concept of reciprocity when in 1913 he said,
"We demand that big business give the people a square deal; in return we
must insist that when anyone engaged in big business honestly
endeavors to do right he shall himself be given a square deal." Perhaps
this attitude had something to do with the nation entering a period of
unparalleled economic expansion during the twentieth century.

I have seen many corporate executives very disappointed when they discover that in spite of their loyalty to their workers and their communities, this loyalty is not reciprocated. Many times, these companies are simply viewed as a never-ending source of jobs and taxes. Little thought is given to the business environment created by the community or state and its impact on the companies. These same communities then feel shocked and betrayed when these companies pack up and move. One example involved a small town of approximately five thousand people in a rural area. Just outside of town was a manufacturing plant that was the largest private-sector employer in a three-county area, employing over five hundred people. The plant had been in the town for over seventy-five years since its founding, but it was now owned by a major US corporation. I was asked to look at the financial advantages of relocation options, including Mexico.

When I asked the reason for the move, the CFO indicated that the plant was old and did not have a fire-suppression system, which was contrary to corporate safety policy and also created insurance problems. The CFO said the company would be willing to pay for a fire-suppression system and extend a water main with adequate water pressure from the town limits, approximately two hundred yards away. No approval for the water line was forthcoming, even after the company pleaded with the mayor and county board president for over eighteen months.

Since the water with adequate pressure had to come from the community, and the water line had to be located in a county easement, we needed both community and county approval. We discovered that these two political leaders, both in their midsixties, had a long-standing, deep dislike of each other and never agreed to cooperate on anything. The conflict dated back to high school when, as football heroes, they fought over the local homecoming queen who, upon graduating, left for college and never returned. I contacted both gentlemen and outlined the company's plan to relocate if the problem was not resolved immediately. I received essentially the same response from both: "The Company had been there seventy-five years and the problem would be taken care of when the time was appropriate." The CFO and I assumed this meant when one of them was voted out of office or died. Both had held office for over twenty years and looked to be in good health. I was told to find a new location.

Since the company preferred not to relocate, I called the governor, whom I had worked with previously. With the governor's assistance—a governor willing to fight for every job—the problem was resolved within two weeks, at no cost to the company. In fact, the company was given tax abatements, job-training assistance, and a grant to cover the installation of the fire-suppression system.

Generally, I find little connection or communication between business and most political leaders. At the state level, too many political leaders have the same attitude of indifference toward corporate problems as local politicians do. Major corporations are armed with legions of Washington lobbyists who focus on specific large-scale issues and are often successful in getting their clients' wishes understood and addressed. This doesn't often occur at the state and local levels with the same intensity. Many manufacturing and office-related operations are lost at this more local level. As an increasing number of these local companies are acquired or merged into large, multinational corporations without ties to a particular community, we find these companies have little patience for dealing with local problems or unions and are quick to pull the closure or relocation trigger.

While most political leaders profess government's need to partner with industry, partnership implies a give-and-take on both sides. This is simply not the reality with most governmental bodies, and industry knows this. At the local level, regional and local economic development organizations, counties, and communities must take greater responsibility for keeping the jobs they have and encouraging local job growth. There are community and regional economic development groups that have performed this task in an exceptional manner. The Greater Omaha Chamber of Commerce and the Charlotte Regional Partnerships are two such organizations. The key to their success is that they have community and business leaders who understand twenty-first-century global competition for jobs. They are constantly monitoring their competition, making improvements to their organizations and programs. They also work at educating their legislators, and they stay in contact with their existing employers to address their issues before they become problems. It is much easier to help an existing company grow and add jobs than to attract a new employer. Sounds logical, but most states and communities spend little, if any, time working on their relationships with local companies.

Myth Number 35: Our community just does not have the money to compete in the international marketplace for jobs. As a location and economic development consultant, I often hear many economic development organizations and communities claim that they don't have the resources to compete for jobs. A community doesn't have to be large, nor does it need to be wealthy, to compete in today's global marketplace—it just needs to be smart. For example, Osceola, Arkansas, a community of fewer than ten thousand, understands what it needs to compete and how to generate the funds necessary to do it. Led by a savvy mayor, the community purchased Caterpillar generators in order to sell electricity during peak periods to the local utility. This allowed the community to amass an economic development war chest that made it a national competitor for jobs. The Arkansas Economic Development Department would never hesitate to recommend this community, as the community has not only the financial resources to compete but also the leadership and business savvy to play in the big leagues.

Staff reporter Norichiko Shirouzu, in a February 1, 2006, *Wall Street Journal* article, singled out Osceola with the following, "In 2003, Osceola persuaded Denso Corp., an affiliate of Toyota Motor Corp., to locate a new plant in town producing car air-conditioning and heating systems. The usual bevy of financial incentives aided by their war chest helped, but for Denso, there was a clinching factor: Osceola's efforts to improve local education by creating a charter school." Denso recognized that here was a town that saw the link between industry and education, a town Denso could partner with.[1]

Will state and local political leaders ever "get it"? The answer is, some already do, like the governor mentioned above (water line) and the mayor of Osceola. My experience tells me that there are so many political leaders who are either risk-averse, unimaginative, or simply ignorant of the need to fight for jobs that they allow jobs to slip out of their states and communities or to bypass them. Some of them will never understand that the most important component of a healthy economy is keeping people employed in good, well-paying jobs. Unemployed people do not pay their share of taxes relative to their cost to society.

In another example, we worked with a large county that had been bypassed by employers several times because it did not have a shovel-ready manufacturing site. With our assistance, the county commissioner managed to sell and lease back a county building in order to raise the cash needed to develop an industrial park, which would make the county considerably more competitive. Don't misunderstand me; this is not necessarily the best economic development tool for every community.

In addition to having the resources to compete, communities and states need to understand that they are in a very competitive world and need to promote their advantages. In general, when it comes to marketing, most states and communities do a terrible job. If you are to compete for jobs in the twenty-first-century global economy, you need to create a competitive advantage. You must then have a strong, creative campaign to draw attention to your advantages in a manner that will be remembered.

I have advised many mayors not to base their communities' marketing campaign solely on quality of life. Doing so is a red flag indicating that you have little else to offer businesses. In over thirty years, I have yet to meet a mayor who did not brag about his community's quality of life. Excellent quality of life does not compensate for a weak business environment, and if you truly have a good business climate, you need to promote it.

Prior to the 1990s, the commercial real estate industry was dominated by entrepreneurs, unlike today, when most large commercial property is owned by large real estate trusts and institutions. I like to think of these earlier times as the "Wild West" days of commercial real estate. Commercial real estate developers and brokers of the day were cowboys—they were characters, they took chances.

In the early 1980s, I had a client who needed a new manufacturing operation in Detroit. I picked up my clients at the Detroit airport. These two partners were from a small town in Indiana, where they had their manufacturing operation. We had six buildings to tour that day. Generally, the building owner or his real estate broker would meet us to conduct the tour. As we approached the second building, I explained that Tom (pseudonym), the owner, could not meet us but would have someone else show the building. The property was located in an old, heavily industrialized area. As we pulled up in front of the building, my clients noticed a young woman on the opposite corner waving at the truckers who drove by. Many of these drivers would wave back and honk their horns.

Pulling up to the curb, I heard one client say, "Oh, no," and the other said, "Maybe we should go." Looking back, I saw the young woman approaching our car, motioning me to lower my window. She was quite a sight—about six feet tall in her red patent leather stiletto heels, red patent leather micro-mini-skirt, and small red patent leather jacket. On her head was a rather large red wig. On the red color palette, with auburn at one end of the spectrum and fire engine red on the other, hers leaned toward fire engine.

She looked in the window and said, "Hi, boys, I'm Ruby, and you must be Ron. Follow me. Tommy asked me to show you the building." Coaxing my clients along, we went inside, where Ruby gave us a flyer with all the building specifications. As we toured, Ruby rattled off the specifications like a professional, indicating ceiling heights, column spacing, roof condition, power availability, and loading dock features (never once looking at the flyer). In addition, she began telling stories and jokes, and by the end of the thirty-minute tour, she had the three of us so entertained that we stood outside the building and talked and laughed for another fifteen minutes before I could drag my clients away to make our next appointment.

That evening, as we had dinner and reviewed all six buildings, I noticed that as they described or tried to recall the features of each building, they were all compared to "Ruby's building," which they remembered in great detail. In reality, of all six buildings, "Ruby's building" ranked third in terms of meeting all their requirements, but they kept it in second place to the very end as we eliminated properties. It ended up as runner-up.

Two years later, I picked up the same clients at the Buffalo, New

York, airport, where we were looking for another building. They immediately started to talk about Ruby. I asked if they could describe Ruby's building, and sure enough, their memories of her building were still very vivid. My memories of the building were still very good, and I had been in over a hundred buildings since that day in Detroit. As I drove to our first meeting, I thought, *Tommy, you SOB—you're a marketing genius.* I am not suggesting that every community or state hire Ruby as an emissary, but you certainly need a marketing strategy that will make you stand out and be remembered. Your marketplace is no longer the adjacent community or state. Your twenty-first-century competition is national and, most likely, international.

WITCHES' BREW—CONGRESS, LOBBYISTS, AND PORK

Myth Number 36: The federal government simply does not have the funds to support economic development at the local level. A little common sense would help provide funding for job creation. When speaking of government spending, nothing seems to agitate the public as much as congressional pork-barrel spending. A pork-barrel project is a line item attached to an appropriation bill that designates tax dollars for a pet project of a specific congressperson or group of congresspeople. Certainly, some of these pork-barrel projects generate jobs; however, the jobs generated are too often for unnecessary projects that waste the taxpayers' money and would rarely receive funding if not as an earmark.

The private, nonpartisan, nonprofit Citizens against Government Waste (CAGW) monitors pork-barrel projects. Even a recession and a record $1.5 trillion budget deficit have not slowed Congress's business-as-usual culture of doling out the pork. While American families are responsibly bringing their own budgets under control, Congress is earmarking as if the economy were as hot as it has ever been. In fiscal year 2009, Congress stuffed 10,160 projects worth $19.6 billion into the twelve appropriations bills, a 14 percent increase over the fiscal year 2008 total of $17.2 billion, belying claims of reduced spending. Since 1991, the first year *The Pig Book* was produced, CAGW says it has identified items of federal pork that have cost US taxpayers $290 billion. Repeated attempts to control the deficit through the use of line-item vetoes have failed.

During Bush's second term, the president signed a $286 billion highway bill, which contained more than six thousand pet projects tacked on by politicians on both sides of the aisle. The pork-barrel projects for this bill alone cost over $24 billion.[2] One provision in this bill allocated more than $223 million to build a bridge taller than the Brooklyn Bridge and nearly as long as the Golden Gate Bridge connecting the Alaskan city of Ketchikan (population eight thousand) to Gravina Island (population fifty).

This now well-known "Bridge to Nowhere" was eventually removed (thanks to pressure from the press) from the highway bill because it was labeled a symbol of greed, waste, and misappropriation of funds. Alaska's senator, Ted Stevens, who chaired the Senate Appropriations Committee, threatened to resign if his "Bridge to Nowhere" was removed from the bill. In the end, the appropriation was removed, but it was agreed that Alaska would still receive the $223 million to spend as it wished.[3]

One of Senator Stevens' biggest opponents was Senator Tom Coburn of Oklahoma. Senator Coburn is an unusual politician in that he does not ask for any pork for his own state, and he opposes the pork-barrel projects of other politicians. When ABC News featured Senator Coburn in its *20/20* series on pork-barrel spending, Senator Coburn said, "The oath that we take has no mention of our state. The oath we take is to do what is in the best interest of the country as a whole." In trying to stop Congress from spending $500,000 on a sculpture park in Washington State, he sardonically said, "And we're going to take money from housing and urban development and we're gonna build a sculpture park."

Bringing home the bacon helps raise campaign funds and shows the voters that their congressperson has political clout. In the early 1990s, the average number of pork-barrel projects was fewer than 1,800 per year versus the approximate average of 9,500 per year in recent years (see figure 3, on page 175). Most important, the dollars have risen from approximately $3 billion in 1991 to a peak of over $29 billion for 2006. Both parties aggressively seek their share of pork.

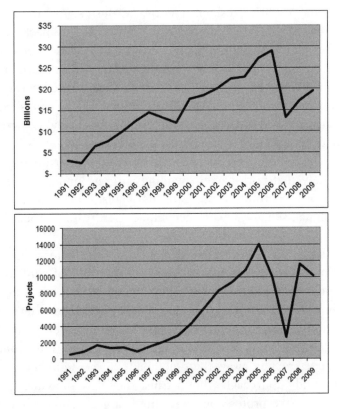

FIGURE 3: Federal Pork Barrel Projects 1991–2009

Source: Citizens against Government Waste

The reduction in pork-barrel spending in fiscal year 2007 (figure 3) can be attributed to Senator Tom Coburn (R-OK), Jim DeMint (R-SC), and Jeff Session (R-AL), who prevented enactment of nine appropriation bills and created a moratorium on earmarks by the House and Senate Appropriation Committee in H.J. Res. 20—the bill that funded the government for the remainder of 2007. By fiscal year 2008, Congress was back in full force, increasing earmark projects by 337 percent over 2007.[4] To further show that many in Congress have absolutely no shame in spending money, the 2008 bailout that was to address one of the nation's worst financial disasters was loaded with over $100 billion in pork before Congress would pass it (see chapter 17).

In September 2007, President George W. Bush signed the Honest Leadership and Open Government Act, a wide-ranging package that requires the names of sponsors of earmarks to be disclosed. When United States Representative Jeff Flake was asked if disclosure of legislators who sponsor earmarks would help reduce waste, his response was: "That works if we have some shame. I think we're beyond shame."[5] Representative Flake's statement would also apply to how Congress is manipulated by the more than thirty-four thousand lobbyists who are spending $8.9 million per day to influence them. Unfortunately, it is highly unlikely that pork-barrel spending will end under the Obama administration. According to the Citizens against Government Waste, while a freshman senator, Obama accounted for fifty-three special earmarks, totaling over $97 million.

Republicans and Democrats alike will promise voters that their party, and only their party, will cut the size of an out-of-control government and return the real power in government back to the American people. They will also promise to balance the budget by cutting unnecessary spending, and, of course, members of the other party have almost made this impossible. When the media packs up their cameras and the reporters put away their notepads, these Republicans and Democrats buddy up to each other because they have the same agenda. It is very much like professional wrestling—a great show—but don't think for a moment that the hostility is real. Republicans and Democrats join together as a team to ensure that everyone gets enough pork. With an adequate amount of pork flowing back to their districts, they are assured of getting reelected. There is nothing that unifies the two parties more than spending your money.

On March 4, 2009, President Barack Obama signed a $410 billion bill to fund most government operations, but warned that Congress must stop jamming spending bills with lawmakers' pet projects. Arizona senator John McCain, an outspoken critic of earmarks, dismissed Obama's comments, calling them "his usual excellent rhetoric," but saying the message was "virtually meaningless" and "toothless." "What he should have done was say he was going to veto this bill, that he wanted the $8 billion in earmarks removed and then he would sign it," McCain said.[6]

Republicans saw the bill as too costly and loaded with 7,991 pet projects—even though Republican as well as Democrat lawmakers added them to the bill. There's $190,000 for the Buffalo Bill Historical Center in Cody, Wyoming; $238,000 to fund a deep-sea voyaging program for native Hawaiian youth; and agricultural research projects. Senator Tom Harkin (D-IA) backed $1.7 million for pig odor research. Senator Carl Levin (D-MI) promised $3.8 million to preserve and redevelop part of old Tiger Stadium to help revitalize a distressed area of Detroit. Under a long-standing tradition, the minority party—Republicans in this case—are limited to about 40 percent of the earmarks.[7]

AGRICULTURAL SUBSIDIES—MORE PORK THAN BACON

Without question, the king of all pork is agricultural subsidies. Each year the United States Department of Agriculture distributes, as direct government aid to farmers, over $22 billion. Not only is the agricultural industry heavily subsidized, the industry also makes sure it gets its share of pork-barrel projects. No other industry has such control and ability to protect its interests.

Rural areas have been hit hard by manufacturing losses. According to the Federal Reserve of Kansas City, rural factory jobs rose 3.3 percent during the period from 1991 to 1998, 50 percent faster than urban areas. However, over the period 2000–2004, rural areas lost 570,000 factory jobs (approximately a 12 percent drop)—a considerably greater percentage than in metropolitan areas. In 1930, only 30 percent of farmers had off-farm work or income. Today that figure is 93 percent. Farmers and their families now must rely on nonfarm income. Nationwide, only 2 percent of total income in rural counties comes from agricultural production. Overall, farm and farm-related employment accounts for 14 percent of total US employment.[8]

Professor Michael Porter of Harvard Business School's research group has shown that, contrary to what some believe, agriculture is a relatively small part of rural economics; even in counties with the highest reliance on agriculture, this sector accounts for a modest proportion of employers.[9] The Department of Labor reports that there are 5.5 million workers in agriculture and related work; of these, only about one million are self- or family-employed farmers, accounting for less than 1 percent of the US workforce. By contrast, the number of people in manufacturing has slipped to approximately fifteen million. While the federal government and most states have done little to protect manufacturing jobs, billions are spent each year to protect profits of large agribusinesses.

Myth Number 37: Small family farmers receive most federal subsidies, without which they could not survive. The wealthiest 10 percent of farmers receive 72 percent of taxpayer-financed subsidies. Eligibility for subsidies is determined by crop and not by income or poverty standards. Growers of corn, wheat, cotton, soybeans, and rice receive more than 90 percent of all subsidies. Growers of nearly all of the other four hundred crops in the United States receive virtually nothing.[10]

Between 2000 and 2006, the federal government paid people in the United States approximately $1.3 billion not to farm. This equates to shutting down all the farming in Wisconsin, Indiana, Ohio, and Michigan, or about forty million acres of land.[11] Among the one hundred wealthiest zip codes in America, seven are located in the city of Chicago or its suburbs. Between 1995 and 2005, the 769 "farmers" in these wealthy neighborhoods received over $9.7 million in agricultural assistance.[12]

The nation's powerful agriculture lobby is siphoning off federal dollars that could be used for building a strong national manufacturing and research and development base, thus preserving millions of jobs. According to the Center for Responsive Politics, during the 2008 election cycle, the agribusiness industry as a whole contributed $49 million from individuals, soft money, and PACs.[13]

Considering the financial problems the nation had in 2008, you might think Congress and the Bush administration would have wanted to cut off the agriculture industry. Not so. The 2007 Farm Bill was passed in 2008 and is certain to be recognized as a crowning achievement of Washington lobbyists and another disgrace for Congress. The Farm Bill will provide $307 billion over a five-year period. According to the Congressional Budget Office, approximately $209 billion will go to nutrition programs, like food stamps and food banks—certainly much-needed programs. The rest will go directly to the agriculture industry. Agribusinesses growing select crops like wheat and corn can avoid almost all risk by using overlapping subsidized loans, insurance, and payments. How many other American businesses receive this kind of risk protection?

Of course, Congress did place a means test on receipt that applies to couples with a $1.5 million annual income. A good accountant could likely avoid this test. The agriculture department has indicated that most of the largesse will go to commercial farm households having average incomes in excess of $229,920 in 2008.[14] Instead of saving the small American farmer, the subsidy system is helping to destroy it. The system Congress and the agribusiness lobbyists have created encourages big farmers to buy out small farmers, drive land prices up, farm marginal land, and require greater automation, resulting in the requirement for costly equipment and fewer jobs.

If alleviating farm poverty was the real purpose of subsidies, for just $4 billion per year of the roughly $20 billion yearly subsidies that go directly to the agriculture industry, every full-time farmer in the United States could receive $34,873 (for a family of four), which is 185 percent of the federal poverty level. Of course, if this were to occur, Willie Nelson would no longer need to put on Farm Aid concerts. But alas, the nation's wealthiest farmers and agribusinesses would no longer receive the other more than $16 billion in subsidies Congress grants each year. Add this $16 billion to the $20 billion in pork Congress spends each year, and invest it in R&D, science education, and automating the nation's manufacturing base, and we could save millions of jobs and generate billions of dollars for our economy. Agriculture subsidies are another example of lobbying at its worst for the American people and a Congress that refuses to bite the hand that feeds it.

Among the most aggressive proposals in President Obama's 2009 budget was a plan to save more than $9.7 billion over a decade by putting strict limits on agriculture subsidies. Obama's grand ambitions ran into a political brick wall. The budget finally approved by the House and Senate did not include any limits on farm subsidies. Did the president simply want to tell the voters he tried, knowing, as everyone in Washington knew, it was a useless attempt?

Myth Number 38: If we don't provide financial subsidies to the agriculture industry today, it will start to collapse like US manufacturing has. The only US industry that has, and will, benefit from the rapid growth of India and China is the agriculture industry. US agricultural exports are increasing at about 10 percent per year. The salvation of this industry for the United States is twofold. First, it is highly automated and requires relatively little labor (little advantage for low-cost labor), and second, agricultural land cannot be exported. Both China and India will continue to increase their imports of agricultural products as their populations grow and continue to strain their ability to feed their citizens.

Why does an industry like agriculture that is doing so well and has a bright future relative to manufacturing receive so much from the government, while manufacturing desperately needs help and receives so little? It's simply a matter of lobbying. The agriculture industry is unified and has developed lobbying into an art form.

The lobbying efforts of multinational corporations are generally fractionalized. Each has its own agenda relative to trade policies, along with the money and the powerful Washington lobbyist to push its personal agenda. It is not the responsibility of the multinational corporations to look after the well-being of the American people. Certainly, they have a responsibility to provide their workers a safe workplace, reasonable hours, pay, and benefits. It is the responsibility of our political leaders to look past political contributions to make sure that legislation and trade policies proposed by lobbyists truly benefit the American people.

CHAPTER 11

A NATIONAL ADDICTION TO DEFICIT SPENDING

I don't make jokes. I just watch the government and report the facts.

—Will Rogers
1879–1935

FEDERAL BUDGET DEFICIT

We are the largest debtor nation in the world. We have the highest federal budget deficit and the highest trade deficit, and Americans are struggling under the highest personal debt they have ever experienced. This and the following chapter will explain how all this debt is growing, and how it has begun to cause a lower standard of living for the typical American family.

President George W. Bush did an outstanding job of driving the national debt into the stratosphere, and President Obama is following. According to the nonpartisan Congressional Budget Office (CBO), the Obama booster rocket will push the deficit from $455 billion in 2008 to $1.1 trillion in 2010. This deficit would be 7.9 percent of GDP—the largest deficit as a share of GDP since 1945.[1] Much of the red ink is the result of the recession, including the cost of bailing out the financial industry and the cumulative effect on GDP, and consequently on tax revenues and interest on the debt.

Overall, federal spending rose over 40 percent during the Bush administration. Then Treasury secretary Paul O'Neill, fearful of the growing budget deficit and further Bush tax cuts, said that he tried to warn Vice President Dick Cheney of the threat posed to the US economy. Cheney cut him off and stated, "You know, Paul, Reagan proved deficits don't matter. We won the mid-term election, this is our due." O'Neill was speechless. A month later, after disagreeing again with the administration about another tax cut, Cheney, who was instrumental in bringing O'Neill into the administration, asked the secretary to resign.[2] It would appear that, as long as you can win elections, the state of the economy and its long-term impact on the American public is of little importance.

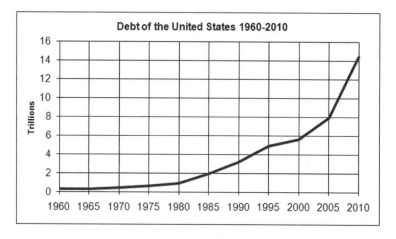

FIGURE 4: Gross National Debt of the United States 1960–2010

Source: Bureau of Public Debt and President's Office of Management and Budget

Figure 4 illustrates the growth of the gross national debt in the United States between 1960 and 2010. In recent years, the debt has continued to rise by over one-half trillion dollars per year. Prior to 1969, the economy continued to grow faster than the deficit.

We all know that if we are spending more than we earn, we need to either earn more or spend less if we want to gain control of the situation. If you don't get control, a growing portion of your income will go to your credit card company or bank. At the federal level, the principle is the same—the numbers are just considerably larger. Raising taxes in a fragile US economy is not a good idea, nor is it popular with the voters. Raising revenue through international trade is not in our future, as the Clinton and Bush administrations and Congress opted to create a trade deficit of monumental proportions. Even if the Obama administration wanted to increase our exports and decrease imports, it would take decades to rebuild our industrial base. Unfortunately, reducing expenditures as a method to reduce the federal deficit has never been a favorite of either political party, in spite of considerable rhetoric by both sides.

The United States has a gross national debt that will exceed $10 trillion by the end of the decade, as shown in figure 4. There are a lot of gigantic numbers used to describe the nation's debt. Figure 5 provides somewhat more detail about the debt. The numbers you hear or see often depend on who is relaying the information. Those in public office and in control will talk about the "national debt" or the "debt held by the public." While this is certainly a very large number ($6 trillion by 2010), it is substantially smaller than the gross national debt, a number used by the party out of power and by those opposed to the way the government is run. Both the national debt and gross national debt are important to understand.

All US debt is owed by the "General Fund" that is financed by US taxpayers. The big question is: How do we get from the gross national debt to the national debt? This is accomplished through "debt held by government accounts," which the Bureau of Public Debt defines as "Government Account Series securities held by government trust funds, revolving funds and special funds; and Federal Financing Bank securities." Included in these are such significant sources of income as the Social Security Trust and Medicare, which, under long-range budget projections, are expected to disappear faster than they can be replaced. All of these securities are then deducted from the gross national debt to get to the national debt.

Figure 5 provides a look at how the President's Office of Management and Budget perceives the national debt from 2005 to 2011. The national debt was only $3.4 trillion in 2000, and the gross national debt was 5.6 trillion. The national debt grew approximately 120 percent in a single decade (1996–2009). For the years in the decade of the 1990s, most of which were during the Clinton administration (1993–2001), the national debt grew 50 percent and the gross national debt increased 75 percent. Between 1990 and 2011, the national debt increased an astounding 285 percent and the gross national debt increased 330 percent.[3] For either Republicans or Democrats to claim that their party is fiscally responsible is simply not true and is nothing more than campaign rhetoric.

	2005	2006	2007	2008	2009	2010	2011
Gross National Debt	$7,905	$8,451	$8,950	$9,985	$11,875	$13,786	$15,144
Debt Held by Government Accounts	$3,313	$3,622	$3,915	$4,183	$4,331	$4,888	$4,645
Debt Held by Public (National Debt)	$4,592	$4,828	$5,035	$5,802	$7,545	$9,298	$10,498
National Debt as a Percent of GDP	37.5%	37.1%	36.9%	40.8%	53.0%	63.6%	68.6%

FIGURE 5: Federal Government Debt 2005–2011 (in Billions)

Source: President's Office of Management and Budget, Overview of the President's Fiscal Year 2011 Budget

Some may say that during the Clinton administration the budget was balanced. This is true. The cold war ended in 1991 and military spending was winding down. We had a booming economy with huge gains in the stock market and the dot-com bubble, which brought in unanticipated tax revenue from taxes on capital gains and rising salaries. In fiscal 1999, there was a budget surplus of $1.9 billion and $86.4 billion in fiscal 2000. The federal budget was balanced and there was a temporary surplus. Keep in mind, a budget deficit occurs in a given year when more money is spent than is taken in. The national debt is the total amount of debt the government accumulates and owes over a period of years. In other words, your family may spend exactly all that you earn in a year and thus you have a balanced budget for the year. You may still have family debt in terms of a house mortgage and loans on the family cars. The debt the government owed was reduced for 1999 and 2000, but by no means erased, under Clinton.

Myth Number 39: The national debt is a nonissue as long as the GDP continues to grow faster. There are those who have labeled the rising national debt as a "phony" or a "nonissue," arguing that the real concern is what percent it is of the GDP (gross domestic product). After all, if our debt is rising slower than income, we're not doing so badly. In 1981, the gross federal debt's percentage of the nation's annual income reached 32.5 percent, the lowest point since 1931. For the period 2005 to 2010, the gross federal debt as a percentage of GDP will have climbed from 64.6 percent to 98.1 percent.[4]

As figure 5 illustrates, if we separate the gross national debt from the national debt and use it to determine percent of GDP, we still have a high percentage increase. For the period 2000 to 2010, it is estimated to have grown from 35.1 percent to 67.1 percent. It really doesn't make any difference how you look at the nation's debt, if you ran your household as Congress runs the nation's economy, you would be considered extremely irresponsible. As will be explained in the section of the next chapter titled "Phantom GDP," there is some question as to how accurately the government's estimate of GDP truly reflects the nation's economic growth and productivity. If, as some economists believe, GDP is overestimated, then relative to GDP, the national debt may be growing at a higher rate than the above numbers indicate.

NATIONAL DEBT'S IMPACT ON AMERICANS

Myth Number 40: As long as the cost of living continues to drop due to cheap imported goods, my family stays ahead of the game. If we compare the growth in debt to real median household income, as defined by the United States Census Bureau, we see a different picture. During the period of 1990 to 2000, real median household income increased on average .98 percent per year (figure 6, on page 186). For the period 2000–2008 (latest data available at the time of this writing), real median household income decreased on average .52 percent per year. This 2000–2008 decrease in the rate of growth occurred at the same time we experienced an approximate 3.2 percent average annual increase in the cost of living. If household income continues to fall or stagnate and the cost of living (Consumer Price Index) continues to rise at or near its current average annual rate of 3.2 percent per year, our ability to maintain our standard of living will continue to diminish. There is no indication that we will see any significant increase in real median household income in the near future. It is also highly unlikely that we will experience a decrease in the cost of living that will compensate for decreased incomes.

The reality is that, for the decade, middle-class incomes have remained reasonably stagnant, while our government has opted to more than double our total national debt. If we consider that individuals now pay over 85 percent of the nation's tax burden, is it any wonder that as a nation and individually we are in trouble? It's obvious that the taxpayers cannot possibly keep up with our political leaders' ability to spend money. The only solution is to substantially cut spending; an admirable thought, but the odds of this happening are highly unlikely. Not all Americans are experiencing losses in their ability to maintain a high standard of living. The wealthiest 1 percent of Americans receives approximately 15 percent of all income; nearly double the 8 percent they received in the 1960s and 1970s.[5]

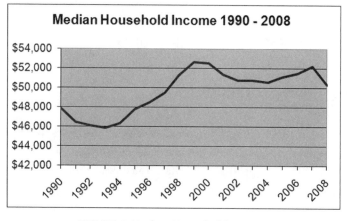

FIGURE 6: Median Household Income

Source: United States Census Bureau, Historical Income Tables—Household Income in 2009 CPI-U-RS Adjusted Dollars

Just prior to leaving office in January 2006, former Federal Reserve chairman Alan Greenspan said that good, short-term prospects for the US economy should not detract from huge, looming fiscal strains that pose significant economic risks. He stated, "Our budget position will substantially worsen in coming years unless major deficit-reducing actions are taken." He warned that "tax increases of sufficient dimensions to deal with our looming fiscal problems arguably pose significant risks to economic growth and the revenue base." He reiterated his conviction that the government should "close the fiscal gap primarily, if not wholly, from the outlay side."[6] It is obvious that his message of fiscal restraint has had no effect on Capitol Hill. Even after passing the Bush 2008 bailout and the 2009 Obama administration bailouts, Congress has not curbed spending. The 2009 Democrat-dominated Congress raised discretionary nonmilitary spending 8 percent in the 2009 budget and another 7 percent in the 2010 budget.

In February 2010, President Obama unveiled a $3.834 trillion 2011 budget, designed to balance the need to create jobs with an effort to cut huge deficits. The budget the White House sent to Congress included a three-year freeze on nonsecurity discretionary spending, billions of dollars in new job-creation packages, and extra education and home-land security spending. The budget, as proposed, foresees a 2011 deficit of $1.267 trillion, down from a record $1.556 trillion in 2010. While Republicans and some conservative Democrats have raised the alarm at high government spending, which has swelled the deficit, both parties will very likely contribute to increase discretionary spending.

In late 1998 and into 1999, budget tightening, in large part due to a reduction of military spending in the immediate post–cold war era and an economic boom, resulted in the first balanced budget (Clinton administration) since 1969. A balanced budget was maintained through most of 2001. Unwilling to endure a balanced budget, the Bush administration, supported by a Republican Congress, went about making a concerted effort to spend more than the income our nation could generate.

Many in government believe that as long as there is an excess of savings in the global economy to fund the US deficit through the purchase of our treasuries and other securities, the US deficit should not place the national economy in danger. US treasury securities are negotiable US government debt obligations, backed by its full faith and credit. They are issued by the United States government in order to pay for government projects and to pay interest owed on government debt. The money paid for a treasury bond is essentially a loan to the government. Repayment of principal is accompanied by a specified interest rate, which is exempt from state and local taxes, but not from federal taxes. US treasury securities are sold by auction in the primary market, but as marketable securities they can be purchased through a broker in the secondary market.

Since Congress is making no effort to reduce the deficit by budget cuts, we remain dependent on foreign investors to buy our treasuries. If that doesn't work, we must risk inflation by printing more money. We entered the twenty-first century with the world's most powerful economy, yet today the future viability of our economy is dependent on foreign investors, and there are many danger signals indicating that foreign investor interest is waning.

Warren Buffett and many economists, including former Federal Reserve chairman Paul Volcker and Nobel Laureate Paul A. Samuelson, have warned that one day the dollar might begin falling in value even more sharply than it already has. This they believe will occur if foreigners decide to increase their diversification into other currencies and begin cashing in their holdings of US stocks, bonds, and treasury securities. If this were to occur, it would likely send US stock prices plunging and interest rates surging more than they did in the wake of the 2008 financial meltdown.

For over half a century, the dollar reigned as the hegemonic international currency. Since its peak in 2002, the dollar spiraled downward, losing over 30 percent of its value by 2010. Given the United States' need to borrow in order to finance its consumption of foreign goods and services, the dollar's fall is not surprising.

By continuing to buy treasury bonds denominated in dollars, China can keep the dollar strong compared with the yuan, thereby keeping Chinese exports cheap relative to US exports.[7] The fear of many foreign investors is that, as the United States continues to run up its debt, it is increasing the risk of defaulting on its obligations through inflation or currency devaluation. If these countries were to just dump the dollar, it would only intensify its decline and thereby adversely affect their investment. A safer method would be to slowly wean off the dollar as a reserve currency.

In spite of a great deal of talk about the value of the dollar, federal officials have acted as if they have little or no concern about its journey into a black hole. By running a huge current account deficit, the government has left the dollar and the American economy vulnerable. Those countries that peg their currency to that of the dollar (China, oil-rich Gulf states) need to allow their currencies to rise if they hope to curb inflation and support rebalancing the global economy. Continued acquisition of the dollar would have to be at a much slower pace. Of course, as this happens, the dollar's eminence would wane, as it is replaced by other, more stable currencies.[8]

As long as foreigners are willing to exchange the products they make or raw materials for US dollars, there is little concern that foreign investors will dump dollars rapidly. The problem we face is that, as the Chinese and Indian middle classes continue a rapid spiral upward, and our middle class shrinks in size and buying power, these countries will focus increasingly on their own markets and will be less prone to help finance our economy. Such a development would have very negative repercussions on our economy.

UNRAVELING OF OUR ECONOMY

The Bush administration inherited a federal budget surplus (1998–2001) and, with the assistance of Congress, managed to turn it into one of the largest budget deficits in US history. In the administration's last fiscal year 2008, the US government paid $454 billion just on interest payments on the gross federal debt.[9] To put this number into perspective, we typically spend only $61 billion on education and $56 billion on transportation—areas in which the United States is in desperate need of improvement.[10]

The loss of jobs, capital, and technology will continue to have a negative impact on wages in the United States in the coming decades. We still have the same mortgages, credit card debt, transportation, food costs, and taxes, but we are finding them increasingly more difficult to afford.

Since nearly 85 percent of the annual US tax burden is paid by individuals, what does the future hold for the American middle and lower classes? Can we expect this percentage of the tax burden that has been rising to continue upward as we lose more employers that actually pay taxes? A decreasing tax base will result in an inability to maintain entitlement programs, infrastructure, and the military at current levels.

The unraveling of our debt-ridden economy could occur in a number of ways. As long as the Federal Reserve is able to maintain interest rates at low levels, most people can manage. As prices continue to rise, the Federal Reserve must protect against inflation by raising interest rates. If interest rates don't rise with prices, we face the risk that the dollar will lose its value to foreign investors, as well as to major pension funds and banks, upon which we also depend to buy our bonds.

The United States is addicted to foreign money—an addiction that it appears will not be broken by the United States but rather by foreign investors. The allure of the dollar was shaken by the 2008 financial industry collapse. Foreign investors are concerned that government guarantees to support the system may tempt the government to inflate away its debt by simply printing more money. Investors in US securities have been attracted by the size of the US economy, its liquidity, and its transparency when compared to other markets around the world.

The question is at what point do America's economic problems cause a loss of interest as a place to invest? The euro's capital markets are comparable to those in the United States in size and liquidity. Had the 2008 US financial industry problem not become an international problem, investors may have shifted their investment to the euro. We have become so dependent on this foreign borrowed money that if it were to stop coming in, the dollar would plummet in value and US bond yields would rise. This would constrain capital expenditure in the United States and further slow the US economy.

China has simply been recycling its surplus US dollars from its US trade surplus back into our bond market. Originally a simple ploy to keep the Chinese currency undervalued, it has stimulated the resulting huge balance of trade surplus. This ploy has resulted in a powerful economic and political tool for the Chinese to hold off any response by the United States to China's unfair trade practices. The added beauty for China is that it is exporting products to the United States that were at one time made in the United States.

How would we react if we discovered a powerful foreign navy stationed offshore that could blockade our ports and shut down our financial markets by jamming our communication systems? These actions would devastate our nation's economy. Suppose this action could be threatened and taken at any time, for any reason, and the United States was powerless to resist? Of all foreign holders of US treasury securities, China holds approximately 23 percent and therefore could cause such devastation without the use of a single warship. China would only need to sell off all of its US treasury bonds to cause such devastation. Such an action is often referred to as the "nuclear option." Interest rates would shoot up dramatically, and mortgage rates and inflation would also spike. The stock market would be devastated, and the value of the dollar would drop into the basement.

When Lesley Stahl, CBS correspondent on *60 Minutes*, asked Gao Xiqing, president of China Investment Corp., a sovereign wealth fund with $200 billion to invest in the United States if the nuclear option was possible, Xiqing said, "Philosophically, everything's possible in this world." Mr. Xiqing went on to say that such an action was unlikely. On the same *60 Minutes* episode, economist Peter Navarro said China has over $1.5 trillion in reserves that it can spend buying US companies. The danger is that it could then strip these companies of jobs, research, development, and technology. Navarro went on to tell Stahl that while this was not a present danger, it was a clear and future danger.[11]

Right now, there is no real need for China to start buying US companies. American companies are already moving millions of jobs to China, investing billions of dollars to grow in China, and developing new technology there. Even the American aspect of this globalization could, in time, be eliminated if the Chinese government in Beijing decided that would be in its best interest. As Peter Navarro states, they could simply start taking control of US companies.[12] But why take this action as long as the flow continues? Perhaps the old saying "Why pay for the cow when you can get the milk for free?" is appropriate.

Myth Number 41: China would never stop the purchase of US securities since China would be harmed as much as the United States. A very important consideration is that the Chinese are in a position to select the time to use the nuclear option due to their powerful centralized government. Their government's motivation can come from strategic thinking rather than profit motivation. They are also in a better position to withstand the shock to their economy.

If America's demand for Asian exports were to decrease, the growth in Asia's exports and output would decrease. The impact, however, would not be as great on Asia as some believe. The greater part of Asia's and especially China's growth has been due to internal demand in both consumption and investment. The increase in consumer spending in China and India now adds more to global GDP growth than that of the United States.[13] Asia's economies, and especially that of China, can withstand a downturn in America's economy because they have small budget deficits or, in some cases, surpluses. The annual prerecession growth in China's exports fell 35 percent from its peak during 2000–2001, with less than a 1 percent slowdown of GDP. While one-third of China's manufacturing workers are in export-oriented sectors, this is only 6 percent of the nation's total workforce.[14] The bottom line is that China's economic growth will not be affected dramatically by a further downturn in the US economy.

Even a moderate decrease in the purchase of bonds by pension funds and banks, if not made up immediately by foreign investors, could force the United States Treasury to raise interest rates to make buying the US debt more attractive. This would, in turn, cause interest rates on homes with floating rate mortgages to escalate, pushing even more home owners toward default. A decision by China to move out of US government bonds, for economic or political reasons, could lead to a sell-off by other investors.

While the Bush administration and the Republicans should take their share of the blame for the state of the economy, the Clinton administration certainly helped set the nation in the wrong direction by raising the banner of free trade at any cost. It's a sad situation when America finds that it can be manipulated into a position of extreme weakness by its trading partners, but more significantly, by its own government.

Clearly, the Chinese know we are at their mercy. The quote below is excerpted from a longer piece, "United States Caused World Recession," that appeared in the *China Daily*, October 6, 2005. Not much appears in Chinese newspapers without government approval. It's interesting to note that the article predicted the bursting of our housing bubble and the recession. The article indicated that even a country like South Korea, which buys considerably fewer US treasuries than China, could push us into recession or a depression. It states that we have been living way beyond our means for much too long, that we have become dependent on the central banks of Japan, China, and other nations to invest in US treasuries. This, they state, is necessary in order to keep American interest rates down, which, in turn, keeps American consumers snapping up imported goods. The article goes on to state that any economist worth his salt knows that this situation is unsustainable. The Chinese recognized in 2005 that "the United States is now clearly in huge trouble, economically, socially, politically, and internationally." They predicted long-term interest rates would rise, creating the bursting of the greatest property bubble the world has witnessed. For the Chinese, they said, "the good news is that when the country is in deep trouble, the United States will not have the energy to pick on China." The article went on to say that when it is necessary for the United States to start another war to divert people's attention, it would pick one with a smaller and weaker country, like Iran.[15]

By the end of 2009, China was selling US treasuries and became the second-largest foreign holder after Japan. Whether this is a temporary or a permanent trend is yet to be determined at the time of this writing. The drop may suggest that China is moving forward with plans to diversify out of US assets. About 70 percent of China's $2 trillion plus reserve stockpile is estimated to be in US dollars. China may be concerned about the growing US debt load, or the shift may be the result of rising tensions between the two countries. The Obama administration had been taking a somewhat tougher stand, relative to duties on Chinese imports. China may be sending an economic and political message to the United States. It has long claimed the United States imposes itself on China's internal affairs, and it may also be a warning to the Obama administration to back off in its efforts to revalue the yuan. If China continues on this diversification process, it is likely to be gradual, given the few attractive alternatives to the US dollar as a reserve currency.[16]

Selling Out a Superpower

The accumulated US debt grew by 44 percent during the Clinton administration and by 75 percent during Bush's two terms. If our own experts and even the Chinese recognize how fragile our economy is, why did our political leaders refuse to take action before the financial markets collapsed in 2008? It took them years of mismanagement to create a financial disaster.

A National Addiction to Deficit Spending

The United States is no longer the manufacturing and technology powerhouse it was during much of the twentieth century. Without this strength that's necessary for a strong twenty-first-century economy, recession recovery periods are likely to be long and deep. Our soaring federal budget and trade deficit are not reflective of some complicated economic theory that looks bad but is really good for the nation—as some politicians and their lobbyist pundits would like us to believe. It looks bad and it is bad.

It doesn't take a Nobel laureate in economics to figure out that if a nation consistently spends more than it earns, and its ability to increase income is diminishing, it is in financial trouble. Certainly all businesses and the typical American family recognize this. I recognized this in fifth grade. You can't continue to survive indefinitely on borrowed money if you don't have the ability to pay it back.

When in grade school in the 1950s, like many Catholic kids in Chicago public schools, my friend Jimmy and I attended Wednesday afternoon catechism class at the local Catholic school. We'd walk together from our grade school to the class. Like every Catholic school in Chicago, the nuns would have an annual raffle and the students were given books of chances to sell. As sales manager for her students, Sister Mary Grace didn't accept anything less than a stellar performance.

After receiving our mandatory allocation of chance books, Jimmy told me he could sell all of them and more. Jimmy's father was a police officer in another part of Chicago. He would sell to other officers in his precinct and to the merchants in his patrol area.

The next week, as Jimmy and I walked to catechism class, he said he sold all the books and would ask Sister for more. This was amazing, as most parents wound up buying the mandatory allotment of books just prior to the close of the raffle sale period. As we walked past Boffa's Drugstore, Jimmy said, "Let's stop and have a sundae." I said, "I don't have any money, and we'll be late for catechism." Jimmy said, "I'll pay and I'll take care of Sister." We were late for class, but as we walked in, Jimmy yelled, "Sister, Sister, I'm sorry we're late, but I stopped and sold my last chance book on the way over." Like Congress, Jimmy knew how to deflect and spin the news. As Sister had already begun to hear the excuses for slow sales from the class, Jimmy's news changed her mood. Jimmy was a hero, inspired by his guardian angel. When Sister collected the sold-out chance books with numbered stubs, Jimmy said he forgot the money (not an uncommon response).

On the way home, Jimmy said we should buy some comic books. Again, Jimmy said he would buy. I said to Jimmy, "You know you're going to get caught." He said he wouldn't, as he was only borrowing the money and would pay it back when he had extra money. I asked him how he would get the money. He said he didn't have to worry about that now. I reminded him of what Sister told us about God knowing everything, and that God was able to talk to the pope. After all, Jimmy had stolen the pope's money. I said the pope is probably calling Sister Superior right now. While Jimmy thought he could handle Sister Mary Grace, he knew that Sister Superior (the principal) couldn't be conned—the best had tried and failed. In spite of this threat, Jimmy was not deterred from spending as much of the pope's money as he could. By the end of the following week, Jimmy's spending spree came to a harsh end when Sister Mary Grace sent him to Sister Superior's office to explain where the money was. Jimmy's parents ended up paying the pope his money, and Jimmy had to deliver newspapers until he paid his parents back.

Despite the looming fiscal disaster, many in Washington, like Jimmy, have not lost their enthusiasm for spending and spinning the bad news. You would hope that after years of rising federal budget and trade deficits, our political leaders would have a better understanding of how to run the government. How long will we be able to survive on borrowed money before we have to see Sister Superior?

Our trade policies have created a massive loss of jobs and trade deficits, and at the same time the size of government spending has never been higher. The simple truth is that we are in trouble financially, and nobody in Washington wants to take the action necessary to correct the situation. Our leaders, both Democrats and Republicans, have put us in a situation where raising revenues through taxes from a populace with decreasing revenues is difficult and unpopular, and cutting spending is a concept foreign to Washington. Steve Forbes and Elizabeth Ames clearly state the problem in their book *How Capitalism Will Save Us: Why Free People and Free Markets Are the Best Answer in Today's Economy*. "The Real World truth is that deficits are not created by tax cuts. And they can't be fixed by either tax cuts or tax increases—if the size of government keeps growing."[20]

CHAPTER 12

WHY FREE TRADE DOESN'T MEAN FAIR TRADE

The greatest danger for most of us is not that our aim is too high and we miss it, but that it is too low and we reach it.
—Michelangelo
1475–1564

FEDERAL TRADE DEFICIT

The trade deficit, like the federal deficit, is something we should worry about today, yet our government often persists in downplaying its importance. The US trade deficit represents the amount in resources that the United States is transferring into the hands of foreigners in exchange for foreign oil, cars, and other products that Americans are purchasing. When foreign companies sell us cars, clothes, and other goods, those businesses are willing to be paid in dollars. As previously seen, some of that money is then invested in US stocks, corporate bonds, and treasury securities.

As illustrated in figure 7, the US prerecession trade deficit soared to an all-time high of over $700 billion by the start of 2008. That takes about $2 billion per day to finance. Prior to President Reagan taking office in 1981, the trade deficit was reasonably stable. During the Reagan years, the trade deficit grew from $16 billion to $114 billion by 1989. During President George H. Bush's four-year term (1989–1993), the trade deficit actually dropped from $114 billion to $39 billion. With the Clinton administration (1993–2001), the trade deficit began soaring like a NASA rocket, increasing $340 billion in eight years. During President George W. Bush's term, the trade deficit hit a high of $760 billion, with a term increase of over $316 billion. This shows in stark terms the speed with which the country is becoming indebted to the rest of the world, and reflects the rapid offshoring of American jobs.

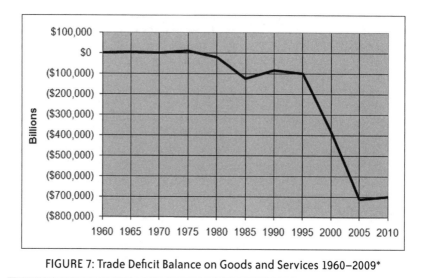

FIGURE 7: Trade Deficit Balance on Goods and Services 1960–2009*

---

* Seasonally Adjusted 1960–2009, United States Bureau of Economic Analysis

Myth Number 42: We have a huge trade deficit, but this is good, since it reflects a strong US economy that demands more products than we can produce. The recent Bush administration contended that the soaring trade deficit reflected a US economy that was growing faster than that of the rest of the world, pushing up the need for imports. In reality, much of what we have been importing was previously produced in the United States by American workers. In addition, a huge amount of resources has been transferred into the hands of foreigners in order to finance this trade deficit. This transfer has begun a long-term lowering of living standards in the United States. In a January 2006 speech at the University of Nevada, Reno, Warren Buffett warned, "If we don't change the course, the rest of the world could own $15 trillion of the United States. That's pretty substantial. That's equal to the value of all American stock."

That the trade deficit is out of control is exemplified by a walk through any major department store. You would be hard-pressed to find "Made in America" labels on merchandise. Nonprofit television service PBS first aired a *Frontline* program on November 16, 2004, featuring Wal-Mart, with emphasis on its business practices. One of the most troubling aspects of the PBS story was the fact that even in 2004, through the port of Long Beach alone, we were receiving $36 billion per year in consumer products from China, while shipping out only $3 billion, mostly represented by raw materials.[1] Sadly, Long Beach is not the only port experiencing this imbalance; it is characteristic of all US ports. As any college student who has taken introductory economics can tell you, a country that imports most of its finished goods and exports raw materials is characterized as a third world country.

By year end 2008, the US trade deficit with China was $268 billion, running 219 percent higher than in 2000.[2] During 2009, the Chinese trade surplus began a slow decline to approximately $226 billion by year end, due primarily to the recession and US consumers cutting back on spending. Of the total amount of trade between the United States and China, our exports to China account for less than 20 percent. The United States would have to increase its exports by five times or cut imports from China by approximately 80 percent just to stabilize the trade deficit. This can't happen, as we no longer manufacture enough to accomplish this, nor are we providing enough high-end professional services to make up for the loss in manufacturing. Exacerbating the deficit is the fact that prior to the recession, import prices were running about 10 percent higher each year. This was the result of the growth of international markets, including China's and India's, and that will continue to drive prices up.

The average American worker is no longer able to maintain a middle-income standard of living without going into debt. Still, during the Clinton and Bush administrations, many of our political leaders, both Democrats and Republicans, wanted us to believe that free trade and offshoring of American jobs was somehow good for America. With a recession in place and double-digit unemployment, the Obama administration has refrained from any positive rhetoric about offshoring jobs but still advocates free trade. There are simply too many lobbyists with major financial backers whose lifeblood depends on free trade.

When we buy foreign goods, services, and natural resources, we put trillions of dollars a year in the treasuries and businesses of foreign countries. Some of this money is invested in our financial markets, which amounts to IOUs to these foreign investors. Like its citizens, the United States government is surviving on borrowed money.

Why Is Our National Debt So High?

1. Congress has been unable and unwilling to control spending.
2. Fighting an expensive war on terrorism.
3. Fighting two foreign wars, though winding down on one.
4. Record-high household debt and bankruptcies.
5. Americans are trying to maintain a standard of living they can no longer afford.
6. Since we no longer produce much in the United States, we are buying record levels of foreign goods on credit.
7. We no longer produce much in the way of goods or services that foreigners wish to buy from us, other than raw materials.
8. We have poorly negotiated free-trade agreements that continue to perpetuate the trade deficit.
9. Other countries maintain trade barriers while successfully insisting that we eliminate ours.
10. We have no effective national program to maintain existing quality jobs and expand quality job growth.
11. We are a financially unattractive place to conduct business operations.

What would happen if China no longer held its currency at artificially low levels and the cost of its products soared? What would happen if the value of our currency continues to decline, making imports even more expensive? What would happen if China and others decided to stop buying our treasuries and wished to sell? Many have argued that a decrease in the value of the yuan would boost the cost of Chinese products, and Americans would then buy American products. The problem is that we no longer produce the consumer goods that our nation requires. It would take many years before we could rebuild our manufacturing base to a point that we could again supply our own needs, much less become an exporter. If the value of Chinese currency rises and the dollar declines, Americans will have little choice other than to pay higher prices for foreign-made consumer goods. This would only hasten the decline of our standard of living and that of the middle class. The recent recession-triggered slowness in the growth of the trade deficit is the result of Americans buying fewer goods (both foreign and domestic), rather than from selling more goods offshore, as some free trade advocates would like us to believe.

PHANTOM GDP

Myth Number 43: Free trade is good for America, as it has stimulated US economic growth. Supporters of free trade like to answer their critics with statements that show that the United States' prerecession economic output was growing at about 3.3 percent annually. This growth, they point out, took place during a period in which the trade deficit grew at an unprecedented rate. They also like to point out that domestic manufacturing was growing, although, they must concede, at a very slow rate.

Michael Mandell of *BusinessWeek* reported that offshoring has inflicted greater damage than government statistics imply. He points out a significant flaw in the way federal statistics treat offshoring. In essence, the growth in domestic manufacturing has been substantially overstated in recent years. The result is that economic growth and productivity have also been overstated, creating "phantom GDP."

This helps to explain the discrepancy between weak wage growth for most Americans and government statistics that claim that US companies are becoming more efficient. In the past, when productivity has risen, the American workers' income has also increased. Since 2001, compensation for the majority of workers has trailed productivity and labors' share of the nation's income has fallen. Where has the income gone? As noted earlier, the top 1 percent of Americans receives about 15 percent of all income, up from about 8 percent in the 1960s and 1970s. Only the best-paid 10 percent of the population have experienced increases in compensation in excess of average productivity growth.[3]

According to the Bureau of Labor Statistics (BLS), import price data does not measure goods as they shift from domestic to foreign production. The phantom GDP is the result of improvements in the global supply chain that are incorrectly attributed to United States growth. In essence, four factors account for this error:

1. Productivity improvement and cost reduction for US companies that occur in other countries are sometimes shown as US GDP growth.
2. When US companies shift R&D and design efforts offshore, the resulting reduction in costs are counted as increases in US productivity.
3. Product improvement and cost reductions that result from subsequent generations of a product that has been offshored are credited to the United States, even when offshore production efficiency and R&D are the cause.
4. If a US company cuts its costs by shifting production from Mexico to China, the resulting savings may show up in US GDP.

Until the Bureau of Labor Statistics develops the methodology for accounting for these significant discrepancies, we will continue to have Phantom GDP growth.[4]

By *BusinessWeek*'s rough estimate, in recent years phantom GDP could account for as much as 40 percent of the gains in manufacturing output. Government statistics show that mid-decade productivity on output per hour has been growing at a rate of about 1.8 percent. Taking phantom GDP into consideration, the actual prerecession rate should be closer to 1.6 percent or the equivalent of the rate in the 1980s.[5] There is no reason to believe that this will change in the post-recession period.

US corporations are supplying their offshore suppliers and subsidiaries with many forms of assistance, including training, research and development, and management, that are not being picked up by federal statistics. In return, these offshore producers are supplying low-cost products. Since the cost savings are not coming from domestic production of goods and don't represent increases in productivity attributable to US workers, it should be no surprise that US workers are not benefiting as their employers become more efficient. Can we continue to downplay the nation's rapidly growing trade deficit based on the false assumption that domestic growth has remained reasonably strong?

CLINTON'S AND BUSH'S FREE TRADE POLICIES

Myth Number 44: Bringing China into the World Trade Organization (WTO) has helped the American economy. Both the Clinton and Bush administrations (1992–2008) have given the Chinese a series of concessions in intellectual property rights and contract laws but have not held them to any standard of reciprocity in trade negotiations. The Clinton administration confidently forecasted that the huge trade deficit with China would improve if Congress would ratify the agreement to bring China into the World Trade Organization. President Clinton said that the agreement was "a win-win result for both countries," pointing to growing exports to China that "now support hundreds of thousands of American jobs" and that "these figures can grow substantially with the new access to the Chinese market the WTO agreement creates."

Within two years of China's entry into the WTO in 2001, the trade deficit increased 50 percent and has continued to rocket upward ever since. Within the same two-year period, 234,000 production jobs were lost in the United States—more than twice the rate of the preceding four years, when only 105,000 jobs were lost.[6] With China in the WTO, was it that difficult for the Clinton administration to foresee that US companies would realize it made better economic sense to produce products within the Chinese market where eager workers would work for 60 cents to $1 per hour, or less?

The problem with our trade policy is that it lacks balance, but worst of all, it can be bought. Free trade, as perceived by the Clinton and Bush administrations, has had a negative impact on the US economy and the American people. Also, as Pollina Corporate Real Estate research has shown, the federal government and far too many state governments do not understand what is necessary to keep companies healthy and growing in the United States. The combination of these two forces has been deadly for American manufacturing and the American worker.

In 1994, the Clinton administration, along with other proponents of the North American Free Trade Agreement (NAFTA)—including both Democrats and Republicans—said that the results of NAFTA would bring 170,000 new US jobs per year. In reality, by 2004 over one million jobs were lost as a direct result of NAFTA, with 660,000 being in manufacturing, according to the Economic Policy Institute.[7] In addition, the US trade deficit in goods with Mexico and Canada had risen from $12 billion in 1993 to a prerecessionary $143 billion in 2008.[8]

NAFTA, CAFTA, WTO, and FTAA must be reevaluated. In fact, we should reevaluate all our trade agreements and our view of free trade as a whole. NAFTA, and later the WTO, both of which were pushed by the Clinton administration, were the beginning of the free trade movement. The banner for free trade was then passed on to the Bush administration, which managed to turn a national budget surplus into a $410 billion deficit (fiscal year end September 2008).[9] This budget deficit did not even include the cost of the wars in Iraq and Afghanistan, estimated at about $170 billion for 2007.[10]

Professor Alan S. Blinder of Princeton University, an avowed free trader and part of President Clinton's Council of Economic Advisers, helped sell NAFTA to Congress and the nation. He has since changed his message. Today he believes that the downside of free trade in today's economy is deeper than many realize. By ranking 817 occupations, described by the Bureau of Labor Statistics as to each occupation's likelihood that it could move offshore, he estimates that thirty million to forty million jobs are at risk over the next two decades. Important to note is that his estimate of jobs lost is not confined to low-skilled jobs but includes most high-skilled jobs that can be delivered electronically.[11] A loss of forty million jobs, based on a US total workforce of approximately one hundred fifty million, represents a 26 percent loss.

What is the Obama administration's position on trade issues? As a candidate, Obama threatened to punish the Chinese for manipulating the value of their currency to boost their exports at the expense of US business. He also promised to renegotiate NAFTA and he opposed President Bush's free trade agreements (FTAs) with Colombia and South Korea. Within months of stepping into office, the president's treasury secretary issued a report that did not indicate that the Chinese were manipulating their currency. Obama also assured the leaders of Canada and Mexico that he would not be changing NAFTA. By April of 2009, he had told the president of Colombia that he should be moving FTAA forward.

Hillary Clinton, during her bid for the presidency, was even more protectionist than Obama. Since taking office as secretary of state, she has placed diplomatic priorities with countries like Colombia and South Korea first, as has the president. It would appear that the administration would now like the entire trade issue to vaporize, possibly until the next election, when winning the American workers' votes takes priority again. A look at the White House Web site agenda of national priorities does not even list trade as an issue (as of January 2010).[12] Trade policy, or the lack thereof, has contributed to the loss of multimillions of quality jobs in the United States that, in turn, has contributed to the recession and will inhibit a full recovery for America's economic future.

Myth Number 45: What's good for American companies, when it comes to international trade, is good for the American people. What is good for US companies in terms of outsourcing offshore is not necessarily good for the US economy. International trade benefits each country when each trading partner is producing different items that their partners need. In the case of China and India, these partners are concentrating on producing the same products and services that we do. If we are not exporting goods and services, our buying power will continue to shrink and with it, our standard of living.

FREE TRADE'S IMPACT ON AMERICA

Paul A. Samuelson, Nobel Prize–winning economist and professor emeritus at the Massachusetts Institute of Technology, in an article published in the prestigious *Journal of Economic Perspectives*, dissented from many other mainstream economists regarding the impact of free trade on America. He disagreed with those who support free trade when they stated that "the gains of the American winners are big enough to more than compensate for the losers." Samuelson wrote, "For it is dead wrong about a necessary surplus of winnings over losings." He contended that low-wage nations like China and India, through the development of technology, can compete with America in such ways as to cause a reduction in United States per-capita income. He noted that low-cost global competition would put pressure on wages.[13] In an interview with the *New York Times*, he said, "If you don't believe that low-cost global competition changes the average wages in America, then you believe in the tooth fairy."[14]

Most important to consider when looking at trade deficit figures is the impact that the loss of jobs and earnings will have in terms of other jobs and earnings lost to the United States. Each job lost has a multiplier effect, taking money out of circulation, causing the loss of other jobs, and generally depressing economic activity. Multipliers vary by type of job. For example, the US Department of Commerce calculated various industry multipliers for the state of Connecticut. For the telecommunications industry, it calculated an employment multiplier of 2.16, which means that for every job gained or lost in this industry, there are another 1.16 jobs either created or lost, respectively. There is also an earnings multiplier to consider. In the case of a telecommunications worker, the multiplier is 3.16, which means that for every dollar invested in local telecommunications, there is an additional $2.16 in earning power created in the local economy.[15]

For the 2007–2008 financial year, India's software offshoring (export) business reached $40.4 billion, up 29 percent over the prior year, and was expected to reach $60 billion for the 2008–2009 financial year. Their biggest customer by far is the United States (70 percent of revenue).[16] India's National Association of Software and Services Companies (NASSCOM) estimated as early as 2005 that the outsourcing industry employed one million programmers and other skilled workers with an employment multiplier of 3.5.[17] Therefore, for every job in the industry, there were 2.5 other people employed as retailers, police officers, government workers, teachers, carpenters, lawyers, and so on.

If we were to step back and assume that if only half of those one million Indian programmers and other skilled workers employed in the Indian software industry were offshored from the United States, the actual loss in US jobs would not be 500,000 but 1,750,000. If we consider the impact of the multiplier effect, it's easy to explain the significant impact of offshoring or the relatively prerecession slow job growth in the United States. No one, not even the US government, knows how many high-tech and professional jobs the United States has offshored, and therefore we have no way of telling where our economy and standard of living would be today had we not been so eager to make it attractive for our companies to offshore them.

It would be a false assumption to believe that wages in the United States, India, and China will become comparable within the foreseeable future. If we compare an Indian software programmer making $30,000 per year and a programmer in the United States making $140,000 per year, you need to understand that the income differential is in large part a reflection of cost of living and not necessarily skill or training. Two things would have to happen for these incomes to become equal: First, until such time that the population of India is pulled out of poverty and achieves a standard of living comparable to that of the United States, wages will remain lower in India. Second, achieving this leveling off would be more realistic if the standard of living in the United States were to decrease, bringing the two standards of living closer. In recent decades, millions of Indian and Chinese have risen from poverty to form a rapidly growing middle class, while the US middle class is in a slow decline. Considering the sheer size of the Indian and Chinese populations and the level of poverty in these nations, these two countries will have a wage advantage for decades.

Myth Number 46: The US middle class is as strong as ever and shows no signs of weakening. Throughout the twentieth century, the United States had the world's largest middle class, a group that grew rapidly during the century and was responsible for the unparalleled accomplishments of our country. There is no standard definition of middle class, but if you took the pretax income of $25,000–$99,999 per household (or a group occupying roughly the middle half of the census income distribution as seen in figure 8), you would have a good representation of the middle class. Rather than a continuation of the middle-class growth that occurred during the twentieth century, the twenty-first century has begun with a decrease of our middle class.

I have used the table shown in figure 8 in speeches, and members of the audience often question the $100,000 starting point for the upper class as being much too low. I believe many people have a difficult time admitting that they are affluent. Much has to do with where you live in the United States. For example, the median household income in Mississippi in 2008 was $36,446, while in New Hampshire it was $66,176. The fact is that the "median" income for the United States was $50,303 (latest data available at the time of this writing). The median is the income that equally divides the number of incomes that are larger and smaller. There were nearly twenty-nine million households (average 2.6 persons per household) in the United States in 2008 with incomes of less than $25,000. President Obama has talked about taxing households with incomes of over $250,000. This group represents approximately 2 percent of all households, and many in this group earn well in excess of $250,000. The US income gap between the rich and the poor is increasing. Among developed countries, the United States, Germany, and Poland rank among the countries with the most rapidly growing gap between top and bottom wages.[17]

In 2008 CPI-U-RS Adjusted Dollars		
	2000 % of households	2008 % of households
Lower Class: $0–$24,999	22.6%	24.8%
Middle Class: $25,000–$99,000	56.4%	54.7%
Upper Class: $100,000+	21.0%	20.5%

FIGURE 8: United States Household Income by Class

Source: United States Census Bureau, Historical Income Tables—Households: Table H-17
Classification: Pollina Corporate Real Estate Inc.

The World Bank estimates that globally the size of the middle class will grow from 430 million in 2000 to over 1.15 billion by 2030. In 2000, developing countries had 56 percent of the global middle class, but by 2030, that figure is expected to reach 93 percent. China and India alone will represent two-thirds of the expansion, with China contributing 52 percent of the increase, and India 12 percent. It is the expectation that of the nearly 700 million new middle class by 2030, approximately 350 million will be in China. Considering that the entire population of the

United States is estimated at 304 million, we can easily see why China's market is so attractive. As China's middle class grows and ours diminishes, so go the respective markets for products. China's dependence on the United States as a marketplace for Chinese products will continue to diminish.

In prerecession 2006, our trade deficit hit its high point of $760 billion by year end. The inability of our nation's political leadership to recognize that a massive trade deficit financed by borrowing foreign capital to buy foreign goods is a formula for a rapidly weakening economy is foolish at best and self-destructive at worst. We are a nation that can no longer produce products for our own consumption, much less for export, and our highly skilled service sector is following in the same footsteps as our manufacturing sector. Perhaps it's time to take our heads out of the theoretical clouds and become the tough, global competitor we were in the twentieth century.

CHAPTER 13

THE ELEVENTH COMMANDMENT
For Some Presidents, It's a Matter of Faith

*The great enemy of the truth is very often not the lie—
deliberate, contrived and dishonest—but the myth—
persistent, persuasive and unrealistic.*

—John F. Kennedy
US president, 1961–1963

RICARDO'S ELEVENTH COMMANDMENT VS. THE SOOTHING SCENARIO

The argument is often made that America's free trade policy reaps enormous benefits. While this is true for our trading partners, it has not been true for the United States. Historically, no nation has ever become an industrial leader under the banner of unrestricted free trade. This is the case today with the rapid rise of China as a world leader in industrial production. The same was true with the rise of Japan and the United States. All have sheltered their industries from foreign competition through the use of tariffs or through less imposing but equally effective obstacles. Free trade and fair trade are defined differently for each country, and the definition can change radically, depending on the people to whom political leaders are talking. When talking to and negotiating with US trade representatives about opening US markets, you can be assured that foreign governments use the term "free trade," but when talking to leaders of their protected home industries they speak of "fair trade."

When speaking on the subject of the trade deficit to groups around the nation, the question I am often asked is, "How does the government justify its trade policies?" There are essentially two directions these discussions can go. First is the economic theory approach that is based on David Ricardo (1772–1823) and his Doctrine of Comparative Advantage, and second is more of a humanitarian approach. Let us first look at the economic theory approach.

Anyone who has read anything about offshoring and free trade has seen references to David Ricardo and his Doctrine of Comparative Advantage. Advocates of free trade, including Presidents Clinton and Bush, held up this theory as if it were carved into the tablet as the eleventh commandment Moses brought down from the mountain. With a trade deficit that is growing by leaps and bounds, something must be wrong with it (see figure 7, on page 198).

No discussion of international trade is complete unless David Ricardo's doctrine is examined. Having had the misfortune of teaching economic theories to college students, I know that this is where many of you may start to groan. I will therefore try to keep it as clear and easy to understand as possible. Most often attributed to Ricardo, the Doctrine of Comparative Advantage was explained in his 1817 book, *The Principles of Political Economy and Taxation*, by using the example of wine and cloth production in England and Portugal. He explained that the relative cost of producing these items is different in these countries. It's difficult to produce wine in England and moderately difficult to produce cloth there, while in Portugal, it's easy to produce both. Therefore, while it's less expensive to produce cloth in Portugal, it's more economical for Portugal to produce excess wine and trade it for English cloth. England benefits because its cost for producing cloth has not changed, but it can buy wine at a cost closer to that of cloth. The point of Ricardo's example is to illustrate the counterintuitive result that specialization and trade will lead to greater well-being for *both* countries, even if one country has the ability to produce all goods at a lower cost.

You're not alone if you just said, "Huh?" However, who are we to question such a doctrine if two recent US presidents have used it to justify their trade policies? Unfortunately for most people, if a concept or theory is difficult to understand, it's simpler to agree with it than to question it. This is especially the case if experts say that you have to understand that it is counterintuitive but true. We are expected to accept this eleventh commandment on faith. What better theory could the Beltway economists and their lobbyists use to justify free trade agreements that support their clients, whether they be US corporations or foreign governments?

What is most amazing is how many politicians, journalists, and authors invoke Ricardo's doctrine as the primary, if not the sole, justification for US free trade policy. What they often ignore are the facts about the repercussions of the Clinton and Bush administrations' free trade policies (see figures 7 and 9, on pages 198 and 223, respectively).

If we are to believe Ricardo's doctrine, we must believe that free trade will create enough economic gains that, when distributed widely enough, will benefit everyone. The doctrine, however, neither predicts when—or if—this will occur. In the interim, the doctrine makes no mention of the fact that large segments of the population may lose their source of livelihood and that entire communities and regions could be economically devastated—as has been the result of free trade in the United States. It's true that some communities and regions rebound, but many don't. States like Michigan, long the nation's automobile hub, struggle as large numbers of automobile parts manufacturers have offshored or have been replaced by offshore suppliers. The southeast United States is also struggling to replace employment opportunities lost as a result of the offshoring of furniture manufacturing, textiles, and shoes.

Myth Number 47: If we support capitalism in China through free trade and we're patient, in time the people will demand democracy and the communists will be forced to concede. Let's go back to the original question about the justification for our trade policy. "How does the government justify its trade policies?" The second attempt at justification is easier to understand than Ricardo's Doctrine, although it is more disturbing. As Americans, we hold democracy very close to our hearts. If you want to convince the American public that something is good for them, tell them it is also good for democracy. Many of our leaders in politics, big business, the media, academia, and Beltway think tanks have been telling us that we must sacrifice to build China's economy through free trade. In the end, we are told by these free trade advocates: This will be good for democracy and America.

Why is a nation—with a one-party Leninist system of government that is known for its heavy-handed suppression of any form of dissent—embraced and protected by American leaders? After all, China has given comfort and even support to unsavory regimes such as those of Robert Mugabe in Zimbabwe and Kim Jong Il in North Korea. Beijing has supported Burma's repressive military government and the Sudanese government for its military actions in the Darfur region. China has consistently blocked efforts by the UN to classify Sudan's actions as genocide and enact sanctions. Granted, in an effort to improve its image, China does occasionally work with the international community to bring pressure to bear on some repressive regimes.

In his book *The China Fantasy: How Our Leaders Explain Away Chinese Repression,* James Mann does an excellent job of explaining how American free trade advocates justify our relationship with China. Dating back to the Nixon administration, which opened the door to China in 1972, a collection of ideas, phrases, illusions, doctrines, and, most important, rationalizations began to emerge. Mann refers to these as the "Soothing Scenario." This scenario was created in an effort to paint China in a positive light and to deflect attention from its repressive method of governing and justify our one-sided trade policies. Every administration since Nixon's has supported the Soothing Scenario.[1]

Well-meaning but self-serving American multinational corporations, with the acquiescence of the Chinese, have sought to keep the United States trading with and investing in China. How do you spin in a positive light a nation with a history of repression? The image of China as a nation of dynamic change was the answer. What better spin could you put on it than to say China is a nation that, through capitalism, will transform itself into a democracy? When we are concerned about the repression in China, jobs lost to China, our trade deficit with China, or its control over our economy, we are offered the Soothing Scenario. A democratic China would benefit America, from a political, economic, and security perspective.

We are warned that China is fragile and that if it is not handled with kid gloves, capitalism could collapse into chaos and with it any hope of democracy. Consequently, critics of China's human rights abuses should not to be too outspoken. President Obama, like his predecessors, has found himself backtracking. Clinton understood soon after taking office that American attempts to force change in China would not work. In less than a year, he changed his mind about making China's low tariff trade terms dependent on China's human rights progress. President Obama succumbed and declined to meet the Dalai Lama during a visit to Washington, DC, in October 2009. Secretary of State Hillary Clinton has said that Chinese human rights should not interfere with US and China discussions on the recession, climate change, and security issues. Clearly, the Obama administration is signaling that human rights in China are not a top priority. President Bush, who claimed it was his policy to support democratic movements, ignored the fact that when he visited China in 2005 the government rounded up dissidents. During the Bush administration, trade with China nearly tripled, with the United States ending up with a huge trade deficit. While our presidents have been ignoring human rights issues in China, anti-Western nationalism protests have increased in China.

Lobbyists for multinational corporations doing business in China tell us that there is no point in upsetting Chinese authorities. They have learned that this only makes them harder to deal with, and the Chinese will not hesitate to punish offenders (see chapter 4).

For those who don't buy the Soothing Scenario, Mann says we are offered the "Upheaval Scenario," which states that China is headed for some sort of disaster.[2] This will cause an economic or political upheaval, which will result in liberalization and democracy. China has certainly been through many trying times, economically and politically, yet the Communist Party always comes out in full control. Since the protests of Tiananmen Square in 1989, China's security force has gotten much better at suppressing any attempts at large-scale demonstrations and the use of the Internet by protesters.[3]

We are told that rapidly growing upper and middle classes are the principal forces for democracy. But as Mann points out, democracy could allow the masses of poor Chinese peasants to undo the privileges that the relatively small Chinese upper and middle classes have enjoyed under the protection of the Communist Party. After all, these classes have the most to lose if the nation falls into a period of upheaval that may simply result in another authoritarian government.

The third scenario offered by Mann is one that few proponents of China or America want to think or talk about, and that is that the one-party system remains in place and does not change in any fundamental way.[4] Are we being sold the Soothing Scenario and the Upheaval Scenario because we do not want to believe that in twenty or thirty years a much richer and more powerful China will be as authoritarian a state as it is today? Americans want to believe that prosperity and trade with the United States will create an atmosphere in China that will demand democracy. Somehow, we believe that no people can resist this great system if only exposed to its advantages. This belief kept us in a prolonged war in Vietnam and most recently a war in Iraq. Wearing blue jeans, drinking Starbuck's coffee, or eating Kentucky Fried Chicken does not make people yearn for democracy; it makes them want more jeans, coffee, and chicken.

We have helped the Chinese to become capitalist, frankly, to the point that we could learn a lot by studying their methods. China is a master at currying favor with the West when it wants something, giving hints of reform that rarely materialize. In an era when capitalists are welcomed into the party built by Mao, it should be apparent that the Chinese communists can adapt and position themselves to gain more power both in China and internationally.

If China's political system stays repressive over the next twenty-five years, will it mean that the American people have been sold a bill of goods again by our own political leaders? If human rights are not a priority and if democracy in China is no closer than it was twenty years ago, why do we reinforce the fallacy about China becoming a democracy? If we are to look at Ricardo or China's democracy as reasons to support free trade with China, Ricardo has a better argument for free trade.

What we must caution against is painting China as an enemy rather than a formidable competitor. China has the ability to control our playbook and manipulate our companies, economy, and political system. I don't believe the Chinese see any advantage in being our enemy when they are doing so well as a competitor.

FREE TRADE REALITY

Myth Number 48: Ricardo's Doctrine of Comparative Advantage holds up as well today as it did in 1817. Since the world has changed considerably in the nearly two hundred years since Ricardo's death, can we assume his 1817 theory is still valid? The most important element on which Ricardo developed his doctrine was that political measures would not change the natural factors of production. He assumed that, in the absence of interference from governments, the international division of labor would result in every country finding its place in the world economy. Obviously, Ricardo did not consider twenty-first-century trade policies, protective tariffs, reciprocating agreements, cartels, monetary policies, intellectual property laws, and enforcement. Nor could he have considered the impact of transportation systems and the transfer of knowledge and technology, afforded by the Internet, when developing his doctrine. In the twenty-first century, capital and the fruits of labor move between nations as was never before possible. Ricardo's Doctrine of Comparative Advantage is based on many assumptions that are not valid in today's very imperfect and complex global economic system.

Two very important points should be noted regarding Ricardo's theory. First, Ricardo says, "Under a system of perfectly free commerce." In today's world, we are a far cry from having such a system of free commerce, and there is no reason to believe it will ever come to be. Second, Ricardo states "But if in consequence of the diminished rate of production in the land of England, from the increase of capital and population, wages should rise and profits fall, it would not follow that capital and population would necessarily move from England to Holland, or Spain, or Russia, where profits might be higher." Unlike in 1817, today both capital and population move relatively freely internationally, and both certainly are following profits. If capital could flow as easily across borders in 1817 as it does today, there would be no advantage to invest in cloth or wine in England. In addition, the doctrine does not consider the impact that shifts in production can have on political decisions, the environment, and social inequities.

Viewing international trade as it ought to work in theory rather than how it actually works has gotten the United States into a difficult and dangerous situation. We have either bowed to special-interest lobbyists who fear trade retaliation against their clients' personal interest, or we have behaved in a naive manner, assuming that if we make concessions, our trading partners will reciprocate.

Understanding the world beyond our country is essential to our economic future and to our very survival. From a trade perspective, we are considered weak—you need only look at our balance of trade to have that verified. Not only do our trading partners bully us as a nation, but our companies are also bullied. The worst part is that we have brought it on ourselves; we have set ourselves up as an easy target. We're viewed as weak and thus are subject to being bullied.

President Teddy Roosevelt once said, "Speak softly and carry a big stick." Roosevelt used this proverb to define his foreign policy, including US trade and financial interests around the world. It would appear that in recent decades our "big stick" (world's largest economy and market) is getting smaller as our government's rhetoric relative to free trade gets louder.

To have faith in Ricardo, you must believe that governments don't concede to special interests and that the impediments to free trade deliberately introduced by nations can be eliminated in order to free the movement of goods and services. The following are some examples of politically imposed impediments that complicate the Doctrine of Comparative Advantage or any other attempt to justify free trade:

Difference in taxation. According to the Tax Foundation, the United States now has the second-highest corporate tax rates among Organisation for Economic Co-operation and Development (OECD) nations. There are nations that charge no corporate income taxes in order to improve their competitive advantage.

Restriction on the flow of intellectual property. How long could we survive if other nations had free access to all US R&D to use as they pleased? In China alone, bootleggers selling DVDs for 75 cents cost US studios $3.8 billion per year.[5]

Tariffs and import quotas. These and their offshoots, including border taxes, antidumping procedures, and voluntary limitations of exports, are utilized by most advanced nations. They are used to protect national security (defense industries) fledgling industries, and critical industries (agriculture) and to counteract governments that subsidize certain industries to gain market share.

Health, fair labor, safety, and environmental standards. The United States and other nations attempt to impose their standards on developing nations that effectively place obstacles in the way of trade for these nations. American and Western European countries are quick to highlight the inhumane working conditions and environmental degradation in developing countries. Will all nations incur the costs to ensure the same environmental and safety standards and work conditions for their workers that Western nations have?

Restrictions on free movement of services. The United States, as well as other countries, restricts the right to provide professional services, such as medical, financial, and legal. There are state monopolies on telecommunications service and restrictions on foreign airlines, enforced by limiting landing permits. Can we expect that the powerful trial lawyers' lobbyists will allow Indian lawyers into the United States to file class action suits for contingency fees substantially lower than those of American trial lawyers?

Restrictions on the flow of international labor. This is a common practice in economically advanced countries, including the United States. These restrictions take the form of work permits and student visas, or they are evident in the practice of simply not recognizing diplomas or other certifications of professional expertise.

Restrictions on the flow of capital. There are countries that restrict the flow of capital out of their country on the assumption that the funds will be invested domestically if not allowed to go offshore. Many nations, including China and India, at times have placed restrictions on the purchase by foreigners of certain domestic assets, including real estate, securities, and all but a minority interest in domestic companies. Foreign companies have the privilege of providing all the capital, technology, and experience, but they still may be required to take a minority partnership role. In spite of uneven restrictions, capital now flows internationally like never before.

Undervalued currency. Officials in most economically advanced countries have long complained that China should let its currency rise with the market. Harvard economist Dani Rodrick estimates that China's yuan is about 50 percent below what it should be trading at when compared to other developing countries, which gives China an unfair trade advantage.[6]

Restrictions on the cost of labor. Among other advantages of keeping the value of the Chinese yuan pegged low relative to the dollar has been the advantage of keeping Chinese investments in China, where the yuan would buy more. Of course, keeping the value of the yuan pegged below the dollar has ensured that Chinese wages would remain substantially below US wages and that their products would be priced lower.

In November 2008, G-20 leaders signed a pledge to avoid protectionist measures. By March 2009, many countries, including seventeen of the G-20, implemented forty-seven measures that restrict trade at the expense of other countries, according to a World Bank study. For example, Russia raised tariffs on used autos, China banned importation of various European items like Belgian chocolate, Italian brandy, and Spanish dairy products, and India banned Chinese toys. Some countries approach the free trade issue from a different direction by subsidizing key industries, such as the automotive industry. By April 2009, over $48 billion worldwide was given or loaned to this industry by countries such as the United States, Canada, France, Germany, the United Kingdom, China, Argentina, Brazil, Sweden, and Italy. The fact is, stimulus money given to banks, agribusiness, or other industries is in effect a form of a protectionist trade barrier.[7]

In August 2008, after fourteen years of discussion, the Chinese government imposed a broad antimonopoly law. Many found this to be somewhat surprising, since the country is loaded with government-imposed and government-controlled monopolies. In March 2009, China used the law to stop the merger of Coca-Cola and Huiyuan, China's largest privately owned juice producer. This should not be surprising, in spite of the fact that China is very vocal about other countries opening their markets to Chinese investment and trade.

In June 2009, China placed restrictions on the export of nine critical raw materials (bauxite, coke, fluorspar, magnesium, manganese, silicon carbide, silicon metal, yellow phosphorus, and zinc). The United States and European Union claimed that China was breaking World Trade Organization rules. China argued that it was within the rules, as these restrictions were in keeping with China's environmental and energy conservation measures that are allowed under WTO rules.[8]

Obviously, other nations as well as the United States do not truly practice free trade, yet each insists that the others must. We have the "big stick," but for fear of alienating trading partners who may threaten retaliation against special-interest groups in the United States, we most often refuse to use it. Our "big stick" from a trade perspective is not our military power but rather the power of our market. Each year, as we increase our national and personal debt, lose our best jobs and industries, and decrease our ability to supply ourselves with goods and services produced in the United States, we shorten our stick. If we are bullied into weak trade policies now, what will it be like when we become less attractive as a market for foreign goods and services?

THEORY VS. EMPIRICAL EVIDENCE

Since the days of Ricardo, economic, political, and technological conditions throughout the world have changed considerably. In the twenty-first century, the United States will continue to slip as long as capital and technology are moved offshore to pursue a virtually limitless supply of skilled, low-cost labor and high-growth markets. Huge supplies of low-cost labor in China and India will continue to cause wages in America to fall faster than Asian wages will rise. Senator Charles Schumer and economist Paul Craig Roberts, in a January 6, 2004, *New York Times* article, "Second Thoughts on Free Trade," claim that in the eighteenth century, Ricardo's "factors of production" were not as mobile as they are today. They state that, in Ricardo's day, the critical factors of production—soil, climate, geography, and most workers—were immobile. Today, key production factors of capital, technology, and ideas are easily moved across borders, thereby undermining Ricardo's Doctrine of Comparative Advantage. The result, per

Schumer and Roberts, is that "some countries win and others lose," as new jobs are created overseas at the expense of jobs in America. They did not propose old-fashioned protectionist measures but rather a new era of "new thinking and new solutions." Still, they were criticized as "protectionists."

Myth Number 49: If all nations supported free trade, the US economy would grow, as would every country's economy. The most common Ricardoian argument is that, according to the Doctrine of Comparative Advantage, different countries each produce different products that they can produce most efficiently. Productivity is improved for each country, and thus the size of the pie grows larger. The question that is not addressed by the critics of Schumer, Roberts, and others who have favored Ricardo is how this pie is distributed among the countries. Can one country end up with a substantially smaller piece of the pie? It should be quite obvious that the average American's share of the pie is getting smaller.

In the time of Ricardo, many of the factors of production were immobile. Countries had different relative costs, geography, climates, and economic systems, most of which were based on agriculture. Knowledge moved slowly geographically. And adding all these factors together affected trade. Today, knowledge is bounced around the world instantly via the Web, and the limitations on producing crops in certain parts of the world have changed through the use of technology. Now, capital and business move quickly and quietly across borders. Materials and finished products move freely and cheaply around the world. In relative terms, the only item of production that does not move as freely is labor, and that is in large part due to political restrictions. As long as Asia maintains its huge supply of low-cost workers, it will have an absolute advantage. (But as we've seen, that is far from the only reason that China has an advantage.)

Supporters of Ricardo also argue that there will be jobs left for Americans, viewing this not as a short-term but a long-term result. They believe there will be a structural change in the US economy, which is not explained, and that with specialization and an overall larger economy, the United States will be better off. They argue that while many Americans will lose their jobs, they will simply be reeducated and trained for new jobs, although what these jobs are to be is not made clear. Thus far, we have not found any jobs that Chinese or Indian workers could not be trained to do as well as Americans, and at a considerably lower cost. There are also those who argue that buying cheap, foreign goods outweighs lower wages here in America. In reality, lower wages have resulted in a lower standard of living for Americans.

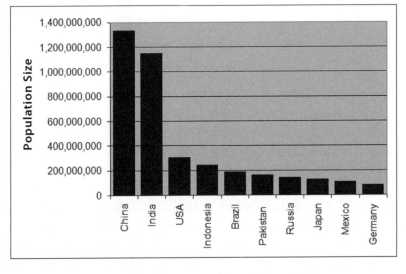

FIGURE 9: Select Nations' Populations, 2009

Source: CIA—*The World Fact Book*, 2009

There was a time when free trade proponents made the argument that free trade would open huge markets in China, India, and elsewhere in the world for American companies. There is no question that these markets are developing rapidly and that many American companies are benefiting. The problem is that those markets will be supplied not by American workers but by Asian workers, because we shipped our production capability offshore along with our jobs, leading to a huge trade deficit, rather than a surplus.

The ultimate free trade argument is that there are industries and jobs yet to be identified that will replace those lost in offshoring to China and India. The baffling part of this logic is why or how one could assume that these industries or occupations would not also be lost to an endless supply of well-educated, highly skilled foreign workers who are willing to work for considerably less than Americans.

Some may argue that free trade, per the comparative advantage argument, gives the United States an advantage in high-wage industries due to our superior entrepreneurial spirit. This belief does not take into consideration that America is falling behind educationally, nor does it recognize the sheer size of the foreign populations with whom we compete. The Chinese and Indian populations total 2.4 billion, while the United States is 308 million (12 percent of China and India) (see figure 9, on page 223). Technological leadership is fleeting; it can be distributed around the world in seconds, pirated, improved, and sold. Even then, it may only have a shelf life of six months before a new and better technology is sent around the world.

The fact is that the comparative advantage argument is a powerful analytical tool that can be used to explain much of the world's international trade. However, when applied to a world of imperfect competition with significant market distortion, resulting in unbalanced international trade, Ricardo's theory must be questioned. Certainly, a nation such as the United States should not base its foreign trade policy on a two-hundred-year-old economic theory. To allow our trade policy to be dictated by special interests with different objectives than the American public is equally short-sighted and dangerous for our future. As a result of free trade, we have been selling off America's best jobs, our manufacturing base, and technological leadership. Even if we have received some questionable benefits or the assurance of a democratic China, the long-term prognosis does not bode well for the American worker or her standard of living.

CHAPTER 14

THE HIGH COST OF FREE TRADE

Qui se fait brebis le loup le mange.

He who makes himself a sheep must expect to be devoured by the wolf.

—General William Eaton
1764–1811

FREE VS. FAIR TRADE POLICY

There was a time, as Teddy Roosevelt stated, when we could expect that our children and our children's children would have a better life. The Chinese, Indian, Japanese, and Russian governments want the same. So to believe that any of these nations want anything less than to bump the United States out of first place is naive. Be assured that the only economic theory they adhere to is the one that will put them in first place. If this means driving the American standard of living down in the process, some would view this as an added bonus. There are political leaders around the world who would view an America with diminished economic power and with a resulting decline in political and military power as a significant benefit. Our competitors encourage the United States to continue believing in free trade rather than fair trade because they profit from our folly.

Myth Number 50: If we don't continue our free trade policy, we'll be called protectionists, and this will harm our trade negotiations. The only way to diminish our dependency on imports and boost job growth is to switch from a free trade to a fair trade policy. Fair trade does not mean protectionism. Free trade agreements in the 1990s promised US workers a chance to export their products to new markets around the world. In reality, the only thing exported was their jobs.

When the concept of "free trade" is defined, it generally refers to a lack of governmental barriers and protectionist policies, such as tariffs, quotas, export subsidies, currency manipulation, and multiple exchange rates. Under free trade, governments do not discriminate against imports or interfere with exports. In theory, the producers of goods or services in trading partner countries all have the same practices. On the other extreme are "protectionists," who believe there should be rules to protect markets and workers from imports.

In essence "fair trade" looks beyond individual, corporate, or industry interests, giving precedence to national interests. Under fair trade practices, when a government determines that an unfair trade practice is being used by another country, they can offset it through higher import duties, quotas, or other restrictions, thus keeping competition open between foreign and domestic companies.

Myth Number 51: We can solve the loss of American jobs to offshoring problem if Americans would simply buy American-made products. When pressed about the offshoring of American jobs, many politicians used to profess the mantra "We should all buy American." Today, these same politicians have finally come to the realization that we can't "buy American" anymore. At best, you might find a product assembled in the United States from parts produced abroad. Even our so-called American-made cars and pickup trucks, while assembled in the United States, are increasingly being made from parts produced in Canada, Mexico, and China. What could be more American than the Ford Mustang? Assembled in America, 45 percent of the Mustang's parts are from other countries. The Japanese Toyota has a higher percentage of its parts made in the United States than the Mustang.[1] Ninety-six percent of all clothing sold in the United States, including from our own designers, is imported. These politicians asked us to "buy American" to diffuse the situation, drawing attention away from their inept trade policies directed by special-interest lobbyists.

We hear politicians and commentators claim that free trade has resulted in lower-priced goods and that this allows labor and resources to be used for other things to improve our standard of living. This theory makes sense, only if free trade is not at the expense of jobs. Currently, debt-ridden Americans must have lower-cost consumer goods since they can't afford anything else. As markets grow in China, India, Eastern Europe, and elsewhere, the United States will compete for these foreign-made goods, with the result that prices will be raised. The problem is that American incomes will not be rising if we proceed in the same way we've been going.

Senator Byron L. Dorgan (D-ND) in a Senate hearing quoted a report submitted to Congress by President Bush that said, "When a good or service is produced more cheaply abroad, it makes more sense to import it than to make or provide it domestically." Senator Dorgan, who has taught economics and is familiar with Ricardo's Doctrine of Comparative Advantage, argues against such a trade philosophy and states that "in my judgment, our country is injuring itself and is not doing what it needs to do for our own self-interest by allowing this kind of trade to continue." He continues that those who speak out against free trade are called "protectionists, some sort of xenophobic isolationist stooges who just don't get it." Senator Dorgan makes the point that we too often rush into trade agreements that are not mutually beneficial.[2] These free trade agreements have a lot to do with producing benefits only for stockholders of international corporations, and in the long run, they weaken the country.

SIXTEEN YEARS OF PING-PONG TRADE POLICY

In 1994, President Clinton promised the American people that if Congress ratified the WTO treaty, the average American family would experience a $1,700-per-year increase in income.[3] William Greider, in his book *One World Ready or Not: The Manic Logic of Global Capitalism*, suggests that this is like promising that everyone on the block will get richer if one neighbor wins the lottery.[4] In reality, as international trade has grown, gains have gone to the wealthiest segment of the nation, wages for the majority have stagnated, and for many, wages are falling.

The exporting of America's jobs is a relatively recent phenomenon, starting in earnest during the Clinton administration. Many Democrats and Republicans continue to assure us that this is the result of the postindustrial economy that will inevitably result in a stronger America with a higher standard of living for all. Since the established facts do not reflect these claims, the question must be asked: Who is providing our political leadership with the research on which they base their claim? Are they not reading the newspapers or their constituents' letters or their own federal and state employment statistics? Again, keep in mind that this downward spiral of jobs and income began to occur long before the recession began.

Myth Number 52: Ross Perot was wrong in 1992, as a presidential candidate, when he referred to the "giant sucking sound" caused by US jobs leaving for Mexico if we supported the North American Free Trade Agreement (NAFTA). Ross Perot recognized that our trade policy was being developed by lobbyists for the benefit of corporate special-interest groups. He wrote, "Ultimately, NAFTA is not a trade agreement, but an investment agreement. NAFTA's principal goal is to protect the investment of United States companies that build factories in Mexico. This is accomplished by reducing the risk of nationalization, by permitting the return of profits to United States businesses, and by allowing unlimited access to the American markets for goods produced in Mexico."[5]

Corporations, particularly today's global corporations, wield tremendous influence on government trade agreements. When it suits them, these advocates of free trade can also be adamant protectionists. As Greider points out, at the same time the Clinton administration was pushing NAFTA and the WTO, it was helping develop a worldwide aluminum cartel to raise prices by limiting production.[6]

In his January 2004 State of the Union Address, President Bush said, "My administration is promoting free and fair trade to open new markets for America's entrepreneurs, manufacturers, and farmers, and to create jobs for American workers." In March 2002, that same president, pushed by steel industry lobbyists, announced the imposition of tariffs of up to 30 percent on imported steel in an effort to shore up the industry. After twenty months and the threat of a trade war with European countries and Japan, Bush repealed the tariffs on steel.[7]

By the end of the Bush administration (2009), we had sixteen years of a ping-pong trade policy. Both the Clinton and Bush administrations were professed free trade advocates, but both made many exceptions. We have no game strategy; in essence, our trade policy has bounced back and forth, controlled primarily by the lobbyist or foreign trade partner that is serving the ball the fastest. The one common element has been a lack of planning to achieve what is best for the American people and our economy.

Sixteen years of weak foreign trade leadership has placed the American economy in a perilous position. Neither administration held to a consistent policy with a vision and with the goal of helping the American public and improving our economy. We have not had a consistent trade policy, and our trading partners and the K-Street lobbyists know this. We have gotten ourselves into an international trade game where all the players, both in the United States and abroad, are calling the plays to benefit their individual interests, while the American workers and the economy suffer.

There are many tools the United States can use to help improve our trade deficit, including tariffs. There is nothing wrong with tariffs if they are applied consistently and for a purpose other than solely to raise profits for stockholders. If a US industry is in trouble, and the profits resulting from the tariffs are reinvested in updating plants and equipment so that the industry, in time, is able to compete internationally without the aid of tariffs, then tariffs make sense. Other countries have successfully used this tool to help develop new industries and protect critical industries like agriculture and defense. The biggest problem for the United States is that we do not use this tool properly, nor do we have what it takes to withstand the pressure from foreign governments or lobbyists.

STEEL INDUSTRY TARIFF

The steel industry tariff signed by President Bush in 2002 is an example of the misuse of tariffs. The history of the US steel industry is a fascinating one. To understand why the steel industry tariffs alone wouldn't work, you need to understand the history of the industry and how and why it got into trouble. One of the nation's greatest business leaders, Andrew Carnegie, was instrumental in the early development of the industry.

Under Carnegie's leadership, Carnegie Steel dominated a highly competitive American steel industry. Carnegie took great pride in creating better technology to reduce costs and improve productivity and profits. This effort involved the expenditures of enormous sums of money and the constant return of profits into the business, but it produced results in the form of better products and greater market share and profits.

Carnegie's success also came from management practices that today are commonly followed, including recruiting top executives, vertical integration (all stages of production from acquisition of raw materials to retailing), acquisition, and development of modern plants and technology. In 1901, the Carnegie Company was sold, and US Steel Corporation was established. With the transition came a change in management philosophy—the dominant philosophy became stability with emphasis on short-term profits and a lack of interest in long-term research. Incredibly, the head of research for US Steel in 1927 said on behalf of the President James Farrell, "Research is needless because the corporation already knows substantially all they need to know about steel in order to make it at a profit."[8]

In spite of this philosophy, US Steel products hit their height in 1947 when the company produced 56.7 percent of the world's output. By 1982, US production dropped to only 9.2 percent, with a higher unit cost than Japan, West Germany, France, and the United Kingdom. The Japanese and Europeans began to restructure their steel industries in the 1950s, and US steel companies continued to maintain their short-term philosophy and their old technology. Along with better technology came higher quality and lower prices. United States steel producers were excluded from foreign markets, not because of tariffs, but primarily because of quality and price.

The US steel industry, with its huge plants, also initially ignored the mini-mills that began to be a significant force in the country during the 1960s. High productivity at these mini-mills was the result of a number of factors, including a high reliance on scrap metals and resulting lower energy costs. In addition, these facilities were relatively small and more geographically dispersed, thereby cutting transportation costs and delivery time. Very important was the fact that, due to their smaller size and investment, they were constantly able to adopt the most recent technology, unlike the huge plants on which the US steel industry continued to rely.

With the imposition of President Bush's 2002 steel tariffs came immediate complaints from domestic steel consumers and foreign steel producers. The tariff was initially to last three years to allow the industry to reorganize, but the tariffs lasted less than two years. Trade retaliation threatened by the European Union and Japan forced Bush to back down. While some reorganization took place, with some struggling companies being bought by larger ones and some jobs being cut, the industry did not begin the radical change it needed to become a global competitor. The lobbyists did achieve their goal of keeping profits up and union workers employed for a little longer, but the real issues of the industry were not addressed.

When the administration was finally hit with the WTO ping-pong paddle, they responded by rescinding the tariffs on December 4, 2003.[9] The European Union and the Japanese know our system and how to manipulate it. They threatened trade retaliation against other US industries, and then waited for the lobbyists from these industries to bang on the White House and congressional doors. By the time the WTO was ready to take action, President Bush, under pressure from the lobbyists, was ready to rescind the tariffs.

The United States has tended to use tariffs to protect investors and workers when pressured by industry and labor union lobbyists, with little or no emphasis on turning the industry around. Plowing profits into automation with a resulting improvement of productivity has not been a popular process with stockholders or unions. Few would argue that the US steel industry was not distressed. The question that should have been addressed was whether steel tariffs would allow the industry to reinvest in itself and become more competitive in a global market. Lobbyists working for their large steel industry clients focused the blame for the industry's problems on imports and the need for protective tariffs. While this was happening, over half of the decline in large, integrated steel production in the United States was attributable to the growth of domestic mini-mills.[10]

Steel is an industry that is certainly worth saving. Tariffs alone were not going to save the industry, even if they had been kept in place for six years, rather than the originally planned three years. It would have been more beneficial to implement tax credits for research and development, low-interest or forgivable loans for new state-of-the-art mini-mills, grants for retraining employees, and improved infrastructure. The burden need not have fallen entirely on the federal government. There are some progressive states that would have helped with these improvements in order to gain jobs.

The steel industry, like the US auto industry, is burdened with "legacy costs"—the benefits promised retired workers. These costs place a greater cost burden on the older, heavily unionized US steel industry as opposed to the newer mini-mills. This burden makes it difficult for the industry not only to compete but also to reorganize. No investor wants to buy a company with such liabilities. Continued industry bankruptcies will shift much of this legacy cost to the government.

President Bush's initial instinct to help the steel industry was correct, and I would even argue that temporary tariffs should have been a part of the strategy. The problem was that the tariffs were too little, too late. It was placing a Band-Aid on a mortal wound. Certainly, the tariffs provided relief to the industry, which allowed some reorganization to take place and even the implementation of some new technology. However, the administration and the industry did not address the real problems of legacy costs and antiquated plants and equipment. Had the industry, with federal and state assistance, taken significant steps to make it competitive in the international market, then President Bush should have kept the tariffs in place in spite of the pressure to rescind.

However, considering the lack of a comprehensive program to significantly improve the industry, the tariffs were ill conceived. We cannot have a steel industry that survives only when the economy is strong and demand is high, and then slides into financial difficulty when there is a dip in the economy and/or in demand. The nation needs a steel industry that can hold its own and be competitive in the international marketplace of the twenty-first century. The story of the steel industry illustrates an administration willing to react to the problem as outlined by industry lobbyists (loss of profits) and not to the root causes of the problem.

ISOLATIONIST TEMPTATION

The knee-jerk reaction to our current balance of trade and job loss situation is to move toward isolationism. A major segment of America's population has always supported isolationism. Both sides of the isolation debate have, and continue to make, strong arguments. An isolationist attitude in trade is not the solution to improving America's economic prospects for the twenty-first century. As a superpower we need to be involved globally, especially relative to international trade and in terms of strategic alliances with other countries.

In spite of all the protectionist activity and the decline in world trade resulting from the recession, most companies have become so dependent on their worldwide tentacles and markets that protectionist policies will adversely affect the domestic production we have maintained. For example, the US automotive industry asked for bailout money, not tariffs. In addition to being dependent on parts supply chains from Mexico, China, and elsewhere, their foreign competitors already operate major assembly plants in the United States, and they see foreign markets as critical to their survival.

The weakest argument for avoiding trade isolationism is that we will lose our friends and the support of the international community. After nearly sixteen years of free trade under Clinton and Bush and intense involvement in world affairs, we have found ourselves with few friends. Most of Western Europe disagrees with much of what we do, including our positions in the Middle East and the war in Iraq. China, Japan, and India have taken our best jobs, and some in the Arab world would be pleased to see the United States implode. Isolationism is, however, not the solution to the situation. The situation we are in is the result of poor leadership and a lack of long-term strategic planning along with neglect of the process of alliance building. To look to isolationism as a solution is to admit the United States lacks the leadership necessary to correct the situation.

It's a good thing that the rest of the world is growing economically. India, China, eastern Europe, Brazil, and Mexico, as well as many other nations, should be proud of what they have accomplished. The fact that the middle classes of these and other countries are growing should help to stimulate economic growth and prosperity internationally. Our government, however, has steered us down a path where this growth has been occurring at the expense of most Americans. This does not have to be the case. We need to understand this growth and why it is occurring, and then develop a national strategy to harness this surge in economic growth to benefit our nation as a whole.

Today, we allow special-interest groups to map out a multitude of uncoordinated trade strategies that benefit individual companies or industries, with little, if any, thought given to the long-term impact on the American people. In addition, our political leaders, at the federal and state levels, just do not grasp the simple and most basic economic concept—that capital goes where it is needed and stays where it's well treated.

Protectionism is not the solution. We're in the twenty-first century—a century of global economic activity like we have never experienced before. We cannot look to the past and expect the same for the future. With economic growth comes disruption. Industries will change, some will disappear and others will be created. We must make sure we're on the cutting edge of the best of those new industries. Today, we're truly in an economic war and rapidly positioning ourselves to lose. In economic warfare there are losers, but there can also be many winners. We entered this new century an economic superpower, and if we don't exit it as such, it will be due to our own weak strategic planning, mismanagement, and leadership. We must not hide from globalization but embrace it in a manner that will benefit all Americans.

There are many ways to isolate a nation; trade is only one. To isolate a nation based on politics or religion can be more divisive and enduring. We moved a long way toward isolating the United States politically during the Bush administration. We isolated ourselves because we lost the respect and support of other nations.

Most important, we lost the support of Europe, a part of the world that we long counted among our closest friends and allies. The British, French, or Germans individually may not become superpowers comparable to China or America, but as part of the European Union, they have achieved that status in economic terms. In Brussels, the capital of the EU, politicians and strategists are increasingly seeing themselves as the fulcrum between America in the West and China and India in the East. Europe is able to play all sides and, as a result, has positioned itself to profit extremely well in the twenty-first-century global market.

The EU represents the world's largest market. In spite of setbacks in some member countries such as Greece and Spain, it is still considered as one of the safest places to bank and invest money, especially if America and China were to begin a conflict. The euro is likely to become the currency of choice if the dollar's value becomes less stable. If investors scrambled to switch into more stable and secure currency, we would be unable to slow or stop the decline in the value of the dollar.

As European economic and political influence grows, US influence wanes. America continues to lose its political influence and friends, while the EU continues to add new nations to its sphere of influence. Increasingly, the poor of the world are looking to the EU Dream rather than the American Dream. After 9/11, we turned our backs on the world's best and brightest by making it difficult to study in the United States, so they turned increasingly to European schools. Many of these students will remain in Europe (as many once had done in the United States), and those that return home are destined to become their countries' leaders. We are not educating them, so they will find it increasingly difficult to understand and identify with the United States.

Myth Number 53: If you ask anybody in the world where they would like to live, they will tell you, America. For over a year, I made a point of running an informal survey. When I was in a cab or a research facility anywhere in the United States and I met a person who was from another country but living in the United States, I asked the same question: If your relatives and friends in (Europe, the Middle East, Africa, Asia, South America, or Russia) were given a choice of living in America or the European Union, which would they choose? The most common choice by far was the EU. The last four people I asked were a young engineer with an MBA, an accountant with a CPA, a journalist with a master's degree, and an assistant professor with a PhD. All had received their degrees in the United States. The MBA and PhD were from western Europe, the CPA from central Europe, and the journalist from China. The general consensus of the four was that their friends and families would be unanimous in selecting the EU. Some of the comments they recounted from their friends and family were, "Ten years ago I would have picked the United States; not today." "If you're educated and work hard, your chances for advancement are better in the EU." "Why get paid in dollars when the euro is worth so much more?" "The economy and standard of living in the EU are improving and in the United States they're on the way down." If the rest of the world can see what is happening, why is it that we Americans have such a hard time understanding what is happening to our country? Another common comment is that many people around the world are no longer enthralled with our politics or our political system. In previous decades, if you were to ask people throughout the undeveloped part of the world what kind of political system they would like to live under, they would clearly have favored the American system. Today, they view our system as having a single powerful leader and therefore prefer the parliamentary system.

Europe, China, and India understand the impact of globalization better than we do, and they are making the necessary effort to integrate it into their economic and political systems. Europeans have a long-term view, which is true for their political leaders and companies. The Bush administration lectured the rest of the world about advancing "American values." The rest of the world doesn't care about American values. While the Europeans are making friends throughout the world, we did a spectacular job of creating enemies.

Are our political leaders really delusional enough to believe that the nations in the rest of the world want a single leading nation to protect them and guide them in economics, culture, and political thinking? As a nation, we don't get it. In the twenty-first century, the rest of the world will resist centralized power in favor of globalization. If we do not understand this, we will become increasingly isolated.

Our American companies recognize how important it is to be a part of the twenty-first-century global economy and what needs to be done to be a dominant force. Our government has had a difficult time comprehending this. Embracing this concept is not about being liberal or conservative. It is about survival. If a nation does not have friends in the world, it *will* become isolated, and once that occurs, it makes no difference how powerful its military is—that nation will not survive for long. We need friends, but we must also recognize the competition for what it is.

In President Obama's 2006 book *The Audacity of Hope*, while discussing the competition that existed between the great powers that had dominated the nineteenth and early twentieth centuries, he states, "That world no longer exists. The integration of Germany and Japan into a world system of liberal democracies and free-market economies effectively eliminated the threat of great-power conflicts inside the free world." He goes on to say, "Today, the world's most powerful nations (including, to an ever-increasing extent, China)—and, just as important, the vast majority of the people who live within these nations—are largely committed to a common set of international rules governing trade, economic policy, and legal and diplomatic resolution of disputes, even if broader notions of liberty and democracy aren't widely observed within their own borders."[11]

I would argue that if President Obama still maintains this philosophy, he is proceeding in a naive and perilous direction. The competition that existed between nations in the nineteenth and early twentieth centuries never really disappeared but rather was suppressed by the power that the United States gained in the latter half of the twentieth century. It should be clear that the rest of the world did not become committed to a common set of rules governing trade, economic policy, and legal and diplomatic resolution of disputes. They were forced to bend to the will of the United States—we intimidated them. We made the rules and had the ultimate economic and military power to back them up. It should also be clear that we did not make a lot of friends. As we have entered the twenty-first century, with the rise of other powers in the world and the decline of the United States, I would expect that memories will be long and the new powers of the world will rise with a bit of vengeance in their hearts. The Obama administration has a lot of bridge-building to accomplish with our enemies, as well as those nations that we have considered our friends. Chinese general and highly regarded military strategist Sun Tzu (sixth century BCE) is credited with the statement "Keep your friends close, but your enemies closer." This is excellent advice, provided you recognize who your enemies are.

CHAPTER 15

THERE'S NO SUCH THING AS WIN-WIN NEGOTIATING

Negotiations are a euphemism for capitulation if the
shadow of power is not cast across the bargaining table.
—George Schultz
US secretary of state
1982–1989

LOSE-LOSE NEGOTIATIONS

The failure of our government to do what is right for the people and our future is not taking place just at the federal level, but also at the state and local levels. After years of representing companies in relocation and negotiating state and local incentives, I continue to be amazed at the lack of realization on the part of political leaders that they could lose existing local jobs. This was particularly true during the years leading up to the recession, and it has not changed in many states even during the recession. There was a pervasive approach that I call lose-lose negotiations, in which a state, community, and company all lost because each side didn't believe the other side had options. The following is only one of my numerous experiences that demonstrate how state and local governments and unions drive jobs offshore.

Several years ago, a European client purchased a company in the United States. The company had been established and located in the same small town for over ninety years. The company, with over eight hundred fifty employees, was the largest private employer in a rural three-county area. In spite of an earlier reduction of one hundred fifty employees and other attempts to cut costs, the company was headed for bankruptcy. The major problem was that the company was unable to compete with offshore competition utilizing low-cost labor. Our client believed that fully automating the plant would make the operation competitive in the international market. This program would involve a considerable capital investment in new equipment and the retraining of employees; it would result in the reduction of two hundred fifty jobs over a thirty-six-month period.

The company hired my firm to examine the short- and long-term advantages and disadvantages of (1) remaining at their current location; (2) relocating to a more pro-business location in the United States; or (3) relocating to Mexico. Key to alternatives 1 and 2 was the support of local and state governments relative to the capital investment required for automation. This assistance was necessary to offset substantially lower Mexican labor costs.

The lowest-cost solution was alternative 3, moving to Mexico, followed closely by alternative 2, another location in the United States. The only advantage to alternative 3 was lower labor costs. We were able to identify two US locations that were willing to provide up to $38 million in state and local incentives, including fully improved sites for free real estate, sales and income tax abatements or credits, training assistance, and cash grants or forgivable loans for new equipment, among other forms of financial assistance. In addition, the new US locations would have provided lower-cost labor and better access to customers.

The state and community where the company was originally located went into "stall mode," beginning the process of lose-lose negotiations. The mayor said that the company had been there for ninety years and wasn't going to go anywhere. The governor, concerned about the reduction of two hundred fifty jobs and the union's reaction, chose to remain uninvolved. We didn't find this to be an unusual reaction and had warned our client in advance.

Our client was concerned with the potential disruption in serving customers that relocation might create, as well as some short-term loss of profitability caused by moving an already marginal operation. The company's executives opted to stay at their current location. With many years in the business, we've learned to recognize red flags, and we warned the client of potential problems. The almost complete absence of state and local assistance indicated a lack of investment in the success of the operation—usually the first and most obvious sign of a problem. Of course, we received the standard statement "We love you, and you're vital to the well-being of the community and the state" from the governor and mayor, and the union passed on a guarded offer of support. Our client wanted to believe in the political leaders and the union.

Within less than a year, we were called back by the company. As the new equipment came in, retraining occurred and some employees were let go. The entire plant began to slow down, and some of the new equipment was damaged after being set up. We were asked to talk with the state and local political leaders, who refused to become involved for fear of alienating the union and the employees. We made it clear to all parties that if something was not done soon to alleviate the situation, the company would relocate. The message was ignored, and it didn't take long before the company announced it was closing the plant and relocating.

Political leaders suddenly were now more than willing to become involved in any way possible. In fact, they offered to better any offer from another state or community. We were asked repeatedly to arrange meetings with the CEO. The CEO said simply, "When we wanted to talk, when we needed help, nobody was interested. We need to go where our jobs are appreciated."

The ripple effect on the community went far beyond the loss of potentially six hundred well-paying jobs. With few other job opportunities, many of the younger families would relocate out of the area, teachers would lose their jobs, retailers would be adversely affected, and the tax base of the area would show a marked decrease. In essence, the area would slip into a recession.

In a final meeting with the mayor and the lieutenant governor, they pleaded for a meeting with the CEO. "We never believed they would really move," was the mayor's final statement. The company had no choice if it was to survive. The press was told that the facility was closing due to changes in international market conditions.

In the end, everyone concerned lost—the workers, the community, and the union. The company experienced approximately two years of losses before relocating. At its new location, in a relatively short period of time and with state and community financial assistance, the company was profitable and growing.

WIN-WIN NEGOTIATIONS

Myth Number 54: If we enter all our trade negotiations with the intent of achieving a win-win situation, we'll all be winners. There are learned people who believe that free trade creates a win-win situation. Win-win negotiating is the perfect method of negotiation if you are managing a dispute between your children. In the world of international trade negotiations, you are starting from a distinct disadvantage if you enter those negotiations believing this is your goal. Such a philosophy will lead to disaster for the country you represent.

Early in my career as a corporate real estate consultant and broker, I was fortunate to have an older gentleman nearing the end of his career suggest that I read a book titled *Winning through Intimidation* by Robert Ringer. He said that after thirty-five years of negotiating large commercial real estate transactions, he was amazed at how much he agreed with the author's assessment of three types of negotiators. In this 1973 book, Ringer indicates that there are only three types of negotiators, and all three intend to take as many of the chips on the table as you will allow them to take. The difference between them is that, when they grab all the chips, Type 1 isn't sorry, because he warned you ahead of time that this was his intent. Type 2 isn't sorry, in spite of the fact that she told you ahead of time that it was never her intention to try to take all your chips. Type 3 is sincerely sorry he took all your chips, but he had no choice when you gave him the opportunity.[1]

After over thirty years as a high-stakes negotiator, my experience tells me that if either party enters the room truly believing his intent is to ensure that both sides win, he shouldn't be in that room. The bottom line is that, given the opportunity, if the stakes are high, all professional negotiators will grab as many of your chips as you will allow. Only the most naive negotiators truly believe the other side really wants them to win. There are many negotiations in which both sides walk away feeling they have won, but that is not to imply that either side didn't try to grab as much as possible.

In 1981, when I started my corporate real estate company, I was thirty-six years old and was fortunate to have as a client a new technology company that was growing extremely fast. During this period of growth, I ran all over the country, putting together major office transactions for this client. One of the transactions was a large lease in the Washington, DC, area. In today's dollars, the lease would be valued at over $65 million. In the early 1980s, lease negotiations took place in person across a conference table, unlike today, where computers and e-mail dominate. The building selected was owned by one of the nation's largest developers, then based in the Washington, DC, area.

I arrived at the developer's offices and was immediately ushered into a huge conference room where I was greeted by the developer/owner, his general counsel, the head of construction, and another staff attorney. I was told we were waiting for Rex King (pseudonym) and his staff, who would be representing the developer in the negotiations. Mr. Rex King, I was informed, was a senior partner with one of Washington's largest law firms. He was delayed, and we would start as soon as he arrived. Eventually, he arrived with two associates.

I stood and walked around the table to shake hands just as he slipped away to make a call at the other end of the conference room. After shaking hands with his associates, I went back to the other side of the table to sit and wait while Mr. King completed his very important call. He was impressive, tall, tan, with a great head of perfectly combed white hair, a powerful voice, and a suit that was worth at least seven times more than mine. As we sat and waited, I looked across the table at what I am sure was meant to give the impression of an NFL defensive line. I was supposed to feel like a 160-pound high school quarterback facing the Chicago Bears Super Bowl XX defensive line.

When Mr. King completed his call, he came around the table, motioning me to stay seated. While standing behind me, forcing me to turn in my chair and look up at him, he asked where the rest of my team was. I responded that I was it. He then proceeded to tell me that this was not wise. He told me of his vast experience in negotiating real estate leases, as well as many other types of major transactions on behalf of his numerous Fortune 500 clients. One of his associates, at the appropriate time, said that Mr. King was considered the best negotiator in DC. Somehow, he even worked into his lecture his close personal friendship with the president. Mr. King then walked around the table to sit with the rest of the defensive line. The room went silent as I was now expected to respond. I said, "WOW! Your family must really be proud of you. Can we get started now?" With that, the developer burst into laughter and said, "I guess it didn't work this time, Rex," After several days of negotiations, one of his associates told me over dinner that Rex found out I was young, and this was one of his ways of intimidating the opposition. I actually liked Rex; although a bit theatrical, he was definitely a Type 1 negotiator—my personal choice of opponent in a negotiation. It's always best to know where you stand.

Rex was what I would call a sophisticated Type 1. He was threatening and always attempted to intimidate, but he did it with style. I once negotiated a lease with another Type 1 who was more of a Khrushchev-style negotiator. His style was to yell, swear, and bang his fist, all with the purpose of attempting to intimidate his opponent. In the sports world, they would call him a "trash talker." Our negotiations, at his insistence, took place in the bar of a very nice Chinese restaurant, located in a large suburban office building he owned. Starting each day at about 3 p.m., the negotiations would go on until the owner of the restaurant, whom my sparring partner claimed to be a good friend, would throw us out for disturbing his customers. One night we wound up concluding our negotiations on a bench at the local police station as we waited to be reprimanded by the police chief, another of his "good friends."

I can say unequivocally that when there are big dollars at stake, no one cares, nor should they care, about the other side winning. There are no novice negotiators sitting at that table. International trade agreements are big business. The Chinese understand this, as do the Indians and the members of the European Union, and all will stop at nothing to pick up all the chips on the table if they can. Why, then, does our government insist that our trade philosophy be based on achieving win-win solutions? Perhaps their idea of win-win refers to the foreign country and the US special-interest groups. What is good for special-interest groups is not always good for America.

Who wins in international trade when the US structures trade agreements crafted by special-interest-group lobbyists in the same way they push through legislation? Based on what is happening to the American middle class, it would appear that not enough political leaders care if the American people win or lose. A good look at our trade deficit and our trade policies makes it clear that our political leaders are much more interested in their lobbyist friends' special-trade interests.

OUR TRADING PARTNERS ARE BRILLIANT

Myth Number 55: Opening our borders to our trading partners has resulted in a friendlier atmosphere between the United States and our trading partners. Isn't it time that our national and state leaders recognize that we must begin to pursue a policy of fair trade? State and federal governments should, at the very least, stop the offshoring of government contracts.

In 2000, the United States negotiated a trade agreement with China so that China could enter the WTO. As part of that agreement, our negotiator agreed that the United States would impose a 2.5 percent tariff on Chinese cars, and China could impose a 25 percent tariff on US cars. Yes, we allowed China a tariff on US cars ten times higher than our tariff on China's cars. Are we really that terrible at negotiating? As one expression of fairness to their American trading partners, the Chinese car manufacturer Chery Automobile Co. (as reported by *Time* magazine), was alleged by General Motors to have stolen the production-line blueprints of a GM compact car.[2] The identical Chinese-made twin, called QQ, had a sticker price one-third of the GM car.[3]

Chinese pricing is not in keeping with their agreement with the WTO that they joined in 2001. Their currency continues to be undervalued by as much as 50 percent, making their products more attractive on the international market. In addition, the Chinese government subsidizes manufacturers with low interest rates and protects them from foreign competition.

Should we be angry with the Chinese or Indian governments? Absolutely not! They are beating us, and the federal government and many states are standing aside and allowing it to happen. You have to respect those countries that are taking our jobs. Their strategy is brilliant: they understand our political and economic system and know how to use this knowledge to their advantage. How do we fault the Chinese, or our own companies, when we have always preached capitalism to the world? We have opened our doors to free trade more than any other major country, yet most other nations do not like us, nor do they respect us.

Myth Number 56: The fact that so many foreign carmakers have assembly plants in the United States is proof that free trade works. When I and others complain that we are trading away the future of this nation, political leaders like to point to foreign carmakers and the US assembly plants as proof that free trade works. The truth is that these plants are proof of just the opposite.

In 1987 the Reagan administration negotiated a voluntary restraint agreement with the Japanese, limiting imported Japanese cars. Rather than restrict imports by placing a tariff on cars entering the United States, Japan agreed to restrict exports to the United States to 1.68 million and later, 2.3 million. The effect is somewhat the same, except that Japan was able to control the price of its vehicles sold in the United States rather than have the price increased by a tariff that would have resulted in fewer cars being sold. Under this quota system, cars manufactured here did not count toward the quota. The Reagan administration used the same concept of voluntary restraints for the steel and machine tool industries. The US trade deficit with Japan in 1981 for the entire year when Reagan took office was $16 billion. Our current trade deficit with China exceeds $20 billion *per month*. Even taking into consideration the value of 1981 dollars, the Japanese deficit pales in comparison.

The Reagan administration found that only strong threats of retaliation to counter Japan's barriers to fair trade were effective. The Japanese recognized that the administration, Congress, and the American people were unified on the issue and took the threats seriously. Today, the Chinese know that there is no unity of purpose in the United States. Since the Clinton administration, the only voice for fair trade, rather than free trade, comes from the majority of working Americans and a limited number of members of Congress, and even some of them waver under pressure from special-interest groups.

Ronald Reagan and George H. Bush were the last presidents to place the American worker, the American public, and the American companies first. If we examine figure 7, "Trade Deficit Balance on Goods and Services, 1960–2009," it's easy to see that, during the Reagan administration (1981–1989), the trade deficit was reasonably stable, even under considerable pressure from the Japanese. The same was true for President George H. Bush's four-year term. Note that during the Reagan years, there was very little talk of Ricardo's Doctrine of Comparative Advantage. The Reagan and George H. Bush administrations recognized that the key to successful international trade policy for the United States was based on a level playing field and safeguarding the American economy and its workers.

"QUI SE FAIT BREBIS LE LOUP LE MANGE"

Fear of trade retaliation is often mentioned by political leaders who favor offshoring. Special-interest lobbyists preach the fear of retaliation when it comes to all negotiations—other than those of their clients. The United States is generally the nation to back down when threatened, just as we have with the steel tariffs and dangerous consumer goods.

This is not the first time in our history that fear of retaliation and the placating of special-interest groups has been used as an excuse to avoid taking action. America has dealt with threats of trade retaliation for over two hundred years. In 1797, William Eaton was appointed US consul at Tunis, one of the Barbary states, which was a collection of ports stretching from Tangiers to Tripoli along the North African coast. Each state was ruled by a pasha, whose pirate ships would plunder Mediterranean shipping, taking cargo and slaves for ransom or labor. One of Eaton's primary duties was to negotiate the release of Americans enslaved by the Barbary pirates.

England and France, the superpowers of the day—and eventually the fledgling American government—paid tribute to these pirate states to ensure safe passage of their ships. Like the British and French, we feared resistance would create a retaliatory response. We also had special-interest groups who restricted the use of funds needed to develop the naval power necessary to protect our commercial fleet. The Democratic-Republicans, as they were called, wanted the government to spend its limited resources on westward expansion and believed a buildup of naval power would lead to foreign conflicts. Meanwhile, the Federalists believed a strong navy would subdue the pirates and protect US commercial interests and gain the fledgling nation respect internationally. At the time, we certainly didn't have the military power of the British or the French, but, like them, we opted for the easy route of paying tribute.

The taking of American slaves, ships, and cargo, and the payment of tribute was not the limit of indignities perpetrated by these pirates (not that slavery was not an indignity in itself). Our willingness to placate the Barbary states was viewed by them as weakness. In 1800, the American warship USS *George Washington* docked in Algiers with a shipment of tribute for the pasha of Algiers. The pasha commandeered the *George Washington* and forced the captain to take down the American flag and run up the Algerian flag and then transport a shipment of livestock and treasure to the sultan of Istanbul. After the USS *Washington* embarrassment, Eaton wrote the secretary of state, "Hast thou not yet one son whose soul revolts, whose nerves convulse, blood vessels burst, and heart indignant swells at thoughts of such debasement? . . . I would have lost the peace, and been impaled myself rather than yield this concession. Will nothing rouse my country?"

Pasha Yusuf of Tripoli, now assured of the weakness of America, demanded a gift of $10,000 upon President Washington's death, claiming this was the custom when the leader of a tributary state passed away. When the tribute did not arrive, the pasha increased the tribute to $225,000 and an annual payment of $25,000; this was in addition to the other tribute already being paid. Frustrated by constant and ever-growing demands of the pasha, Eaton continued to argue against passive obedience. He warned, "They will find that *qui se fait brebis le loup le mange*. He who makes himself a sheep must expect to be devoured by the wolf."[4]

In 1805, William Eaton led a force of US Marines (hence the phrase "to the shores of Tripoli" in the Marine Corps hymn) and Christian and Arab mercenaries hundreds of miles through the desert to capture

Derna, the second-largest city in Tripoli. Eaton took the city, and President Jefferson ended the war by paying $60,000 to the pasha. During the War of 1812, the Barbary states resumed their harassment of US trade in the Mediterranean. This occurred after accepting additional bribes from the American government and expelling the counsel general. It wasn't until 1815—and the end of the War of 1812—that the United States finally sent a naval force, including marines, large enough to put a final stop to the harassment of our shipping and the enslavement of our citizens. Within three hours of the American peace negotiators making their demands, the Algerian minister returned all prisoners and signed a treaty. The treaty, among other demands, called for the abolishment of all tribute, release of all prisoners, and payment of $10,000 for the seizure of American property. Practically no concessions were made by the American negotiators.[5]

How long will it be before we take the necessary action to protect our international trade and our jobs? What more could our trading partners do to us? They have captured most of our manufacturing and are well on their way to taking most of our high-tech and high-paying service jobs. The worst thing they could retaliate with at this time would be to stop buying our treasuries, making us unable to make payment on our huge debt. This could push us into a deeper recession or depression. If we were pushed into a deeper recession or depression at this time, the value of their treasuries would drop like a rock.

As the years pass and the middle-class markets of India, China, and eastern Europe continue their rapid growth, the relative impact of a US recession on our trading partners has diminished and will continue to do so. The Chinese are already recognizing that the United States may have passed its time to have any negotiating leverage. They seem to realize that our political leadership, with but a few exceptions, is destroying our economy and our way of life. For far too long we have had political administrations so controlled by special-interest groups, and so focused on campaign contributions, that they have lost sight of their obligations to the American people. Until we develop a unified fair trade policy for the benefit of the nation as a whole, and have the nerve to follow through with it, we will continue to be abused by the twenty-first-century pashas of the world. We are now being rapidly "devoured by the wolf."

CHAPTER 16

EASY CREDIT, FAMILY DEBT, AND TAX CUTS
Why You Can't Get Ahead

Just be glad you're not getting all the government you're paying for.

—Will Rogers
1879–1935

FAMILY DEBT—MAXING OUT CREDIT CARDS

Myth Number 57: The typical American family is much better at controlling their personal debt than the government is at controlling the federal debt. According to the Center for Responsible Lending, credit card debt almost tripled between 1989 and 2001 and was up 31 percent over the first half of the 2000–2010 decade alone. According to the Federal Reserve, by 2010 the recession caused a slowing of the growth in credit card debt. But Americans still owed over $900 billion by 2010. Prior to the bursting of the housing bubble, households surveyed in 2005 by the Center for Responsible Lending found that half cashed out home equity and used the money to pay credit card bills. According to the survey, 20 percent of home owners who had paid off some credit card debt with mortgage refinancing prior to the housing crash, had added $12,000 to their mortgage debt and still had average credit card debt of over $14,000. Nearly 60 percent of those surveyed had less than $1,000 in nonretirement savings.[1] The credit card had replaced the savings account for unexpected or emergency needs. Nationwide credit card debt is reported to average approximately $10,678 per household.[2]

Myth Number 58: Unlike loan sharks, the credit card industry is restricted from charging whatever interest rates it thinks the consumer will bear. The exemption of regulated institutions such as banks from usury laws (restrictions on interest rates) in South Dakota (1980) and later by other states allowed the banking industry a "sky's the limit" system of charging interest. In 1996, a US Supreme Court ruling lifted the lid on penalties. The Senate Banking Committee indicated that in prerecession 2006, banks were estimated to collect $17.1 billion in credit card penalties, up 906 percent from 1996.[3] One year later, in 2007, the amount had risen to $18.1 billion.[4]

In 2003, Elizabeth Warren and Amelia Warren Tyagi published *The Two Income Trap: Why Middle-Class Mothers and Fathers Are Going Broke.* The book makes a case for how predatory lending practices of the credit card and mortgage industries are transferring wealth from lower- and middle-class families to giant lenders and their shareholders.[5]

In March 2008, prior to the September 2008 financial market collapse, treasury secretary Henry Paulson (former Goldman Sachs CEO) and Federal Reserve chairman Ben Bernanke agreed that excessive US financial institution deregulation had created a global financial crisis that threatened the US economy.[6] The credit card industry, banks, investment banks, hedge funds, and mortgage bankers let their unbridled greed and arrogance contribute to ruining the US economy. This could not have occurred without the support of Congress. The housing bubble and high rate of personal debt resulting from the deregulation of the financing and credit card industries was a predictable outcome of a system that rewarded those who could persuade Americans to borrow more than they could afford.

Like subprime mortgages, credit card debt is often securitized. About one-third of this debt is resold around the world. According to Innovest Strategic Value Advisors, credit card debt grew by approximately 80 percent between 1999 and 2009. United States credit card debt was estimated at about $1 trillion in 2009. While a collapse in the credit card industry is possible, some economists have argued that a collapse in this market similar to that of the housing market is not likely. The argument is that the credit card industry is only one-tenth the size of the mortgage market, and its percentage of Americans' income has remained relatively steady. In addition, with the bursting of the housing bubble, incomes fell far behind mortgage debt as housing values plummeted. Some homes were worth less than their mortgages. A number of the mortgage holders of those loans were compelled to default on their loans. Since credit cards are not backed by an asset, credit card borrowers felt less compunction relative to walking away from their debts.

Banks are therefore more willing to work with defaulting credit card borrowers to make payments easier.

Adding to the credit card industry's woes is the passage of the Credit Cardholder's Bill of Rights Act of 2009, which will limit the issuer's ability to raise interest rates on cardholders' existing balances and to charge certain fees. How long it will take for industry lobbyists to soften the legislation will likely depend on the duration of the recession. This would not be the first time that limitations were placed on interest rates and fees were eventually eliminated.

Many American families are literally financing their groceries. Unlike citizens of other nations, Americans on average have no savings. With the onset of the recession, Americans have begun to show some increase in savings. Prior to the recession, Americans behaved as though their credit cards and any equity they had in their homes were their safety nets for emergencies.

After the Great Depression, Congress focused considerable attention on regulating Wall Street and the nation's financial institutions for good reason. Congress recognized that the success or failure of this industry would affect the entire economy, and that its success was based in large part on the public's trust. Since this industry was working with the public's money, it needed to be constrained and transparent in the use of this money. Over time, these regulations were viewed as oppressive by the industry, and they were claimed to be responsible for stifling economic growth.

US politics became heavily influenced by Ronald Reagan's response to the welfare choking and heavily regulated economy of the 1970s. Reagan opened the system through deregulation, which ushered in three decades of economic growth and prosperity. During the Reagan and post-Reagan period, pressed by Wall Street and the banking industry, regulations began to fall quickly. As mentioned above, the banking industry, with support from state governments, managed to have usury restrictions eliminated, and many new products were introduced, like collateralized debt obligations (1987) and "liar loans" that contributed to the bursting of the housing bubble. Understaffed regulators could not keep up with fast-paced markets, powerful industry leaders, and their lobbyists.

Deregulation became the mantra of politicians across the nation—after all, it was working. Reagan's banner of less government intervention was easy to take up, especially when you consider that it fell into line with the philosophy of most lobbyists. It was at this time that the lobbyist movement took off in earnest. The result was that the Reagan revolution started to become distorted. The distortion of a good idea begins when, as is often the case in Washington, an entire industry develops to support it. With deregulation, there were millions of dollars to be made by lobbyists pushing a concept in Congress that appeared to always work. Democrats and Republicans embraced deregulation—it was good for the nation, and lobbyists were willing to show their appreciation. The problem was that while all deregulation appeared to be good for the industries pushing for deregulation, not all deregulation was good for the consumer, the taxpayer, or the nation. We need only look at the bursting housing bubble and the financial market collapse to see how unbridled deregulation can create a financial nightmare for millions of Americans.

As time progressed and the depth of deregulation grew, there were many signs that deregulation was causing some industries to drift into dangerous waters. Industry lobbyists convinced Congress that there was nothing to fear, and our leaders assumed the American financial industry was sophisticated enough to self-regulate. They saw it as the financial model the world wanted to emulate.

Even Americans who did not buy stocks, bonds, or other securities were touched by the hand of deregulation. As discussed, the credit card industry was deregulated, allowing unlimited interest rates and penalties. Then there was the final blow in the form of the completely out-of-control residential financing industry that became the trigger for the collapse of the nation's financial industry in September 2008. The collapse of this critical industry affected not only home owners but also the industry's shareholders and employees. Ultimately, the collateral damage rippled throughout the national and world economies.

In the wake of the scandal, Mary L. Schapiro, chairman of the US Securities and Exchange Commission, said her agency would perform surprise inspections on ten thousand money managers to ensure clients were not being ripped off. Later, after meeting with major fund companies, the number of surprise inspections was reduced by over 80 percent.[7]

Ronald Reagan was not wrong at the time in his basic concept of deregulation. But times and circumstances change, and our recent political leaders (Clinton, Bush II, and Congress) failed to adjust their policies to deal with the growing corruption and mismanagement that undermined our financial industry and led to the 2008 collapse. The devil is certainly in the details, and we must caution against a regulatory backlash. Most industries have done an admirable job of self-regulating and will continue to do so. A regulatory backlash can impose unnecessary restrictions that will hinder the growth of industries that we will need to bring the American economic model back to prominence.

Regulation is not a simple black-and-white issue. Lowering barriers did usher in over two decades of wealth and freedom on a grand scale for those businesses that were deregulated. The problem was that a lack of regulation encouraged high risk-taking in some industries, notably banking. The Obama administration must caution against overregulation that will not provide an inoculation against future financial crises. Better government, not more government, is the solution. This means more control in some areas and less in others, and for many industries, it simply means different regulations. Most important, the administration and Congress must guard against having regulations that safeguard the American public and the economy twisted or eliminated by special interests.

BANKRUPTCY ABUSE PREVENTION AND CONSUMER PROTECTION ACT

As the nation's credit card debt soared along with mortgage foreclosures, resulting in a growing number of bankruptcies, why did Washington do so little to control the mortgage and credit card industries? Why did it wait for a complete collapse of the financial markets to occur? The deregulation of these industries, like that of the S&L industry during the 1980s, placed our economy in a precarious position. Yet the only action taken by Washington to address these problems during the last two decades was to change the personal bankruptcy law.

Congress, under the guidance of the National Consumers Bankruptcy Coalition (NCBC), a banking industry lobby group, was successful in restricting the rights of consumers to file for bankruptcy. This reduced the industries' losses due to bankruptcy and allowed banks and other creditors to pursue these consumers indefinitely.

The original intent of American bankruptcy law was to offer a fresh start to families who had financial problems due to job loss and medical emergencies. The banking industry won congressional support for their bill by lobbying hard. They also happened to make more than $60 million in political contributions. This was followed by publicity campaigns stating that the bill would eliminate "bankruptcies of mere convenience," which would put $550 a year into the pockets of bill-paying Americans.[8] Initially defeated in 2002, the Bankruptcy Abuse Prevention and Consumer Protection Act of 2005 was enacted on October 17, 2005.[9] To my knowledge, the $550 per year has not found its way into American pockets.

With the new law in place, individual bankruptcies in 2006 dropped to levels comparable to 1987. How much of this drop was due to the huge number of filings being made before the law went into effect is difficult to estimate. (See figure 10, on page 264.) It's pretty clear that the law has made it much more expensive and difficult to file, and thus the number dropped initially but began rising rapidly due primarily to mortgage delinquencies.[10]

Myth Number 59: Most people who file for bankruptcy are deadbeats.
Persons filing "bankruptcy for mere convenience" will find it difficult to get out from under debt, which is as it should be. But filing for bankruptcy will also be more difficult for families facing a job loss, medical problems, or the loss of a spouse due to death or divorce (the latter accounted for approximately 90 percent of all bankruptcies).[11] A family with high consumer debt, when faced with job loss, medical bills, divorce, or rising mortgage payments, has no buffer against financial disaster. During the decade and a half, prior to the new law taking effect, bad-debt losses and loan write-offs soared in the United States, while profits to the banking, credit card, and lending industry also skyrocketed.

With $60 million in political contributions, it's easy to see that the banking industry had the political clout necessary to push through their legislation. It also had the financial muscle to create a marketing campaign for legislation that would otherwise be unpopular if the public really understood it. The marketing campaign made it much easier for the banking industry's friends in Congress to justify their votes.

When American families have financial problems and are unable to pay their debts because they lost their jobs to offshoring, unexpected medical costs, or death of a spouse, Congress, at the request of the banking lobby (NCBC), made it more difficult for these families to seek relief. When the banking industry and their other friends on Wall Street got into financial trouble in late 2008, Congress decided to give them $700 billion to help them through hard times. It would appear that American families facing bankruptcy did not have powerful lobbyists working to protect their interests.

The new bankruptcy law that the banking industry lobbied so long to enact eventually turned to bite them. Under the old law, troubled borrowers could file under Chapter 7, which was relatively inexpensive and quick. Courts would protect a home owner from foreclosure by mandating lower mortgage payments and order the rest of the borrower's property sold to pay unsecured debt like credit cards and medical bills. When the assets were sold, the remaining debt was canceled and future income could go to make mortgage payments. Under the new law, no part of the debt can be canceled and only low-income borrowers can file Chapter 7. The problem is that many subprime borrowers could not raise the much higher costs of filing Chapter 7 under the more complex new law. The price, which used to be about $800, was raised to $1,400–$2,400. Also, under the new law, the courts no longer had the option of lowering mortgage payments for primary residents. The bottom line for the lenders is that more people were forced to walk away from mortgages they could no longer afford, leaving lenders holding nonperforming assets they couldn't sell in the soft market that they helped create. So bills were introduced that would allow judges to adjust unaffordable mortgages downward, thereby allowing borrowers and lenders to avoid foreclosure.[12]

A generation ago, the average American family couldn't get into financial difficulty as easily as now. A middle-class family could not borrow anywhere near what they can today. You couldn't run up debt anonymously—you had to meet a banker face-to-face to get a mortgage. You had to produce a 20 percent or more down payment, show tax returns, pay stubs, credit references, and family budgets. You had to prove you could repay a loan. The banking industry was highly regulated—there were usury laws. Individuals in financially difficult situations simply did not qualify for loans. After over twenty years of deregulation in the lending industry, home owners were three and a half times more likely to lose their home to foreclosures than a generation earlier, and bankruptcies rose rapidly.

If the credit industry would simply have not made loans to high-risk borrowers (who are much easier to recognize today, due to computerized credit scores, than a decade earlier), fewer families and individuals would have found themselves in a rapid, downward-spiraling plunge due to high interest rates, late charges, and fees. The fact is, with the new bankruptcy legislation, these high-risk borrowers were even more desirable to the credit industry. These are the types of credit card customers who carry the highest balances, are charged the highest rates and highest penalties, and are most likely to never pay off their debt.

Though it's not the credit card industry's responsibility to protect the American public, they should endeavor to be fair to the public. In the end, it's the responsibility of federal and state governments to create the laws necessary to protect the public. Obviously, they have been unwilling to buck their friends in the finance industry.

With more and more money needed to run a campaign, the US Congress and state legislators don't have the will to challenge an industry that provides so much in campaign contributions. According to the Center for Responsive Politics, in the 2008 presidential election, the commercial banking industry contributed over $19.4 million.

On December 15, 2005, Senator William Proxmire passed away. Senator Proxmire represented the people of Wisconsin in the Senate from 1957 to 1989. He was chairman of the Senate Committee on Banking, Housing and Urban Affairs from 1975 to 1981. He pushed for consumer protection laws, notably the 1968 Consumer Credit Protection Act, known as the "Truth in Lending Act," which requires lenders to disclose interest rates and finance charges owed them by borrowers. If the House and Senate had more political leaders like Senator Proxmire, the nation would not be in the situation it is today. In 2005, Bob Schieffer of CBS News said of Senator Proxmire upon his death, "Yesterday's giants have been replaced mostly by good, but smaller men . . . he refused to accept campaign contributions. Let me repeat: He refused to accept campaign contributions. And in thirty-two years in the Senate, he never spent more than 200 dollars on a campaign, and most of that went to buy stamps to return contributions people had sent him."

PERSONAL TAX CUTS—WHO BENEFITS?

Reaganomics introduced the idea that almost all tax cuts would be self-financing. Prior to the Reagan administration, most conservative politicians were not willing to spend more of the government's money than was taken in through taxation. Reagan supported the concept that tax cuts would stimulate economic growth and government would, as a result, take in more tax revenue. The view was correct but also required that spending must be constrained, or the deficit might end up increasing. It was the constrained-spending part that Reagan had difficulty with, and this resulted in raising the deficit.

During the Clinton administration, the economy grew as fast as during the Reagan years, in spite of the fact that taxes were increased. Clinton actually managed to curb deficit spending for a short period, aided by a reduction in military spending due to the end of the cold war and an economic boom. Bush, anxious to raise his ratings with the public and to stimulate a lagging economy, was a Reaganomics devotee. Globalization was working for Bush, as foreigners were eagerly willing to buy US treasuries, thereby allowing the United States to run a massive deficit while maintaining growth. This is why Vice President Cheney was able to tell then-treasury secretary Paul O'Neil, "Reagan proved deficits don't matter" (see chapter 11). The part of the equation that Bush and Cheney also missed was related to constraining consumption. Cutting taxes was simply not enough to overcome the massive spending spree the nation was on—including two wars, along with huge national and trade deficits.

In March 2008, Americans received a notice from the IRS telling them that President Bush had signed into law the Economic Stimulus Act of 2008. The Bush administration felt this tax cut would stimulate the economy and again stave off a recession. The economic stimulus payments would be made to over one hundred and thirty million American households. Individuals could be entitled to as much as $600 $1,200 for joint filings, plus additional amounts for each qualifying child.[13]

President Bush had gone down the tax rebate road before. In 2001, he added refunds of up to $300 per individual. In May 2003, President Bush signed into law a $350 billion tax relief package that was meant to be a financial stimulus to the American economy. While conservative economists say the president's tax cuts and stimulus package helped lay the foundation for economic expansion, they agree with liberal economists that the administration's lack of spending discipline mortgaged the nation's future.

The Bush tax cuts had little impact on the middle and lower classes. While the economy continued to grow, according to Census Bureau data, most families with real median household income showed little or no increase, and credit card and other personal debt continued to grow to an all-time high. American families were and still are haunted by layoffs and the loss of retirement benefits by bankrupt corporations.

Myth Number 60: Tax cuts have significantly helped the American public reduce family debt. When the Bush administration provided the American public with tax cuts in 2003, the majority of the middle and lower class did not pay off credit card debt or put that money away for a rainy day, or put it into retirement accounts. Many Americans went to Wal-Mart and spent that money on consumer products and, in far too many cases, actually used their tax cut and also their tax refund checks to acquire more debt. If you take your $400 tax cut or refund and use it to buy a $1,500 big-screen TV and put the remainder of the cost on your credit card, you have not helped your family's economic situation. Perhaps you believe that a $1,500 purchase has helped the American economy, as President Bush proposed. Part of the $1,500 wound up in Wal-Mart's pockets and the wallets of their sales clerks and other employees. Also, a part went to the truckers who drove that television from the Wal-Mart warehouse to the store and between the warehouse and the port of Long Beach. Part of the $1,500 went to a foreign-owned shipping company who transported that TV across the Pacific. A major portion, however, went to the manufacturer in Asia. The Bush tax cuts, while putting new TVs in American homes, did little to help the typical American family to experience any improved economic health.

DANGERS OF EASY CREDIT

How long will it take for consumer spending to reach prerecession levels? This is an important question, as it will indicate a true ending of the recession. Unemployment rates will need to get to levels that make consumers feel confident in their financial future before consumer spending increases in earnest. Since the early 1980s, consumer spending for goods, services, and housing grew faster than the GDP. This economic engine allowed for the nation's global expansion. Lower interest rates kept Americans above water by keeping payments for housing, cars, and credit cards low. The problem arose when, at the beginning of the new century, incomes began to stagnate and debts continued to rise. This imbalance caused the share of income needed to service personal debt to rise disproportionately to income. Americans, supported initially by rising housing prices, felt safe, and many simply pulled equity out of their homes to help support their lifestyle.

Pressure on consumers to reduce their debts relative to income levels and the value of their homes will cause consumption to be depressed longer than most would like. It's hard to spend when you realize that your income potential is weakened, your wealth has been lowered (housing and retirement savings), credit has tightened, and there is no chance that taxes will be lowered. The nation will need to go through a period of "deleveraging," that is, a period in which income grows faster than consumption. Considering the state of the national economy and our ability to export goods and services, the deleveraging process will be a long, painful one.

It's not just the federal deficit or trade deficit that scares most economists. It's also the personal debt Americans have incurred to maintain a lifestyle that they can no longer afford. Unlike prior generations, the dollars being spent result in a lack of savings. Not only does the typical American save very little, but most have borrowed at record levels to keep a lifestyle that is beyond their means (see chapter 11). While the cost of living is growing at about 3.2 percent per year for the decade, most families have no gain in income (see figure 6, on page 186).

Recovery from the 2000–2001 recession was fed by low interest rates that resulted in American families acquiring record levels of debt. These same low interest rates pushed us into a supercharged housing market that fostered economic growth. Low interest rates and credit cards have also allowed Americans to finance cars, washing machines, furniture, and countless other consumer goods. If we had produced these goods, we would be in a much better economic position than we are today.

Before the housing bubble collapsed, many people, in spite of level incomes, took advantage of the rapidly rising market by buying bigger, more expensive homes. Many Americans became housing speculators, and lenders were more than willing to accommodate them. For example, in the supercharged San Diego market, in order to speculate on the market's ability to continue to rise, two-thirds of the loans issued in 2004 were interest-only mortgages.

Subprime lenders who were not required to follow the tougher regulations of commercial banks made loans to borrowers who often stretched very hard financially to buy a home. Over half of subprime loans were adjustable-rate mortgages.[14] According to the Center for Public Integrity, the top twenty-five subprime mortgage originators spent nearly $380 million on campaign contributions in the ten-year period prior to 2009.

As long as Wall Street could package and sell the securities on which these loans were based, mortgage companies were willing to sell as many as possible. When the market was hot and prices were rising, a buyer facing default could, with the help of a creative mortgage broker, roll their loan into a new, larger loan. As subprime loan defaults increased, the mortgage originators made themselves rich and began closing down.[15]

Nationally, by the middle of the decade, home prices had risen over 50 percent in seven years due primarily to low interest rates. The Federal Reserve has stated that housing price appreciation helped add $5.2 trillion to America's balance sheets during the expansion, or 68 percent of all wealth creation. Many families had shifted from investing in stocks for retirement to investing in homes. New laws made this financing easier. At the beginning of the decade, nontraditional mortgages accounted for less than 3 percent of the home financing market; by mid-decade, loans were granted with no down payments, interest only, and adjustable rates. Nationally, between 25 to 35 percent of all mortgages made during the housing boom period were estimated to be based on adjustable rates.[16] Many of these were high-risk loans, with over 18 percent being made to economically marginal families.

By mid-2009, the International Monetary Fund (IMF) estimated that roughly ten million American home owners still had negative equity. These mortgages pose a roadblock to a housing recovery, as they are more likely to fall into foreclosure and get dumped onto a saturated market. Home ownership had been the single best way for most Americans to accumulate wealth. When home prices are rising, Americans feel financially secure, and they tend to spend more. When home prices are weak or falling, they feel less secure, even if their own house value is stable, and tend to spend less. IMF research shows that of the hundred-odd recessions since 1960, one-quarter were associated with housing busts. These recessions tended to be longer and deeper than other recessions. The road to recovery in past recessions was aided by exports, which is now not going to happen; therefore, savings must be rebuilt and spending increased.

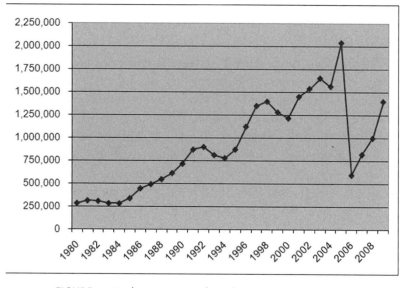

FIGURE 10: Bankruptcy Annual Nonbusiness Filings by Year

Source: American Bankruptcy Institute

Figure 10 illustrates the impact that our highly leveraged society is having on personal bankruptcy. Federal statistics show that about two million people filed for bankruptcy protection in 2005, up from 875,000 in 1989. This jump in bankruptcy was likely due in part to changes in the bankruptcy law passed in October 2005 (see "Bankruptcy Abuse Prevention and Consumer Act," above). After a drop in 2006, filings began to rise rapidly.

So what is the prognosis for the average American family? In his January 2010 State of the Union address, President Obama offered what amounts to a small change package of initiatives for the American family. Initiatives included help for families to pay for child care, save for retirement, pay off student loans, and care for elderly parents. His proposals called for a near doubling of the current $1,000 child tax credit and capping federally backed college loan payments at 10 percent of a borrower's income. He also proposed $1.6 billion for the Child Care Development Fund to help working parents pay for child care. The administration will also streamline the process for employers to automatically enroll workers in 401(k) plans. There was a $102.5 million Caregiver Initiative proposed to ease the burden on families with elder care responsibilities. To offset his programs, Obama proposed a three-year freeze on all nonsecurity discretionary spending in the federal budget, amounting to a savings of $250 billion over the next decade. To accomplish this would require congressional support, something President Obama has found hard to come by.

CHAPTER 17

THE MORPHINE SOLUTION TO ECONOMIC PROBLEMS

The Government's solution to a problem is usually as bad as the problem.

—Milton Friedman
1912–2006

THE MORPHINE SOLUTION

Political leaders tend not to like to hear about complex, intertwined causes for economic problems, nor do they want to hear about complex solutions. Tell political leaders that we are now spending more on interest payments on the national debt than on national security, and they lose patience, as the solution would be complex, difficult, long-term, and unpopular to implement. They prefer to address problems with simple, short-term, popular solutions that can be easily managed. Tell them that a decrease in interest rates or a tax rebate will provide a temporary cure for the nation's ills, and most are very pleased. The fact that such solutions are often nothing more than Band-Aids that mask but do not cure the problem does not attract their attention.

Say, for example, you broke your leg and your insurance carrier said it would pay for one of two options: Your leg could be set and put in a cast. This would involve some pain and a long period of discomfort while you hobbled around on crutches. The second option would be to simply provide the "morphine solution." A shot of morphine would alleviate your pain and would actually make you feel pretty good immediately. With regular doses of morphine, you would need no cast, and you would have no discomfort. Of course, the morphine would, in the short term, be less expensive and more comfortable, and may even create a state of euphoria. On the other hand, your leg would never heal properly, your entire body would be weakened, and you would never regain your full health. You would also likely become addicted to the morphine that, in the long run, would prove to be even more detrimental to your health and more costly to you and society than the broken leg.

Simple policy fixes, like morphine, have an added bonus in that they divert the public's attention from the real problems. They tend to distract the public's attention from other, more complex and troubling problems, such as a loss of jobs, a decrease in the standard of living, or stagnant wages.

If the economy shows the slightest improvement, the politicians will take credit, even if the policy is no more than a morphine solution. If the problem gets worse, then it is their adviser's fault or, better yet, the fault of some other government's actions or inactions. Blame it on China or India, or simply on globalization or the prior administration's policies.

We must guard against quick-fix economic policies that are put forth to serve a political agenda or that of a special-interest group or groups. Many of these quick-fix policies can result in a short burst of improvement, but they seldom result in sustained economic gains. In the end, your leg is still broken. For example, there is a significant difference between personal and corporate tax cuts. If corporate taxes were reduced and offshore shelters eliminated, the middle and lower class would be better served than if insignificant short-term tax relief had been provided, as Bush did. Bush's and Obama's one-time tax abatements are no more than morphine solutions: they divert the public's attention from the real problems and the more difficult solutions.

What Americans need are better private-sector jobs and higher incomes, not a few hundred dollars a year for families strapped with massive debt. Simply reinstating usury laws and reducing credit card penalties would put billions of dollars back into the economy. Taking the Reagan approach to fair trade, as with the foreign auto industry, would bring millions of manufacturing jobs back to the United States. Today, the typical American family is working to support not only themselves but also their local, state, and federal governments and the credit card industry. If anything is left over, they might have enough to pay medical bills, gas bills, and mortgage payments; put some money into retirement savings; give some money to the religion of their choice (many accept MasterCard and Visa); and educate their children.

Likely one of the nation's most outstanding examples of the morphine solution was the welfare system of the twentieth century. With a huge bureaucracy, budget, and the best of intentions, we allowed the system to spin out of control. Today, we need job creation legislation and must be very cautious about adding more safety-net programs at the expense of providing job creation programs (see chapter 8). House and Senate leaders have been quick to address high unemployment by adding to and extending unemployment insurance, food stamps, and health insurance for unemployed Americans. While they are needed, they do tend to add to bureaucracies and create government dependence.

On August 22, 1996, President Clinton signed into law the Personal Responsibility and Work Opportunity Reconciliation Act, a welfare reform law. Under this legislation, states were responsible for implementing their own welfare programs. However, the federal government imposed requirements for states to move families into work and self-sufficiency. Changes to the welfare system moved millions (5.1 million families in 1994) off the welfare rolls into jobs. The nation cut bureaucracies and saved the taxpayers billions of dollars. States were under pressure to develop job-creation programs, and most did.

Today, as has been indicated previously, most states do a terrible job of creating an environment for job development (see chapter 9). Safety-net programs relieve them of this responsibility, much as the welfare system did for much of the twentieth century. Our legislation and money must be used to develop the more complex and longer-term programs (see chapter 8) that will create jobs with wages and benefits that allow families to support themselves.

YOU COULD ALWAYS DEPEND ON AUNT FANNIE AND UNCLE FREDDIE

Myth Number 61: The bursting of the housing bubble and the financial market collapse could not have been anticipated by the federal government, or it would have done something to avert them. Fortunately for many banks, their home loans were sold to two organizations perceived as semigovernment: Fannie Mae and Freddie Mac. Fannie Mae and Freddie Mac are known as government-sponsored enterprises, or GSEs. Just before the financial market collapse in mid-2008, Fannie Mae and Freddie Mac had over $5 trillion of retained mortgages and mortgage-backed securities. Together, the GSEs were involved in more than half of the nation's mortgages.[1]

Fannie and Freddie were set up and sponsored by the government to provide liquidity to the housing market by buying mortgages from banks. They then repackaged these mortgages and used them as collateral for bonds called mortgage-backed securities. Fannie's and Freddie's dominance reflected an implicit federal guarantee that allowed them to be funded at lower interest rates and also gave them tax exemption. In addition, Fannie and Freddie had a formidable lobbying machine behind them and have employed a fair share of ex–Capitol Hill politicians. This muscle was effective in keeping Fannie and Freddie insulated from federal regulation.[2]

In September 2008, with foreclosures rising, the US government took control of the world's largest financial enterprises—Fannie Mae and Freddie Mac. Contrary to what the administration and Congress would have liked the public to believe, the mess was not unexpected. In 2000, Gary Gensler, undersecretary of the Treasury, asked Congress to rein in the GSEs. Gensler rightly believed they were getting too big, and if something went wrong, the results would be devastating to the economy.

Why would our political leaders not rein in the GSEs? It's simple; when the GSEs were on a roll, they used their profits to influence the very politicians that were supposed to oversee them. Between 1989 and 2008, the GSEs' political action committees and employees donated $4.8 million to members of Congress.[3] They were successful in fighting regulations, influencing congressional friends, and intimidating enemies. Congress did create the Office of Federal Housing Enterprise Oversight to keep an eye on the GSEs. Lobbyists for the GSEs made sure the agency was poorly funded, and thus they became dependent on the GSEs to supply information and expertise. When regulators become dependent on the industry they are supposed to regulate, the industry is regulating itself.

Many believe that Federal Reserve chairman Alan Greenspan was partially responsible by keeping interest rates so low for so long, thus triggering the housing bubble. Of course, if he did not keep interest rates low, the American people would have realized sooner that they were living beyond their means. Keeping interest rates low was part of a morphine solution to an economy with a weak foundation.

The Bush administration was quick to spin the impact of the takeover of Fannie Mae and Freddie Mac. The White House announced that there was no reason to account for the GSEs' losses in the federal budget. They claimed the risk was not great enough to require the cost to be reflected in the budget. The GSEs owned or guaranteed over $5 trillion in mortgages in an awful real estate market. These mortgages were roughly equivalent to half the federal debt and would represent a huge increase in the overall US indebtedness if made part of the federal debt.

The taxpayers' biggest risk was not with the banks or the automakers; it was with Uncle Freddie, Aunt Fannie, and AIG. The bailout for this toxic trio has been revised upward several times, after the initial attempt to save it with what amounted to a morphine solution. As incomes continued to stagnate and unemployment and foreclosures continued to rise, the GSEs required more assistance.

It is the taxpayers whose money is at risk, due to the federal government's inability to regulate the GSEs and steward the economy. It could take years to work out the housing problem; by then, the takeover will have easily dwarfed the Savings and Loan crisis of the 1980s and early 1990s that cost the taxpayers, by some estimates, as much as $175 billion.

Yogi Berra once said, "This is like déjà vu all over again." Again our government positioned the taxpayers for another financial mess like the S&L disaster. While there were numerous reasons for the S&L failure, two key triggers were the deregulation of the S&L industry, allowing them to make commercial real estate loans in geographical areas they were unfamiliar with, and their ability to lend up to 40 percent of their assets in commercial real estate loans. Congress and the Reagan administration, under pressure from S&L industry lobbyists, were led to believe that if S&Ls made higher-yielding but riskier investments, they would make more money to offset the long-term damage caused by the industry's low-interest, long-term, fixed-rate mortgages.

Deregulation encouraged high risk taking by the S&L industry, just as it did for the GSEs. After all, the federal government guaranteed the S&L's depositors' savings, just as the GSEs knew the government would cover their losses. An initial $200 billion bailout for the GSEs was a lot for the American taxpayer to comprehend. However, as the TV infomercial pitchmen say, "But, wait! There's more!"

BUSH'S $1.1 TRILLION BAILOUT

In September 2008, it appeared to the American public and the world that within a two-week period, the world's leading capitalist nation was pulled into a Category 5 hurricane. Worst of all, the entire nation appeared surprised and the government overwhelmed. President Bush proposed the Economic Stimulation Act of 2008, often referred to as the Troubled Asset Relief Program (TARP).

The American financial industry was supposed to be the one remaining US industry that was still strong—the bedrock of the nation's economy. Most other segments of the economy were in varying levels of distress. The American financial services industry's share of all American corporate profits jumped from 10 percent in the 1980s to 40 percent by 2007.[4] This was one of the principal service industries that some politicians talked about when arguing that the American economy was strong and not in trouble.

Triggered in part by the bursting housing bubble, financial institutions by September 2008 were failing or threatened with failure. Extreme distress in short-term credit markets and a psychological crisis of confidence were paralyzing the financial system. All of this was threatening to adversely affect the entire economy by tightening credit for households that had become addicted to low-cost, readily available credit, as was true for businesses. The government's plan was to replace troubled assets with an enormous infusion of money into the financial system. The theory was that the quicker the money was injected, the quicker the recovery. Morphine was needed in unprecedented amounts.

Secretary of the Treasury Henry Paulson told CBS News, "We have a system that is way out of whack, where our institutions are too big to fail. We don't have the regulatory authorities and structure in place to protect the American People." here is our secretary of commerce, a financial industry insider, former chairman of one of Wall Street's giants, Goldman Sachs, saying Wall Street and our political leaders have not protected the American people. Perhaps you could argue that this is not Wall Street's responsibility, but it is certainly the responsibility of our political leaders. Assuming Secretary Paulson, with all his industry experience and two years as Secretary of the Treasury, saw this coming, why did the administration and Congress wait until the economy was near collapse before saying the system needed more regulation?

Nobel Prize–winning economist Joseph Stiglitz, as well as others, warned of the danger. Stiglitz told CBS News that it was not only foreseeable, "it was foreseen." Dissatisfied with the bailout, he indicated that Wall Street found the sucker to take these bad assets. He went on to say, "No one in the private sector would touch these toxic mortgages. . . . The sucker is the American taxpayer."[5]

The basic idea behind Paulson's plan was to use $700 billion to buy the worst mortgage-backed securities from financial institutions, thereby taking the toxic assets off their books so they could then start lending again. The $700 billion in junk assets that nobody in the financial community would touch would then be owned by the American taxpayer.

Some economists were of the opinion that the bailout was far in excess of what needed to be done. These economists believed that we should not have succumbed to a "sky is falling" scenario, as those in Washington and Wall Street wanted the nation to believe. In fact, by the beginning of 2010, the government expected to lower the projected long-term cost of the program. It expected the cost to be $200 billion less than previously thought.[6]

Myth Number 62: When the housing market collapsed, Congress said they would do and did everything possible to keep American families from losing their homes. Contrary to some of the spinning by the president and many on Wall Street, the bailout program was designed to solve problems for investment banks and offered little to keep home owners from going into foreclosure. Objections to the plan came from both Democrats and Republicans. Most of these lawmakers seemed more intent on extracting concessions that would give them oversight. This would mean that powerful Congressmen and their parties would determine who gets the money and how much and what reciprocity would be required of the recipients. An overwhelming majority in Congress saw the program as a no-strings-attached Wall Street windfall that could be used to pay down debt, acquire other businesses, or invest for the future. There were questions of how much of TARP funds would be used to support home owners by avoiding preventable foreclosures. Of course, the press also gave its share of criticism, pointing out that banks that received bailout money had paid their top executives nearly $1.6 billion in salaries, bonuses, and other benefits the previous year. According to the Center for Responsive Politics, banks, automakers, and other companies that received TARP money spent $114 million on lobbying and campaign contributions during the prior year.[7] The Center for Responsible Lending nonetheless estimated 2.4 million foreclosures in 2009, and 9.0 million during 2009–2012, so it would appear home owners had little influence in Washington.[8]

As Congress began to examine the details of the bailout, the lobbyists were hard at work pushing to have all types of troubled investments covered, not just bad mortgages. The *New York Times* estimated that lobbyists were looking at hundreds of millions of dollars in fees per year.[9] No lobbyist would be able to look at himself in the mirror unless he was able to pry loose a piece of the pie for his clients, regardless of need. Automobile financing companies, credit card lenders, and student loan lenders, among many others, lobbied to be included in the plan. Initially, residential and commercial mortgages were to be bought, but later, with the assistance of lobbyists; the plan was broadened from "mortgage related" to "troubled assets," thereby including virtually all other financial instruments. In time, the Bush administration was propping up the credit card and auto loan industries. Also, initially only US firms could benefit from the program, but the lobbyists managed to get the language broadened to include any financial institution.[10]

Let no bill pass without an inappropriate amount of money added for pork-barrel projects. Some in Congress, as is customarily the case, can convince themselves to support a bill they are fundamentally opposed to if they receive a little pork on their plate. Pork tends to aid digestion in Congress. Some examples of earmarks added to the bill included a tax break for wooden arrows sold for use by children, tax breaks for auto racetrack owners, a rebate on excise taxes for rum producers in Puerto Rico and the Virgin Islands, tax benefits for plaintiffs in the 1989 *Exxon Valdez* case, and tax breaks for the film and TV industries.

After a good deal of grandstanding and partisan finger-pointing (the election was only weeks away) and the addition of approximately another $100 billion–$150 billon of earmarks, in October 2008, President Bush signed the bill. The morphine solution was in place. Keep in mind that the over $800 billion was in addition to the $200 billion the government put up to save Fannie Mae and Freddie Mac, as well as the $123 billion lent to save insurance giant AIG. Add this $1.1 trillion to the federal debt (which was over $13 trillion by the start of 2010), and you're talking about serious money, even by congressional standards.

Immediately after the financial collapse of 2008, Congress moved into what I refer to as the "Goat Roundup Stage." In government and big business, if something goes wrong, a scapegoat, or even better, multiple scapegoats, must be found and sacrificed. This was certainly the case with the 2008 financial collapse. Politicians blamed a lack of corporate ethics, greed, and a lack of industry regulation. It does seem somewhat ironic that politicians would accuse banking leaders of lacking ethics and of being greedy, especially if we consider the number of politicians who have been accused of the same.

Keep in mind that Congress, pressed by its banking lobby friends, was instrumental in eliminating much of the regulation that could have greatly helped, if not completely avoided, the problem. Congress also ignored all the warning signs that a problem was imminent. It was time for Congress to do what it does best—deflect the blame by finding goats to sacrifice. For the sake of the press, Congress baited the corporate witnesses regarding their high pay, multimillion-dollar sales conferences, and other perks. Yes, it was another successful day in Congress; blame was deflected from those who could have avoided the problem, and numerous goats were found and sacrificed for the sake of the press and the American people.

BAILOUT RAMIFICATIONS

Other than Wall Street, who else was blamed for the biggest economic disaster in eighty years? Many looked at economists. Paul Krugman, the 2008 winner of the Nobel Prize in Economics, has argued that the financial collapse is largely due to the past thirty years of macroeconomics, which was "spectacularly useless at best, and positively harmful at worst."

Many economists saw trouble brewing, and perhaps they can be faulted for not shouting loud enough. For several years before the collapse, I spoke and wrote about the impending disaster reluctantly, for fear of being referred to as "Dr. Doom"—a fear many economists suffer from. I lost more than one speaking engagement at business conferences when I provided a synopsis of what I wanted to speak about. These business organizations said everything was going so well and their members did not want to hear depressing news. The executive director of one business organization, after telling me that many of their members had requested that I speak about the future of the economy, asked if I couldn't spin my predictions to be more positive "so their members would feel better about the economy and themselves." Essentially, this was the philosophy of most political leaders, both national and state.

House Speaker Nancy Pelosi, in an attempt to spin the $700 billion bailout, said, "This isn't about a bailout of Wall Street; it's a buy-in, so that we can turn our economy around." Of course, the fact that the Treasury did not have the money to spend to "buy-in" was not emphasized. Not having the money is not a problem for Congress; it has certainly not stopped them in the past. There was no talk of massive cuts in federal spending, and there was certainly no talk of raising taxes. After all, it was an election year, and the morphine solution was in place.

Where is the money to come from? With a national debt of over $10 trillion at the time, it was obvious we could not simply dig into some federal bank account and pay for the bailout. The Chinese, Japanese, and other investors might lend us the money as they have in the past. After all, if they did not and the American economy collapsed, so would our ability to repay the money we already owed them.

The question of whether the bailout was really needed or that the idea that $700 billion was an absurd amount was not debated, at least not seriously. The reality is that at the time, nobody had a clear picture of what the problems really were, and they didn't know what was needed to fix them, if indeed they should have been fixed with taxpayer funds.

Myth Number 63: Congress will impose a system of regulations on Wall Street that will protect the economy against another financial collapse and safeguard the American people. The collapse was the result of an industry with fragmented government oversight and ineffective regulations. As we have seen throughout these pages, many of the problems the nation faces are the result of regulatory failure. In some cases, it was the result of too little regulation; in others, too much. Some situations required better, more effective regulations, yet other problems were the result of unenforced regulations. Bowing to the public's demands, Congress demanded that Wall Street had to be controlled, and the way to accomplish this was by strict regulation and enforcement. To simply say we need to add more regulations to control the market is an oversimplification of the issues involved and another example of a morphine solution.

One of the best examples of how ineptly and unfairly government agencies regulate is the Bernard Madoff case. Mr. Madoff was alleged to have defrauded investors out of $50 billion in the biggest Ponzi scheme ever. Harry Markopolis, a former securities industry executive and fraud investigator, stated in testifying before Congress that the Securities and Exchange Commission (SEC) "is captive to the industry it regulates and is afraid" to bring cases against prominent individuals. He went on to say, "The SEC was never capable of catching Mr. Madoff. He could have gone to $100 billion without being discovered. It took me about five minutes to figure out he was a fraud."[11] According to *Bloomberg BusinessWeek*, in the wake of the scandal, Mary L. Schapiro, chair of the SEC, said her agency would perform surprise inspections on ten thousand money managers to ensure clients were not being ripped off. As noted earlier, after she met with major fund companies, the number of surprise inspections was reduced by over 80 percent.[12]

Some may believe that the 2010 Dodd-Frank Wall Street reform and Consumer Protection Act, commonly known as the financial reform bill, will finally safeguard the American people against another financial crisis. The Center for Public Integrity estimated that the financial services industries alone hired three thousand lobbyists to influence the reform bill. During the first quarter of 2010 it is estimated that the financial services, insurance, and real estate industries spent $125 million on lobbying.

It is therefore not surprising that many of the measures that offered the greatest opportunity to reshape how Wall Street conducts business were struck out or weakened. Of the two most high-profile provisions, neither emerged intact. The first would have forced banks to stop trading financial instruments with their own capital and give up their stakes in hedge funds and private equity funds. The second would have compelled banks to spin off their derivatives operations into separately capitalized affiliates within their holding companies. Both activities have been highly lucrative, annually generating billions for the nation's largest banks. Important questions—such as the amount of capital financial firms will have to set aside as a buffer between assets and liabilities—are scarcely even addressed.

The bill will create a mechanism for liquidating failing financial firms whose collapse could upset markets, and put in place regulators to monitor firms for threats to the economy. This is expected to create vast new bureaucracies. Regulators will be responsible for implementing the legislation by writing hundreds of rules for financial firms. If history is any indication of the future, Wall Street lobbyists will succeed in weakening the bill's intent during this rule-making process.

We must keep in mind that executive and professional compensation created the motives, while deregulation and a lack of oversight create the opportunity for abuse. In spite of Congress's berating of Wall Street executives, the bill falls short in addressing the problematic nature of modern executive and professional compensation even though it was a primary cause of the recession.

The bill lays out a broad mandate and powers for a new Consumer Financial Protection Bureau. The bureau will monitor banks for credit card and mortgage lending abuses. It does not address how the agency should balance the directly competing goals of greater safety and wider access to financing. If the agency significantly reduces the availability of credit for low-income borrowers, it will lose the support of politicians who have supported easy access to credit.

In general, the bill nips at the heels of Wall Street practices rather than forcing fundamental changes to the industry. Certainly, there is little in this bill that would make you believe it will end the risks of too-big-to-fail financial institutions. The largest banks will continue to enjoy the implicit subsidy that results from the expectation that the federal government using taxpayers' money will bail them out in the event they get themselves into trouble. Congress has created the illusion of security with this new bill.

Eliminated from the original House contribution to the bill was the provision that would have allowed federal judges the power to extent loan terms, lower interest rates, and cut principles for home owners in bankruptcy. By September 2009, according to the Mortgage Bankers Association, 14.4 percent of all US mortgages were either delinquent or in foreclosure. When the housing bubble burst, the recession started and the financial markets collapsed; those in the White House and the Capitol insisted something would be done to stop the foreclosures. Billions were given to Wall Street; after all, these institutions were "too big to fail." With millions of home foreclosures occurring, home owners, on the other hand, must have been "too small to bother with."

OBAMA'S $787 BILLION BAILOUT

President Barack Obama, upon taking office, needed his own morphine solution and so signed the $787 billion American Recovery and Reinvestment Act into law on February 17, 2009. Obama focused his stimulus plan on an ambitious package of federal spending and tax cuts that was supposed to revive the economy and save millions of jobs. The administration contended the stimulus plan would create or save 3.5 million jobs.

Simply put, this is how the bill breaks down: 39 percent was to go to appropriations spending, including $120 billion on infrastructure and science and more than $30 billion for energy-related infrastructure projects. The bill allocates 34 percent for direct spending, including unemployment benefits and food stamps. Approximately 27 percent was to be allocated for tax breaks for individuals and businesses.[13]

Obama's financial rescue plan was light on details and was not a true strategic plan that would provide long-term economic growth and employment stability. Both the Obama and Bush plans were geared more toward an attempt to throw money at a problem in the hope that the problem would go away, at least on a temporary basis. Neither bailout provided true long-term solutions; neither would stop the nation's long-term economic freefall, much less produce quality long-term job growth or bring prosperity to Americans. The only thing that is certain is that they would boost the federal debt.

Also, without question, the program would result in a considerable number of new government jobs being created, adding to the national debt. And once government puts new bureaucracies in place, they are virtually sure to become permanent. How much will the $787 billion stimulus program really cost the American taxpayer after the long-term bureaucratic costs are added on? We do not need more government; we need more manufacturing and high-tech jobs, not more bureaucrats, if we are to have sustained economic growth throughout the twenty-first century.

Job creation was not adequately addressed in the president's program. A more focused program of cutting federal spending, and permanently cutting corporate taxes and loopholes, would boost sustained economic growth. Tax incentives aimed at consumer spending were added and stimulated in the short term the purchasing of houses and cars. Had a moratorium been placed on capital gains taxes, you would have seen more money (nonfederal) flowing into the economy. Providing small businesses and start-up entrepreneurs with working capital to build their businesses is critical to job creation. These are some of the kinds of programs that would boost sustained economic growth. The Obama plan does call for some of the money to be used by state and local governments to help pay police, firefighters, teachers, and government workers' salaries in an effort to preserve jobs, and some will be used for new infrastructure construction, which will create jobs.

According to the nonpartisan Congressional Budget Office (CBO), by the time President Obama's term is halfway through, only slightly more than 17 percent of the money will have been spent. This is very confusing, given that Congress's justification for passing this bill so urgently was to help the economy immediately. Other than building the size of government, I don't see how this stimulus plan will be a tremendous boost to the economy.

So where does the money come from for this spending binge? In essence, the money would need to be removed from the private sector as higher taxes or be borrowed by issuing bonds. For every dollar spent by the government, there is one fewer dollar for private investment and consumption. The bottom line is, do we believe the government will do a better job of spending our money than would the private sector? Will the dollars spent by Congress be more productive in stimulating the economy? Recognizing how little planning goes into spending the taxpayers' money by our government, I believe we have invested in a very high-risk venture.

In contrast to the Obama spending portion of the stimulus plan, tax cuts took effect in April 2009. Estimates are that the tax break saved eligible individuals $400 throughout the rest of the year. To stimulate the economy, tax cuts must be permanent. The Kennedy tax cuts of 1964 and the Reagan tax cuts of 1981 were based on this principle.

As I have repeatedly stated (see chapter 7), permanently cutting corporate taxes while closing tax loopholes is critical to spurring business growth and securing long-term job retention and expansion. The "multiplier" effects on economic growth would be far greater. President Obama's own White House chief economist, Christina Romer, has said that every $1 in tax cuts can increase output by as much as $3. The stimulus of substantial permanent corporate tax reductions would help small businesses, which create about three-quarters of all new jobs.[14]

Senator Lindsey Graham (R-SC) complained that a tax benefit for business was cut from $67 billion to only $4 billion.[15] The plan did extend two provisions of 2008's economic stimulus bill that allowed small businesses to take a bigger up-front deduction for the cost of new equipment. The problem is that companies whose sales are down are not going to make big expenditures for new equipment.

Clearly, the Obama plan focuses on the public sector with few incentives for the private sector. The disconnect between politics and business is clearly indicated by this. Those people who would be willing to take the risks to start new businesses and expand existing businesses and, in turn, build employment, would be given very little assistance. They would still be facing staggering taxes, red tape, and government indifference toward their problems.

President Obama declared that no member of Congress would be allowed to insert into his stimulus bill any wasteful, last-minute earmarks to benefit special interests in their states and districts. "We were told this was going to be a massive infrastructure spending program," says Veronique De Rugy, a senior research fellow at George Mason University's Mercatus Center. She argues that the bill is overflowing, not with needed infrastructure spending, but with hundreds of billions in pork.

Where the pork is likely to be found is in the so-called $308-billion discretionary spending portion of the bill. Of that money, $48 billion would go to the Department of Transportation for infrastructure projects. The remaining $260 billion would go to federal agencies, as well as state and local governments. This is where it gets a bit fuzzy. How much of these funds would be going to help special interests instead of stimulating long-term economic job growth would be a matter of contention. The following are some of the more controversial pieces of planned discretionary spending that might be considered pork as identified by Ms. De Rugy:

1. $300 million to buy "green" cars for federal employees.
2. $98 million for a US Coast Guard "polar icebreaker."
3. $200 million to "design and furnish" the Department of Homeland Security headquarters.
4. $3.4 billion on an old-school, nongreen Fossil Energy Research and Development program that, among other things, seeks to reduce the amount of carbon emitted by the use of fossil fuels. We wouldn't see the results of this investment anytime soon. Estimates are that $3.4 billion is probably only a fraction of what is needed for real clean-coal technology to ever be achieved.
5. $144 billion directly to state and local governments. The true

amount of pork would then depend on the priorities of governors, legislatures, and mayors. There was a list of "ready-to-go" projects released by the United States Conference of Mayors in January, dubbed the "Main Street Economic Recovery." Some projects that might be included are any "stadium, community park, museum, theater, art center, and highway beautification project." A prohibition against funding for such projects was dropped from the final version of the bill. That means that many of the "Main Street Economic Recovery" projects from the United States Conference of Mayors report would be eligible for funding. Such projects included $150 million for parking improvements at a Little League facility in Cidra, Puerto Rico, and $6 million for a "snowmaking and maintenance facility" at Spirit Mountain ski area in Duluth, Minnesota.[16]

Numbers 1–4 may be necessary and justifiable, but they strike me as items that should have been debated and funded on their merits and not in the American Recovery and Reinvestment Act. Number 5 is a potential minefield of waste and misdirected funds. The Republicans lost the fiscal responsibility title by running up war costs, growing government, and providing tax cuts at the same time. Obama has bet his administration on the stimulus bill that will save the economy. If it doesn't work, the impact of the Bush and Obama stimulus packages on the national debt will be hard to hide.

Investment in the nation's infrastructure, while greatly needed, will provide temporary jobs, not long-term permanent employment. Also, while alternative-energy projects will create some new jobs, the industry is not considered labor intensive. The American people will have to content themselves with lower expectations. Road and bridge repairs, green technology, broadband expansion, and a new, more functional healthcare system, while needed, will not lead to full employment or an increase in incomes to compensate for the rising cost of living in America.

Historically, the nation's economy has kicked into high and sustained gear as a result of innovation that touches all aspects of the economy, such as the development of steam power, automobiles, electricity, air-conditioning, computerization, or the Internet. For example, without air-conditioning, the explosive postwar development of the South and Southwest would not have occurred. Short of a new innovation occurring in the near future, the Obama stimulus by itself will not change the long-term free fall of the American economy.

President Obama must do what President Bush did not, and that is to tie the economic stimulus to long-term fiscal reform. President Obama has the opportunity to fix our regulatory system, medical care system, and nonfunctioning tax system at the same time. Such a fix cannot be accomplished with morphine solutions or without upsetting armies of bureaucrats, lobbyists, and their clients and congressional leaders who have gained from the current system. In our history, our greatest reforms have risen from hard times and politically embarrassing scandals.

Realistically, President Obama is in a very difficult situation. He must propose legislation to correct the problems previous administrations have spent decades creating. What we need are big, bold solutions for big problems, including, but certainly not limited to, a major overhaul of our tax system, the manner in which we regulate our financial systems, and the ability of special interests to steer government at all levels to their benefit at the expense of the nation.

President Obama came into office like most presidents with big bold ideas, the first of which was reforming the healthcare system. He hit a congressional brick wall held in place by special interests and their influential lobbyists. The healthcare industry, enabled through its congressional friends, managed to beat the program to a pulp, through the use of their most effective tools: partisan fighting and partisan infighting. Had the McCain-Feingold campaign finance reform bill not hit the congressional and lobbyist meat grinder, Obama might have resolved the healthcare issue to the public's benefit. In addition, the housing bubble and the financial market disaster may not have occurred—both due in large part to deregulation of Wall Street by their lobbyists.

Until Congress reforms itself, the introduction of the bold solutions President Obama needs to propose will be an even greater challenge. The partisanship that has held Congress in a death grip is not likely to ease unless the voters send a clear message that they want a functioning government that is run for the people and not special interests.

The Morphine Solution to Economic Problems

It is easy to see why Congress is afraid to do anything. They have created a massive federal debt that has made our economy very fragile, while creating a business environment that has resulted in a disastrous employment situation. Every American recognizes that we need good, well-paying jobs in order to generate the tax revenue necessary to strengthen our economy. We Americans recognize you can't live on borrowed money indefinitely. We have had two huge stimulus programs based on borrowed money, and still American incomes are stagnating while the cost of living continues to rise.

As more baby boomers retire, the debt will grow at an even faster rate. We want government, both federal and state, to fix our problems, but at the same time, we tell them it must be accomplished by spending less and reducing taxes. Are we delusional to think we can have everything? Certainly, politicians have pandered to the public's illusion that we can have it all. Congress is now in a no-win situation; there is no way to decrease massive deficits without significant cuts in government programs. Which member of Congress wants to be known for cutting Social Security or Medicare benefits—and if not those programs, do we cut national defense or education? At the same time, Congress does not have any desire to vote for the massive tax increases needed to pay for the programs and to get the debt under some semblance of control. Yet if these problems are not addressed, they will worsen and continue to plague our economy and our economic future. President Obama has indicated that we need to stop focusing on the health and welfare of Wall Street and start to focus our attention on what is best for the American people. We need to let Congress know that we expect more from them. Most of us elect them to represent us, not their special-interest friends or the extreme elements of their parties.

Presidents Clinton and Reagan cemented their relationship with the American people when their economic strategies worked. If President Obama is successful at turning around the economy and can create an economy based on strong job growth, decrease the national deficit and trade deficit, and secure our position as the world's number one economic power, he will have achieved an almost unbreakable bond of trust with the American people. He has much to accomplish before the election of 2012.

CHAPTER 18

TWENTY-FIRST-CENTURY ECONOMIC WARS

There is nothing wrong with America that the faith, love of freedom, intelligence and energy of her citizens cannot cure.

—Dwight D. Eisenhower
US president, 1953–1961

WHAT DOES THE FUTURE HOLD?

Our national economic policies have led to short-term gains, the collapse of our financial industry, and the potential for long-term disaster. We shored up our economy with low interest rates, financed by the countries that need us as a marketplace for their products. As these countries' economies and markets grow, they will no longer need to shore up our economy by buying our treasuries. Free trade and very poor economic development policies have resulted in the offshoring of industries and jobs, making the potential for economic recovery difficult and the potential for further cuts in our standard of living likely. Interest rates, housing values, cost and quality of merchandise, wages, job security, stock prices, inflation, the general health of our economy, and potentially our national security are all being driven by decisions made by special interests. These decisions are being made with no regard for what is best for the nation as a whole.

As noted earlier, in a February 8, 2006, speech to the United Auto Workers, Senator Hillary Clinton responded to the question "Senator, why can't we get tough on China?" with "I say, well, every month we have to borrow $60 billion to feed the interest on our debt and deficit. Who do we borrow from? China, Korea, Japan, and Saudi Arabia. So how do you get tough on your banker? Think about it—every month we have to hope the Chinese don't go invest in something else."[1] Senator, and now Secretary of State, Clinton, is without doubt one of the nation's most influential political leaders. This dependency was not a natural occurrence of economic forces over which our political leaders had no control.

Since the American Revolution, this is the most profound change we have ever experienced in our ability to determine our own destiny. For over two hundred years, after casting off the yoke of British dominance, we fiercely defended our right to determine our future. Overall, we have had a strong government that was internationally respected with many leaders with extraordinary visions, both in the White House and Congress determined to make the American Dream a reality for all Americans. Today, we have a government of both parties more willing to sell out our future and our children's future to the highest bidder: a government with no vision and no long-term strategy to protect our future.

For decades we have lectured the Chinese on how to run their economy. Today, their economy is based on job growth in manufacturing and increasingly on technology. They are spending their money on infrastructure and an educational system geared to the twenty-first century. Their economy is in desperate need of infrastructure; with a geographic area approximately the size of the United States, they have roughly half the road mileage, a third the rail mileage, and only 425 airports with paved runways to our 5,174.[2] Here in the United States, we have done our best to export our jobs in manufacturing and technology and have opted for an educational system trapped in the 1950s. Our economy has been based on low interest rates financed by foreign capital. How pathetic it is that we are now justifiably lectured on the weakness of our economy by the Chinese. They are legitimately concerned that we have such a fragile economy that we could cause a worldwide depression. The current state of our economy can be attributed to two political parties—Democrat and Republican—supported by complacent state governments.

Whether or not you have faith in the Obama administration, you must recognize that, as president, he alone does not control the United States Congress. He has little control at the state level. If he is to correct the course that the nation is on, he and Congress must be able to suppress the demands of the special-interest groups and the influence of their contributions. This is not going to happen unless the voters put pressure on Congress to clean up their system of bowing to special interests at the expense of the nation. If significant changes in the direction the nation is moving are not implemented, we and our children will be competing for jobs at substantially lower wages with a resulting lower standard of living.

We are truly a superpower that is being sold out. Our trading policies are leading the United States toward a future of diminished economic and political power that leaves us vulnerable to external forces. We continue to negotiate trade deals that do not consider how they impact the social and economic quality of life in this country. Our objective should be to help raise the standard of living worldwide, but not at the risk of reducing the US standard of living.

Our nation became a superpower because we invested in manufacturing and research and development. We were innovative and we made things. We are rapidly becoming a nation that makes nothing, and we are not investing in research and development as we should for the twenty-first-century economy. We won two world wars and the cold war because we out-produced and invested more in research and development than our enemies, and we had the leadership, knowledge, capability, and will to do it.

What are the repercussions for our national security? Are we already losing the capacity to make autos and weapon systems? As manufacturers around the United States accelerate offshore purchases of engineering, manufacturing, and software development, will we be able to control the supply chains for US military production?

Many free-market economists assumed that movement of jobs offshore was an example of free trade that would benefit Americans and that these jobs would be replaced by knowledge jobs, or that American ingenuity would somehow compensate. The knowledge jobs that were supposed to take the place of manufacturing jobs never materialized, and there is no indication that they will. In fact, the opposite is true. Entire industries have been wiped out as corporations replace American workers with foreign workers.

We need to reassert ourselves as a formidable trading partner, a partner that can be trusted but never taken advantage of. This must be done soon, before we lose our negotiation leverage as one of the world's largest markets. Our political leaders need to stop talking about free trade; it doesn't exist in anybody's mind except theirs. To continue to attempt to practice free trade in a hostile trade environment weakens our ability to negotiate trade agreements that will benefit America. Trade agreements must be formed with input from American companies, but ultimately they must be designed to benefit America and not these companies if at the nation's expense. It would be better to see some companies fail than to see the American economy collapse. We need to make more of an effort with our trading partners to stop currency manipulation, take harsher action against the theft of intellectual property, open more markets for US services and products, and create meaningful penalties for unsafe products sent to our market (see chapters 14 and 15). To do this does not make us protectionist—it says we are a nation that can't be manipulated or taken advantage of.

AMERICA IS NOT RISING TO THE CHALLENGE

In the 1990s, the US economy produced a net of twenty-two million jobs. Between 2000 and the beginning of the recession in 2007, we were adding only a net 900,000 jobs per year (75,000 per month). We need a minimum net of 150,000 new jobs each month to keep up with the growing working population. From the start of the recession in December 2007 to year end 2009, we lost over seven million jobs. But the nation's business model was failing long before the start of the recession.

The recession, disastrous trade policies, offshoring of jobs, high taxes, choking regulations, a decline in research and development, overzealous unions, out-of-control medical costs, and an educational system that has fallen far behind are not the only factors responsible for the failure of our business model and the economy. Most of these problems stem from political leadership that has been unable to perceive and adjust for the rigors of a global economy and the competition it has created. This same leadership is so focused on each election and the funding necessary to win that it has lost sight of its responsibility to the American people.

Of the approximately one hundred thirty million jobs in the United States, only 20 percent pay over $60,000 per year, with the other 80 percent averaging $33,000 per year. These are not the kinds of incomes necessary for a prosperous middle class. Two-income families have become a necessity, as has a lifestyle based on borrowing for most families. The ratio of household debt to household income declined from 0.7 to 1.0 in 1985 to 1.7 to 1.0 in 2008. To maintain the same lifestyle their parents provided, young American families of the twenty-first century must borrow more.

For over thirty-five years I have traveled America's rural areas, small towns, big cities, and their neighborhoods. What I see is a growing number of examples of political leaders failing the American people. Too many people and communities are hurting. As a people and a nation, we must accept our share of responsibility. For example, amid the economic prosperity we have had throughout the latter part of the twentieth century, we failed to invest in education—a critical component of twenty-first-century success. If we are to attempt to maintain our rank as a leader in innovation, we must reevaluate and correct our entire educational system from K–graduate school (see chapter 5).

The cost of higher education must come into line with incomes. There are now hundreds of thousands of Americans who will never recover the investment in their university educations. If middle-class incomes continue to rise slower than the rate of inflation, these college graduates may never dig their way out. If we do not stay at, or near the top of, the pyramid in education and innovation, wages will continue to outpace inflation.

We have not even been able to take the needed action to slow environmental degradation in the United States, much less encourage other countries to do so. We rely on a system to provide electrical power that uses nineteenth-century technology, and we continue to allow the oil and automotive industries to dictate our energy policies. Creating legislation that will require the development and implementation of alternative fuels is essential, but this also has been resisted by special interests. China now spends more on wind, solar, and battery technology than we do. If our nation is to prosper and resist being dragged into conflicts in other parts of the world, we must become energy independent. Research and development tax credits need to be a permanent part of every economic growth package. Such credits must be made available to all, including those outside the energy or environmental industries, if we are to encourage innovation and capital investment.

The nation's infrastructure is crumbling: bridges collapse, levies give way, and water systems and sewerage treatment facilities are overtaxed. We are in desperate need of a high-speed rail system as an alternative to the overtaxed and expensive national air transportation system. Other countries have found such systems to be highly efficient and environmentally friendly. China will spend $200,000 billion on a high-speed rail system during 2010 and 2011. We continue to ignore such needs in part due to lobbyists protecting their own industries. Our political leaders also like to assert that we do not have the money for such programs. We have been engaged in an unpopular war that has cost thousands of American lives and at least $100 billion per year; we spend over $20 billion per year on agricultural subsidies that benefit big-business farmers and the agriculture-related industry. We also bailed out our financial industry to the tune of over $1 trillion, an industry that imploded in large part due to its own greed and mismanagement. If that is not enough, we also spend as much as $29 billion per year on pork-barrel projects for special interests (see chapter 10).

We must also stop deluding ourselves and stop politicians and the press from talking about training Americans for jobs in the new economy when these jobs are easily offshored. The business community recognizes that there are very few jobs that can't be offshored at less cost. We cannot compete with India and China in terms of labor cost, but there are areas where we can compete with them and have made little effort to do so.

Labor costs alone are not what is driving companies offshore. In manufacturing, direct labor averages only 10 percent of costs. Ninety percent of costs are attributable to items such as technology, capital invested, inventory turnover, waste, taxes, complying with regulations, utilities, and transportation.[3] In many of these areas, America could be much more competitive but makes little or no effort. Good, well-paying jobs pay taxes for education and infrastructure and keep an economy healthy and growing, yet our federal and state governments have allowed these jobs to flow offshore.

TWENTY-FIRST-CENTURY ECONOMIC WARFARE

Myth Number 64: You need not worry. The government has a comprehensive plan that will maintain the nation as the preeminent economic leader throughout the twenty-first century, thereby guaranteeing the American people the highest standard of living in the world. Since the beginning of the wars in Iraq and Afghanistan, Americans have been very focused. Our loyalty and concern for our troops run deep, as do our convictions regarding how best to manage these conflicts. Why then do we appear to be oblivious to another war in which we're engaged? This is an economic war that will radically change the American way of life in terms of our standard of living and security, and that of our children and their children's future. Perhaps this war receives little attention because there is no easily recognizable battlefield, no major city or part of the countryside to secure, but rather many skirmishes that few of us see taking place. There is no single enemy, but rather many different nations and special interests (many within the United States) that are involved in these skirmishes. Much like "friendly fire" in combat situations, many of these skirmishes are occurring on a regular basis with US special interests and Congress. In this twenty-first-century economic warfare, it is the cumulative effect of these skirmishes that will determine if we win or lose. Today, if we look at the United States compared with our tough, aggressive world competitors, primarily China and India, we are not doing well.

There are two ways to deal with the current national crises. The first method, favored by most administrations and Congress, is a tactical approach, much like the morphine solution favored by political leaders. As in warfare, a tactical approach is one in which you charge from one battle to another. In the business world, this is called crisis management. The second, much more complex approach is strategic, a comprehensive plan used to organize present plans of action on the basis of achieving future goals. To have a strategic plan, you must define your strategy or direction and make decisions on the allocation of resources to pursue your goals.

The Bush administration opted for the tactical, crisis management approach in running the government, as evidenced by its approach to the war in Iraq and to its handling of the nation's economy. Not to pick solely on the Bush administration. The Clinton administration was not particularly stellar when it came to long-range planning either. Neither administration was good at reading the signs of increasing economic problems, or perhaps chose to ignore them, hoping that they could be postponed until the next administration. Both administrations preferred morphine solutions if the problem became so obvious that it could not be ignored. If they did see the problems coming, they did not take evasive action. Benjamin Franklin said, "By failing to prepare, you are preparing to fail." The Bush administration and Congress could not have missed the fact that home foreclosures were rising at a frightening pace. Unemployment, the national debt, and the trade deficit were only some of the other signs that should have been obvious calls for concern, relative to the 2008 financial meltdown.

Look at how we and China approached the financial crisis. We immediately sought the morphine solution to protect our backsides by tossing huge sums of borrowed money at the problem. Our government was unprepared for the financial meltdown and recession in spite of the warnings and the fact that it was instrumental in creating the problem. When everything appeared to be collapsing, we strapped a NASA booster rocket onto the deficit and let it rip, not worried about reentry or where it would land. We just started tossing money off of our Deficit Rocket at anyone who had the proper Washington connections, whether the money was needed or not. The faster we tossed the money off the Deficit Rocket, the higher the trajectory we achieved. It was clear early in the process that little thought was given to the best use of bailout funds and even less for building the future. We gave billions to Wall Street and within a year they were paying themselves record bonuses.

China, on the other hand, read the signs and was building a budget surplus, had increased interest rates to keep its growth in check, and controlled consumer consumption by limiting credit. When the recession hit, the Chinese government was able to lower interest rates, create massive infrastructure and higher education programs, and order its banks to let credit flow more freely. The lion's share of the Chinese government's bailout investment went toward building a solid base for future growth.

Through good planning they pulled out of the recession quicker and in an excellent position to grow employment and their economy.

The United States, as a result of considerable experience, has become very adept at tactical solutions to economic problems, but totally inept when addressing a strategic approach to dealing with these issues. Our approach is to let the roof fall in before addressing a problem. We have no comprehensive plan to address the nation's economic woes; rather, we wait for a crisis and then attempt to solve it with taxpayer or borrowed money. The bailouts of 2008 and 2009 are examples of tactical approaches to problem solving.

Our political leaders have a problem-solving philosophy based on crisis containment. During the presidential campaign, neither Obama nor McCain could claim to have proposed anything close to a strategic plan for the nation. As was true at the state-level elections, candidates tend to propose disconnected policies that pander to what they believe are the voters' hot button of the day.

The United States simply has had no long-range economic strategy—there has been no coordinated set of policies that would help us avoid financial disaster, much less ensure that we will stay competitive in the twenty-first-century global economy. Our government has not understood or has simply ignored the rising economic power of the rest of the world. It is therefore not surprising that we are falling behind. It is not just the federal government that has been working in this manner; far too many of our state governments have followed.

At the national level, we know that we are facing many crises involving the national deficit, tax codes, federal and state regulations, offshoring of jobs, family debt, Social Security, Medicare, medical insurance, education, immigration, aging infrastructure, and a trade deficit based on a simplistic approach to free trade. They all pose problems that, together and individually, will have a much more severe impact on the American people than the 2008 financial meltdown. The Obama administration has yet to prove that it really has a long-range coordinated strategic plan for all aspects of the economy. If we continue into the twenty-first century allowing special interest to dictate policy and do not develop our own plan, our superpower status will continue to wane and with it our standard of living.

Our political leaders at every level—federal, state, and local—need to understand that the old relationship between government and big business is different than it was in the twentieth century. We can no longer work with big corporations the way we did in the twentieth century. Global corporations' agendas are different; they are no longer dependent on American markets, investors, workers, innovators, scientists, or engineers as they once were. They have moved into the twenty-first-century global economy. They are increasingly dependent on *global* markets, investors, workers, innovators, scientists, engineers, and executives. To continue to believe that these companies are going to perform in a manner that will benefit the United States is not only naive but dangerous to our economy and our future. If these companies are to survive, they must be competitive in the global marketplace. The actions they must take to achieve this goal will increasingly conflict with what is best for the American people.

Until we decide to retake control of government, we will continue to slide into an economic abyss. Members of Congress must be forced to stop selling out to big corporate interests in return for campaign financing (a form of indentured servitude at best and bribery at worst) and start defending the public interest. Only an aroused and activist electorate can make them do what is best for America.

Congress must also learn to understand and be responsive to those thousands of American companies that are *not* global, that do *not* have high-powered, high-priced lobbyists. These small and midsize companies are the backbone of the US economy and are both taken for granted and often abused. This abuse can take many forms, but most frequently they are simply taken for granted as a source of jobs and tax revenue, and their problems and concerns too often completely ignored.

Who is bailing out the small-business owner losing her business due to US trade agreements? Who is bailing out the family that can no longer pay their debts because a spouse has lost his job due to off-shoring, or because they are overwhelmed with unpaid medical bills, or simply because their income has not kept pace with inflation? These are all problems that need a comprehensive strategic plan—a plan that did not exist under the Clinton or Bush administrations.

Any strategic plan would need to be a bipartisan effort that would prioritize problems based on need and not politics. Rather than having many uncoordinated bills, there needs to be a coordinated and prioritized set of legislation. America's chance of winning at twenty-first-century economic warfare without a strategic plan is as good as our chances of winning a military war without a plan. The first battle to be won in our economic war is to keep from destroying ourselves.

A comprehensive strategic plan would force many difficult decisions. The implementation of such a plan would likely be unpopular with some voters, as well as with most lobbyists and their clients. If we ask why the Chinese are doing so well compared to the United States, it is because they have a highly coordinated strategic approach to controlling and growing their economy. I have pointed out many flaws with the Chinese. But somewhere between their approach and ours is a strategic plan that could work for the United States. If we do not get control of our economy, the nation will jump from one crisis to another. This will occur at an increasing rate as we continue our downward spiral, and other nations will take for their own the best parts of our economy. *Oui se fait brebis, le loap le mange.*

EASY TO ELECT, HARD TO KEEP ON COURSE

In recent decades, we have not had the leadership at the national level to make the required course corrections, and with a few exceptions most state leadership has proven less than competent. When I speak of leadership, I speak not only of presidents and governors but also of federal and state legislators, many of whom, despite their rhetoric, either do not understand the problems or are unwilling to take them on for fear of alienating their special-interest campaign contributors. Moreover, many are obstructionists to any progress, just so their party will prevail, even at the expense of the American public.

What we need to accomplish is cutting government spending while increasing revenue. We should be cutting corporate taxes at the same time we plug all the loopholes in our tax code to ensure that companies are all paying their fair share of taxes. We also need to encourage business growth in the United States by eliminating the mountain of regulatory "red tape" American companies must contend with, especially the small to midsize companies that can least afford the army of experts needed to deal with this red tape. This does not mean we eliminate all regulations, just as many as are necessary. The nation must be made more business friendly by having a better-educated labor force, better infrastructure, and a better tax code and regulations that can be complied with at a lower cost and with less red tape than our competitors. Communities need to stop talking about treating industry as a partner and start acting like a partner. What we don't need are more morphine solutions to complex problems.

Many would say that government meddling in the private sector can stifle economic growth and stability. Strange as it may be, the one economy that has handled the worldwide recession the best is China's. It should be clear to most of us that a weak regulatory apparatus has contributed significantly to the causes of the financial market meltdown in the United States. In China, approximately one-half of the economy is controlled by the public sector, or as much as 70 percent, if you include government-owned companies that are allowed to operate as private firms. The Chinese government does manipulate the stock market and banking industry. For example, the government did not allow its banking industry to embrace the exotic financial innovations that caused the overheating of the US housing market, and thus avoided a housing bubble.[4] Somewhere between the Chinese system of regulation and our system is a system Americans can thrive under. The fact is, at one time we had a system of regulation that worked, but it was slowly eroded at the insistence of special interests and with the help of our own Congress.

Washington would like to heap all the blame onto Wall Street. This is a case of oversimplification and trying to deflect blame. Let's start with the trigger of the housing bubble. The Federal Reserve Board, in its wisdom, created the housing bubble and then let it burst. Between January 2001 and June 2003, the Federal Reserve cut its rate from 6.5 percent to 1 percent and then increased the rate in a three-year period to 5.25 percent. Readily available, low-cost funds were thus able to pump up the housing bubble, followed by higher interest rates that were sure to burst it. The Federal Reserve had the power to control the situation but did not do it. Still, the Federal Reserve should not take all of the blame. The Securities and Exchange Commission allowed the banking system to become overleveraged. An unsupervised Fannie Mae and Freddie Mac added to the problem by allowing the free flow of funds to inflate the bubble.

Fueled by lobbyists for the financial industries, a laissez-faire attitude developed in Washington in support of unregulated capitalism. Washington believed that financial institutions would self-regulate, which for many of these institutions meant no regulation. Washington was more than willing to listen to Wall Street; after all, they had spent over $600 million lobbying to get rid of regulations between 1998 and 2008.[5] Washington sold itself to Wall Street, and the taxpayers paid the price. Ultimately, it is Washington that is supposed to make the rules and enforce them through a regulatory system. It is this regulatory system for the financial industry that proved to be next to useless.

Not only must the nation become more frugal in spending our tax dollars, we Americans must learn the value of saving for a rainy day and become less dependent on our credit cards as a financing tool. Of course, the credit card industry would not like this. Here is an industry that thrives when Americans are deeply in debt. With little regulation, thanks to Congress, the industry has grown and prospered on the backs of Americans who now finance all aspects of their life, from buying a home to groceries. Each year a growing percentage of Americans' income goes to finance their debts. Essentially, Americans have three bosses they are working for. The first pays them. The second taxes them—local, state, federal. Finally, their most predatory boss, their lenders, takes much of what is left. The problem is that for most Americans, their incomes are not rising as fast as their debt (see chapter 16).

There is no mystery about what needs to be done. Most of the necessary banking industry legislation was in place, but the efforts of lobbyists and Congress during the last couple of decades have done away with them. The result is that Americans carry more debt than ever in our history and the credit card industry keeps growing.

DO WE HAVE THE LEADERS WE DESERVE?

Most Americans are driving down the center of the road; they don't belong to the "base" of either party, although they may consider themselves Democrats or Republicans. In the 2008 presidential election, approximately 61 percent of eligible voters took the time to vote. In the 2006 midterm elections, only 48 percent of eligible voters went to the polls. Of Americans eligible to vote, 32 percent never registered.[6] Is it any wonder candidates then coddle the ultraright and the ultraleft? They are organized and they vote as a unit, whereas the majority of Americans don't bother to vote. If you're running for office, you have no choice but to play the cards that will win.

In Washington, in the state capital, and in city hall, money talks. During the campaign process, each candidate will tend to move more to the center to garner as many votes as possible. But by this time, the candidates' souls have already been sold to the special interests and their party's "base," without whom they would not have had a chance to become a candidate. And once elected, heaven help them if they displease their "base" and the corporations, special-interest groups, and lobbyists that *got* them elected. This is discouraging, certainly, but all the more reason to step up and make your voice heard by voting and actively participating in the electoral process. If you don't keep yourself informed and work to restore democracy in this country, you are, by default, allowing the lobbyists to continue to advance special interests at the expense of the national interest. Unfortunately, it seems that far too many people find it easier to complain than to vote.

Summarizing some of the major economic indicators discussed in this book, I would assign the following grades on a United States Economic Report Card based on effort made:

United States Economic Report Card

Gross Domestic Product Growth	D
Gross National Debt	F
Trade Deficit	F
Education	C

Quality Job Growth	F
Personal Savings/Family Debt	F
Middle-Class Growth	D
Economic Development	D

Yes, this is still the best country in the world; yes, the competition still has a long way to go to catch up, in some but not all areas. But does this report card reflect a country that millions struggled to come to so that they and their children might realize the American Dream?

History tells us that to win a war, you must have great leadership. Based on our report card, it would appear our leadership leaves much to be desired. If we are to ever have great leadership, we must first regain control of our political system. We must have a government that represents the best interests of the American people and not political parties, the ultra-right or ultra-left, or special interests. Senators John McCain and Russ Feingold had the right idea when they introduced the McCain-Feingold Bill that, if passed as originally introduced, would have helped move the nation in the right direction. This is one of those skirmishes the American people lost to those in Congress and lobbyists unwilling to relinquish power. Until we gain control again of our political system, we will continue to be sold out.

By August 2009, the Federal Reserve announced that the recession was ending. Not all economists agree on the exact definition of recession. In general, it is a slowing down of the economy's many macroeconomic indicators, such as employment, investment, wholesale-retail sales, real personal income, capacity utilization, and business profitability. The most common definition of a recession is two consecutive quarters in which the GDP drops. Simply, when economic output has stopped contracting, the recession is considered over.

Since unemployment was at 9.7 percent at the time and rising, we were told that it was a "jobless recovery." There is an old economist joke that says: If your neighbor loses his job, it's a recession; if you lose your job, it's a depression. For millions of Americans, it was hard to believe that the recession was over. The vast majority of Americans will not, and should not, believe the recession is over until unemployment drops to 5 percent or below—the prerecessionary level for the decade. In addition, income levels for the middle and lower classes should be rising faster than the cost of living. It is not over until the fat lady sings, and she hasn't even arrived for the concert yet.

Having grown up in the post–World War II 1950s, my friends and I were instilled with a strong sense of patriotism. Of the kids I grew up with, many had fathers and uncles who served in the Pacific or European theaters. These were men who seldom spoke of war, but who instilled in us all a sense of dedication to country and the American way of life.

America is in desperate need of a hero—not a sports hero, not a movie star, and not a rock star. We need a political hero with a clear vision for the nation, a leader who will put the good of the nation as a whole above all special interests, a leader that will get us back on a path of economic and political strength and international respect. We owe it to past generations who sacrificed so much for the nation and to future generations whose lives will be molded by our legacy. It might be Obama or it might be someone else. But we cannot continue on the road we are taking.

I have had the good fortune to see America at its best, with a strong economy, good jobs, and a world leader in education—a nation that was respected and envied. There are many Americans today who have not had this opportunity and may never. Franklin D. Roosevelt placed the welfare of Americans above everything. I would suggest that all Americans think about the following quote when deciding whether they have the time to go to the polls.

> *Those who have long enjoyed such privileges as we enjoy forget in time that men have died to win them.*
>
> —Franklin D. Roosevelt

NOTES

CHAPTER 1

1. Kurt Anderson, "Don't Pretend We Didn't See This Coming for a Long Time," *Time*, April 6, 2010, p. 42.

2. "Globalization: Turning Their Backs on the World," *Economist*, February 21, 2009, p. 60.

3. Alexander Mooney, "Poll: Majority against Free Trade," CNNPolitics.com, July 1, 2008, http://edition.cnn.com/2008/POLITICS/07/01/cnn.poll/index.html (accessed on July 15, 2008).

4. John W. Schoen, "Just Who Owns the U.S. National Debt? And Is Growing Foreign Investment in the U.S. Bad for America?" MSNBC.com, March 4, 2007, http://www.msnbc.msn.com/id/17424874/print/1/displaymode/1098/ (accessed on March 7, 2007).

5. Chris Atkins and Scott A. Hodge, "U.S. Still Lagging behind OECD Corporate Tax Trends," Fiscal Fact No. 96, Tax Foundation, July 24, 2007.

6. Elizabeth Warren and Amelia Warren Tyagi, "What's Hurting the Middle Class: The Myth of Overspending Obscures the Real Problem," *Boston Review*, September/October 2005, http://bostonreview.net/BR30.5/warrentyagi.php (accessed on November 15, 2007).

7. "A Time for Muscle Flexing," *Economist*, March 21, 2009, p. 28.

8. "Companies' and Countries' Prosperity Decoupled," *Economist*, February 25, 2006, p. 75.

9. Neil Roland, "G.M. Plans to Export China-Made Cars to U.S.," *Automotive News*, May 12, 2009, http://www.autonews.com/article/20090512/ANA02/905119971/1131 (accessed on May 18, 2009).

10. Fareed Zakaria, "How Long Will America Lead the World?" *Newsweek*, June 12, 2006, p. 42.

11. "Obama's World," *Economist*, November 8, 2008, p. 31.

CHAPTER 2

1. Marlowe C. Embree, "Social Psychologist's Search for Purple America," University of Wisconsin, November 5, 2004, http://www.uwmc.uwc.edu/psychology/purple_america.htm (accessed on May 5, 2009).

2. Michael McDonald, "United States Election Project, 2008 General Election Turnout Rates," Department of Public and International Affairs, George Mason University, January 28, 2009.

Notes

3. Pat Harris, "Tea Party Welcomes Conservative Darling Palin," Reuters, February 6, 2010, http://www.reuters.com/article/idUSTRE6160A520100207 (accessed on February 10, 2010).

4. Carl Cameron, "Tea Party Convention Plans National Organizing Strategy for Elections," FOXNews.com, February 5, 2010, http://www.foxnews.com/politics/2010/02/05/tea-party-convention-purpose-national-organizing-strategy/ (accessed on February 8, 2010).

5. James Pethokoukis, "Obama 2.0: Candidate Starts His Hard Move to the Center," *U.S. News & World Report,* June 18, 2008, http://www.usnews.com/blogs/capital-commerce/2008/6/18/obama-20-candidate-starts-his-hard-move-to-the-center.html (accessed on June 24, 2008).

6. "U.S. Election Will Cost $5.3 Billion," OpenSecrets.org, Center for Responsive Politics, October 22, 2008, http://www.opensecrets.org/index.php (accessed on November 3, 2008).

7. Gareth Cook, "Laws for Sale—Republicans in Congress Let Lobbyists Write Laws," *Washington Monthly,* July–August 1995, http://findarticles.com/p/articles/mi_m1316/is_n7-8_v27/ai_17263138 (accessed on April 19, 2009).

8. Nancy Pelosi, Speaker of the House of Representatives, http://speaker.house.gov/legislation?id=0002 (accessed on October 8, 2009).

9. Barack Obama, "Ethics & Lobbying Reform," Lobbying Reform Summit, National Press Club, Washington, DC, January 26, 2006, http://obama speeches.com/047-Lobbying-Reform-Summit-National-Press-Club-Obama-Speech.htm (accessed on November 18, 2009).

10. President William J. Clinton, Radio Address by the President to the Nation, Oval Office, July 22, 1995, http://archives.clintonpresidential center.org/?u=072295-presidential-radio-address-on-political-reform.htm (accessed on September 22, 2008).

11. Carl Hulse, "Frustrated G.O.P. Tries to Drive Wedge between Obama and Pelosi," *New York Times,* February 28, 2009.

12. US Federal Election Commission, *Major Provisions of the Bipartisan Campaign Reform Act of 2002* (Washington, DC: GPO, 2002), http://fec.gov/press/bkgnd/bcra_overview.shtml (accessed on February 13, 2009).

13. Ellen S. Miller, "No Chance: McCain-Feingold Was Supposed to Bring the Influence of Money in Politics under Control. But the Powers-That-Be Bit Back," *American Prospect,* December 13, 2002, http://www.prospect.org/cs/articles?article=no_chance.

14. Ibid.

15. "Reactions to the Supreme Court Reversing Limits on Corporate

Spending in Political Campaigns," *Washington Post*, January 21, 2010, http://voices.washingtonpost.com/44/2010/01/reactions-to-the-supreme -court.html (accessed on January 24, 2010).

16. Ibid.

17. Jonathan Alter, "High-Court Hypocrisy, Dick Durbin's Got a Good Idea," *Newsweek*, February 1, 2010, p. 15.

18. Lou Dobbs, *War on the Middle Class* (New York: Viking, 2006), p. 37.

19. Lou Dobbs, "Lobbying against America: Corporate Supremacist Lobbyists Control Congress, Passing Corporate Friendly Laws at Your Expense," CNNMoney.com, August 11, 2005, http://money.cnn.com/2005/08/11/ commentary/dobbs/corporate_lobbying/index.htm (accessed on April 23, 2009).

20. "2008 Overview," Center for Responsive Politics, OpenSecrets.org, info@crp.org.

21. Steve Forbes, *Flat Tax Revolution* (Washington, DC: Regnery Publishing, 2005), p. 9.

22. Travis Smiley Show and Connie Rice, "Top 10 Outrages of the Corporate Tax Bill," first broadcast October 20, 2004, by NPR, http://www.npr.org/ templates/story/story.php?storyId=4117683 (accessed on May 18, 2009).

23. Joe Scarborough, *Rome Wasn't Burnt in a Day* (New York: HarperCollins, 2004), p. 8.

24. "Money Wins Presidency and 9 out of 10 Congressional Races Priciest U.S. Election Ever," Center for Responsive Politics, November 5, 2008.

25. Barack Obama, *The Audacity of Hope* (New York: Crown Publishers, 2006), pp. 109–15.

26. Mark Green, *Selling Out: How Big Corporate Money Buys Elections, Rams through Legislation, and Betrays Our Democracy* (New York: Regan Books, 2002), p. 270.

27. Adam Nagourney and Janet Elder, "Only 25 Percent in Poll Approve of the Congress," *New York Times*, September 21, 2006.

28. Ilya Somin, "When Ignorance Isn't Bliss: How Political Ignorance Threatens Democracy," Cato Institute, *Policy Analysis* 525 (September 22, 2004): 4.

29. Ibid., p. 6.

30. President John F. Kennedy, Remarks in Nashville at the 90th Anniversary Convention of Vanderbilt University, May 18, 1963, John F. Kennedy Presidential Library and Museum, http://www.jfklibrary.org/Historical +Resources/Archieves/Reference+Desk/Speeches?JFK/003POF03 Vanderbilt 05181963.htm (accessed on November 7, 2009).

31. Curtis Gans, "Much-Hyped Turnout Record Fails to Materialize;

Convenience Voting Fails to Boost Balloting," Center for the Study of the American Electorate, American University, November 6, 2008, p. 6.

32. John W. Dean, *Broken Government: How Republican Rule Destroyed the Legislative, Executive, and Judicial Branches* (New York: Viking, 2007), p. 187.

33. Yogi Berra, *The Yogi Book: "I Really Didn't Say Everything I Said"* (Workman Publishing Company, 1998), p. 42.

CHAPTER 3

1. Fareed Zakaria, "How Long Will America Lead the World?" *Newsweek*, June 12, 2006, p. 42.

2. Central Intelligence Agency, *World Fact Book*, 2010, https://www.cia.gov/library/publications/the-world-factbook/ (accessed on February 2, 2010).

3. Carsten A. Holz, "China's Economic Growth, 1978–2025: What We Know Today about China's Economic Growth Tomorrow," Working Paper no. 8, Center on China's Transnational Relations, July 3, 2005.

4. "India Needs More Economic Reforms to Widen Benefits from Growth, Says OECD Report," Organisation for Economic Co-operation and Development, September 10, 2007, http://www.oecd.org/document/10/0,3343,en_2649_201185_39452554_1_1_1_1,00.html (accessed on November 18, 2007).

5. "Chinese Companies Earn Higher Returns Than Is Commonly Claimed," *Economist*, October 21, 2006, p. 88.

6. Howard W. French, "International Business: India and China Take on the World and Each Other," *New York Times*, November 8, 2005.

7. Pete Engardio, "A New World Economy, the Balance of Power Will Shift to the East, China and India Evolve," *BusinessWeek*, August 20/29, 2005, p. 55.

8. Titus Galama and James Hosek, *U.S. Competitiveness in Science and Technology* (RAND Corporation, 2008), p. 16.

9. Ibid., p. xvi.

10. "White House 2010 R&D Budget, Presented at AAAS, Offers Significant New Investment," American Association for the Advancement of Science, May 7, 2009, http://www.aaas.org/news/release/2009/0507rd_budget.shtml.

11. Galama and Hosek, *U.S. Competitiveness in Science and Technology*, p. 28.

12. "China Will Become World's Second-Highest Investor in R&D by End of 2006, Finds OED," Organisation for Economic Co-operation, April 12, 2006,

Notes

http://www.oecd.org/document/26/0,3343,en_2649_34269_37770522_1_1_1
_1,00.html (accessed on January 14, 2009).

13. Ibid., p. 116.

14. "American Companies in India," India Business Directory, USINDIA Business Council, 2010, http://www.usibc.com/usibc/membership/default (accessed on January 8, 2010).

15. Satya Prakash Singh, "Silicon Valley Falls to Bangalore," *Times of India*, January 5, 2004.

16. "Educational Trends in Material Science and Engineering—Enrollment, Degrees, Gender, Ethnicity and Research Expenditure," Report 1005A, *Engineering Trends*, September 2005, p. 4.

17. Kevin G. Hall, "Future Work: Engineer Shortage Looms," Knight Ridder Foreign Service, August 15, 2005, http://www.iseek.org/sv/37.jsp ?fwa=fa/fw5752.jsp&id=5752 (accessed on January 5, 2007).

18. Victoria Colliver, "More Who Need Major Surgery Are Leaving U.S.: Overseas Treatments Sometimes Carry Extra Risks, But Can Come at Fraction of the Expense," *San Francisco Chronicle*, May 4, 2008.

19. Hall, "Future Work: Engineer Shortage Looms."

20. Manjeet Kripalani, "Trying to Tame the Blackboard Jungle," *Business-Week*, August 22/29, 2005, p. 94.

21. "Cisco Systems Make Major Strategic Investments in India," News@Cisco, October 19, 2005, http://newsroom.cisco.com/dlls/global/ asiapac/ news/2005/ts_10-19.html (accessed August 5, 2009).

22. Engardio, "A New World Economy," p. 55.

23. Steve Hamm, "Scrambling Up the Development Ladder," *Business-Week*, August 22, 2005, p. 114.

24. Richard Malish and Geofrey L. Master, "Doing Business in China: China Sourcing," Mayer Brown LLP, December 12, 2007, http://www.mayer brown.com/publications/article.asp?id=4046&nid=6 (accessed on January 18, 2008).

25. "Carmaking in China, the Fast and the Furious," *Economist*, November 25, 2006, p. 63.

26. Fareed Zakaria, "Growing Pains: The Truth about Sino-U.S. Relations," *Newsweek*, February 15, 2010, p. 18.

27. Central Intelligence Agency, *World Fact Book*, 2010, https:/www.cia .gov/library/publications/the-world-factbook/ (accessed on February 2, 2010).

28. "China's Battered Image: Bears in a China Shop," *Economist*, January 16, 2010, pp. 14–15.

29. Rob Gifford, *China Road: A Journey into the Future of a Rising Power* (New York: Random House, 2007), p. 276.

CHAPTER 4

1. Zhou Shijian, "China Is Ready to Meet Challenges," *People's China Daily*, October 24, 2004.

2. Office of the Secretary of Defense, *Annual Report to Congress, The Military Power of the People's Republic of China*, 2005 (Washington, DC: GPO, 2005), p. 1.

3. "A Special Report on China and America, Overkill, China Is Piling up More Weapons than It Appears to Need," *Economist*, October 24, 2009, p. 10.

4. US Congress, *2005 Report to Congress of the U.S.-China Economic and Security Review Commission* (Washington, DC: GPO, 2005), p. 2.

5. Ibid., p. 4.

6. US Congress, *2005 Report to Congress*, p. 5.

7. "Trade Surplus Predicted to Hit U.S. $190 Billion in 2007," *The Economic and Commercial Counselor's Office of the Embassy of the People's Republic of China in the United States of America*, January 5, 2007, http://us2.mofcom.gov.cn/aarticle/chinanews/200701/20070104238760.html (accessed on January 22, 2009).

8. Thomas L. Friedman, *The World Is Flat: A Brief History of the Twenty-first Century* (New York: Farrar, Straus and Giroux, 2005), p. 421.

9. Fareed Zakaria, "India Rising," *Newsweek*, March 6, 2006, www.fareedzakaria.com/articles/newsweek/030606.html (accessed on May 23, 2009).

10. "India and Capital Flows: A World Apart," *Economist*, October 31, 2009, p. 83.

11. "China's Fiscal Stimulus, Dr. Keynes's Chinese Patient," *Economist*, November 15, 2008, p. 16.

12. Jonathan Anderson, "Is China Export-Led?" UBS Investment Research, September 27, 2007.

13. "An Old Chinese Myth—Contrary to Popular Wisdom, China's Rapid Growth Is Not Hugely Dependent on Exports," *Economist*, January 5, 2008, p. 75.

14. "Emerging Markets, Stumble or Fall?" *Economist*, January 10, 2009, p. 63.

15. "China's Economy: Bamboo Shoots of Recovery," *Economist*, April 18, 2009.

16. Ibid., p. 75.

17. Melinda Liu, "China, There's Plenty of Blame for All," *Newsweek*, April 6, 2009.

18. "America's Vulnerable Economy, Recession in America Looks Increasingly Likely," *Economist*, November 17, 2007, p. 13.

19. M. Ayhan Kose, Christopher Otrok, and Eswar S. Prassad, "Global Business Cycles: Convergence or Decoupling?" Working Paper WP/08/143, International Monetary Fund, June 2008, p. 25.

20. "Mattel Apologizes to China over Recalls," Associated Press, MSNBC.com, September 21, 2007, http://www.msnbc.com/id/20903731/print/1/displaymode/1098/ (accessed on September 28, 2007).

21. Ibid.

22. "China's Media—Back on the Leash," *Economist*, August 20, 2005, pp. 32–33.

23. "Chinese Manufacturing, Plenty of Blame to Go Around," *Economist*, September 29, 2007, pp. 68–69.

24. Ibid.

25. Ted C. Fishman, *China, Inc.: How the Rise of the Next Superpower Challenges America and the World* (New York: Scribner, 2005), p. 285.

CHAPTER 5

1. Christine M. Matthews, *Foreign Science and Engineering Presence in U.S. Institutions and the Labor Force*, CRS Report for Congress, July 23, 2008.

2. Scott Jaschik, "Lost Dominance in PhD Production," *Inside Higher Education*, July 15, 2005, http://www.insidehighered.com/news/2005/07/15/science (accessed on February 23, 2009).

3. Gary Gereffi et al., "Framing the Engineering Outsourcing Debate: Placing the United States on a Level Playing Field with China and India," Duke University, December 12, 2005, p. 5.

4. Diversity Lottery, US Citizenship and Immigration Services, October 1, 2008.

5. Richard J. Newman, "Can America Keep Up?" *U.S. News & World Report*, March 19, 2006, http://www.usnews.com/usnews/biztech/articles/060327/27global.htm (accessed on March 12, 2009).

6. "India: The Next Wave," *Economist*, December 17, 2005, p. 53.

7. Pete Engardio, "Can the Future Be Built in America?" *Business Week*, September 10, 2009, http://www.businessweek.com/magazine/content/09_38/b4147046115750.htm (accessed September 15, 2009).

8. "The Knowledge Economy: Is the United States Losing Its Competitive Edge?" Task Force on the Future of American Innovation, 2005, p. 1.

9. Ed Frauenheim, "Brain Drain in Tech's Future?" CNETNews.com, August 6, 2004, http://news.cnet.com/Brain-drain-in-techs-future/2100-1008_3-5299249.html (accessed on March 18, 2009).

10. William J. Broad, "U.S. Is Losing Its Dominance in the Sciences," *New York Times*, May 3, 2004.

11. Ibid.

12. Ed Shanahan, "Getting Ready for Work: The New 'Hire' Education," *Reader's Digest*, October 2006, p. 84.

13. Ibid., p. 10.

14. Thomas C. Friedman, *The World Is Flat: A Brief History of the Twenty-first Century* (New York: Farrar, Straus and Giroux, 2005), pp. 264–65.

15. Todd G. Bucholz, "Bringing the Jobs Home, How the Left Created the Crisis—and How We Can Fix It," *New York Sentinel*, 2004, p. 52.

16. Catherine Arnst, "Science? What's Science?" *BusinessWeek*, April 7, 2008, p. 25.

17. John Stossel, *Stupid in America*, ABC News, January 9, 2006.

18. Ted C. Fishman, *China, Inc.* (New York: Scribner, 2006), p. 240.

19. Tom Loveless, "Do Students Have Too Much Homework?" Brown Center, Report on American Education, p. 53.

20. The Project on Student Debt, Institute for College Access & Success, 2009, http://projectonstudentdebt.org/about.vp.html (accessed on June 12, 2009).

21. "Teachers Pay: Better Marks, More Money," *Economist*, May 24, 2008, p. 40.

22. Stephanie Banchero and Tara Malone, "Case of the Missing Juniors," *Chicago Tribune*, November 1, 2009.

CHAPTER 6

1. Naomi Klein, "Outsourcing Government: The Administration's Overuse of Contractors Abroad and at Home Is Leaving the Public Sector Unable to Perform Its Most Basic Functions," *Los Angeles Times*, October 20, 2007.

2. Amy Belasco, "The Cost of Iraq, Afghanistan, and Other Global War on Terror Operations Since 9/11, RL33110," Congressional Research Service, September 28, 2009, pp. 1–8.

3. Jeremy Scahill, *Blackwater: The Rise of the World's Most Powerful Mercenary Army* (New York: Nations Books, 2007), pp. 321–32, 336–37.

4. Contracts to Blackwater USA (FY 2000–2008), OMB Watch, May 6, 2008, http://www.fedspending.org/fpds/fpds.php?fiscal_year=&company_name=BLACKWATER+USA&sortby=r&datype=T&reptype=r&database=fpds&detail=-1&submit=GO (accessed on March 8, 2009).

5. Tim Weiner, *Legacy of Ashes: The History of the CIA* (New York: Doubleday, 2007), p. 512.

6. R. J. Hillhouse, "Outsourcing Intelligence: How Bush Gets His National Intelligence from Private Companies," *Nation,* July 31, 2007, http://www.truthout.org/docs_2006/pinter_073107A.shtml (accessed on August 15, 2007).

7. Ibid.

8. Scahill, *Blackwater*, p. 185.

9. Brian Grow, Keith Epstein, and Chi-Chu Tschang, "The New E-Spionage Threat," *BusinessWeek*, April 21, 2008, p. 34.

10. "Cybersecurity: Beware the Trojan Panda," *Economist*, September 8, 2007, p. 62.

11. John Swartz, "Chinese Hackers Seek U.S. Access," *USA Today*, March 11, 2007, http://www.usatoday.com/tech/news/computersecurity/hacking/2007-03-11-chinese-hackers-us-defense_N.htm (accessed April 8, 2007).

12. Grow, Epstein, and Tschang, "The New E-Espionage Threat," p. 40.

13. Jay Solomon and Siobhan Gorman, "Passport Breaches Fuel Concerns," *Wall Street Journal*, March 22, 2008.

14. Dana Priest and Anne Hull, "Soldiers Face Neglect, Frustration at Army's Top Medical Facility," *Washington Post*, February 18, 2007, http://www.washingtonpost.com/wp-dyn/content/article/2007/02/17/AR2007021701172.html (accessed on February 20, 2007).

15. Bill Adair, "Young Faces Fury in Vets' Scandal," *St. Petersburg Times*, March 2, 2007, http://www.sptimes.com/2007/03/02/Worldandnation/Young_faces_fury_in_v.shtml (accessed on March 21, 2007).

16. Andrew Murr, "Exporting and Reimporting the News," *NewsWeek Business*, May 11, 2007, http://www.msnbc.msn.com/id/18619929/site/newsweek (accessed on May 18, 2007).

17. "Reuters' Offshore 'Experiment,'" Newsmaker Q&A, *BusinessWeek*, March 4, 2004, http://www.businessweek.com/bwdaily/dnflash/mar2004/nf2004034_9957_db053.htm?c=bwinsidermar5&n=link10&t=email (accessed on July 8, 2009).

18. "Big News Covered by Fewer Full-Time Journalists," Media Relations, Indiana University, September 18, 2006, http://newsinfo.iu.edu/news/page/normal/4045.html (accessed on June 24, 2009).

19. Randeep Ramesh, "The Outsourcing of Journalism," *HINDU*, October 8, 2004.

20. Chris Hansen, "Inside the World of Counterfeit Drugs," NBC News, June 4, 2006.

21. Evan Osnos, Michael Oneal, and Maurice Possley, "Why Lead-Tainted Chinese Goods Slip through Despite U.S. Recalls," *Chicago Tribune*, August 5, 2007.

22. Reporters without Borders, Press Freedom Index 2009, http://www.rsf.org/en-classement1003-2009.html (accessed on September 28, 2009).

23. Prashant R. Dahat, "Is the Regulatory Framework for Creating a Media Company in Consonance with the Guarantee in Article 19(1) (a)?" indlawnews.com, http://www.indlawnews.com/display.aspx?4633#_ftn6 (accessed on March 19, 2009).

24. Constitution of the People's Republic of China, *Hong Kong Human Rights Monitor*, March 6, 2009, http://www.hkhrm.org.hk/english/law/const01.html (accessed on April 10, 2009).

25. Jeffery Wartman, "Freedom of the Press and Democracy in China," *Lethbridge Undergraduate Research Journal*, 1, no. 2 (2007), http://www.lurg.org/article.php/vol1n2/china.na.xml (accessed on April 20, 2009).

26. Ibid.

27. "A New Approach to China," *Official Google Blog*, January 12, 2010, http://googleblog.blogspot.com/2010/01/new-approach-to-china.html (accessed on January 24, 2010).

28. Pamela Constable, "Demise of the Foreign Correspondent," *Washington Post*, February 18, 2007.

29. Ibid.

CHAPTER 7

1. Clayton M. Christensen and Michael E. Raynor, *The Innovator's Solution: Creating and Sustaining Successful Growth* (Boston: Harvard Business School Press, 2003), pp. 158–62.

2. Ibid., p. 161.

3. Nanette Byrnes and Louis Lavelle, "The Corporate Tax Game," *BusinessWeek*, March 31, 2003, http://www.BusinessWeek.com/magazine/content/03_13/b3826058.htm (accessed on April 5, 2009).

4. Carol D. Leonnig, "Bailed-Out Firms Have Tax Havens, GAO Finds," *Washington Post*, January 17, 2009.

5. "Senators Dorgan and Levin Release GAO Study: Top Government Contractors Reap Millions, But Flock to Tax Haven Countries," press release issued by Senator Carl Levin, March 4, 2004, http://www.senate.gov/~levin/newsroom/release.cfm?id=218710 (accessed on February 24, 2009).

Notes

6. Scott A. Hodge, "U.S. States Lead the World in High Corporate Taxes," Fiscal Fact No. 119, Tax Foundation, March 18, 2008.

7. Ibid.

8. Sineon Djankov et al., "The Effect of Corporate Taxes on Investment and Entrepreneurship," National Bureau of Economic Research, Working Paper 13756, January 2008, http://www.nber.org/papers/w13756 (accessed on February 22, 2009).

9. Scott A. Hodge, "U.S. Lagging behind OECD Corporate Tax Trends," Tax Foundation, May 5, 2006, http://www.taxfoundation.org/news/show/1466.html (accessed on April 2, 2008).

10. "Overhauling the Old Jalopy," *Economist*, August 4, 2007, p. 62.

11. Steve Forbes, *Flat Tax Revolution* (Washington, DC: Regnery, 2005), pp. 27–29.

12. Chris Edwards, "Tax Policy under President Bush," Cato Institute, August 15, 2006, http://www.cato.org/pub_display.php?pub_id=6621 (accessed on November 19, 2008).

13. Jane Sasseen, "Taxes: Ready to Rumble," *Bloomberg BusinessWeek* (February 1 and 8, 2010): 38–39.

14. Shahira ElBogdady Knight, "The Economic Effects of Capital Gains Taxation," United States Congress, Joint Economic Committee, June 1997, http://www.house.gov/jec/fiscal/tx-grwth/capgain/capgain.htm (accessed on July 8, 2009).

15. Ibid.

16. John Freear and William E. Wetzel Jr., "Who Bankrolls High-Tech Entrepreneurs?" *Journal of Business Venturing* 5, no. 2 (March 1990): 77–89.

17. Coopers & Lybrand, "Generating Economic Growth through Young Technology Companies" (undated).

18. Steve Forbes, *Flat Tax Revolution*, p. 7.

19. W. Mark Crain, "The Impact of Regulatory Costs on Small Firms," Small Business Administration, Office of Advocacy, September 2005, p. 5.

20. Stephen Carrol et al., *Asbestos Litigation: Costs and Compensation* (RAND Corporation, 2005).

21. "Top Industries to Candidates," Center for Responsive Politics, OpenSecrets.org, 2009, http://www.opensecrets.org/pres08/indus_topall.php?cycle=2008 (accessed on October 23, 2009).

CHAPTER 8

1. Don Durfee and Kate O'Sullivan, "Offshoring by the Numbers," *CFO Magazine,* June 1, 2004, pp. 50–54.

2. Kate O'Sullivan, "Offshoring Spreads Its Wings: From East Asia to Eastern Europe," *CFO Magazine,* March 2008, p. 79.

3. US Department of Labor, Bureau of Labor Statistics, Employment and Training Administration, *Displaced Workers Summary, Worker Displacement, 2003–2005* (Washington, DC: GPO, 2006), pp. 1–2.

4. Arlene Dohm and Lynn Shniper, "Employment Outlook 2006–2016, Occupational Employment Projections to 2016," *Monthly Labor Review* 130, no. 11, table 3, United States Department of Labor (November 2007): 97.

5. "Re-training America's Workers—The People Puzzle," *Economist,* January 3, 2009, p. 21.

6. Steven Forbes and Elizabeth Ames, *How Capitalism Will Save Us: Why Free People and Free Markets Are the Best Answer in Today's Economy* (New York: Crown Business, 2009), pp. 169–70.

7. "Public Sector, Unions: Welcome to the Real World," *Economist,* December 12, 2009, p. 31.

8. Dennis Cauchon, "For Feds, More Get 6-Figure Salaries: Average Pay $30,000 over Private Sector," *USA Today,* December 11, 2009.

9. Julia B. Isaacs, "Economic Mobility of Men and Women," Economic Mobility Project, Brookings Institute, November 2007.

10. Robyn Meredith, *The Elephant and the Dragon: The Rise of India and China and What It Means for All of Us* (New York: W.W Norton, 2007), pp. 102–103.

11. David Lee and Alexandre Mas, "Long-Run Impacts of Unions on Firms: New Evidence from Financial Markets, 1961–1999," Princeton University, 2009, pp. 2–3.

12. "A Giant Falls," *Economist,* June 6, 2009.

13. Alix Stuart, "Small Consolation," *CFO Magazine,* December 1, 2009, pp. 31–33.

14. Ibid, pp. 32–33.

15. Brent A. Pollina, "Economic Development Zones: Do They Work for All Corporations?" *Site Selection* (July 2009): 548, 549.

16. Ronald R. Pollina, *Pollina Corporate Top 10 Pro-Business States for 2006, America's Economy in the 21st Century* (Park Ridge, IL: Pollina Corporate Real Estate, 2006), pp. 1–5.

17. Thomas Hughes, *Funding a Revolution: Government Support for Computing Research* (Washington, DC: National Academy Press, 1999), pp. 20–24.

CHAPTER 9

1. Brent A. Pollina, *Pollina Corporate Top 10 Pro-Business States for 2009, Rebuilding America's Economic Power* (Park Ridge, IL: Pollina Corporate Real Estate, 2006), pp. 2–5.

2. Ibid., p. 14.

3. Stephanie Simon, "More States Considering Tax Breaks to Woo Jobs," *Wall Street Journal*, February 2, 2009.

4. Ibid.

5. Ohio Bipartisan Job Stimulus Plan, State of Ohio, http://jobstimulus.ohio.gov/ (accessed on October 5, 2009).

6. "The States' Budgets: The Time to Turn Out the Lights," *Economist*, April 5, 2008, p. 35.

7. Pollina, *Pollina Corporate Top 10 Pro-Business States for 2009*, p. 14.

8. Bill Whalen, "California at the Crossroads, A Blockbuster Budget Crisis," February 5, 2009, http://www.weeklystandard.com/Content/Public/Articles/000/000/016/104juttg.asp (accessed on March 8, 2009).

9. Bureau of Labor Statistics, United States Department of Labor, "Regional and State Employment and Unemployment Summary," November 20, 2009, http://www.bls.gov/news.release/laus.nr0.htm (accessed on November 20, 2009).

10. Joel Kotkin, "Death of the Dream," *Newsweek*, March 2, 2009, p. 37.

11. Pollina, *Pollina Corporate Top 10 Pro-Business States for 2009*, p. 14.

12. Josh Barro, "2009 State Business Tax Climate Index," 6th ed., *Background Paper*, no. 58 (October 6, 2008).

13. Center on Budget and Policy Priorities, "New Fiscal Year Brings Painful Spending Cuts, Continued Budget Gaps in Almost Every State, Reports Update Severe Impact of Recession on State Finances," June 29, 2009 (accessed on July 9, 2009).

14. Sarah Anderson and John Cavanagh, "Top 200: The Rise of Corporate Global Power," Institute for Policy Studies, December, 2000, pp. 9–10.

CHAPTER 10

1. Norichiko Shiroweu, "Making the Grade: As Detroit Slashes Car Jobs, Southern Towns Pick Up Slack," *Wall Street Journal*, February 1, 2006.

2. "Safe, Accountable, Flexible, Efficient Transportation Equity Act: A

Legacy for Users *(SAFETEA-LU)*," August 10, 2005, Public Law 109-59, 109th Congress DOCID: F: Pub. 1059, 109.

3. Lyle V. Harris, "Don't Keep Public in Dark on Pork," *Atlanta Journal Constitution*, September 1, 2006.

4. Citizens against Government Waste, *Congressional Pig Book* (2008), http://www.cagw.org/site/PageServer?pagename=reports_pigbook2006 (accessed on December 15, 2008).

5. "Democrats Take Half Steps to Limit Pork Barrel Spending," *USA Today*, November 15, 2006.

6. "Obama Signs $410 Billion Bill Despite Earmarks," Reuters, MSNBC.com, March 12, 2009, http://expressbuzz.com/edition/story.aspx?Title=Obama+signs+$410+billion+bill+despite+earmarks&artid=kEOYcjt OFqw=&SectionID=XT7e3Zkr/lw=&MainSectionID=XT7e3Zkr/lw =&SectionName=HFdYSiSIflu29kcfsoAfeg==&SEO= Obama,%20bill, %20 government (accessed on March 18, 2009).

7. Andrew Taylor, "Senate Republicans Force Delay on Spending Bill," *AARP Bulletin Today*, March 6, 2009, http://bulletin.aarp.org/yourworld/politics/articles/senate_republicans_force_delay_on_spending_bill.html (accessed on March 9, 2009).

8. *21st Century Rural America: New Horizons for U.S. Agriculture* (Washington, DC: Farm Credit Council, January 2006), pp. 9–11.

9. Michael E. Porter, with Christian H. M. Ketuls, Kaia Miller, and Richard T. Brydan, *Competitiveness in Rural U.S. Regions: Learning and Research Agenda* (Cambridge, MA: Institute for Strategy and Competitiveness, Harvard Business School, February 25, 2004), pp. 18–21.

10. Sacha Zimmerman, "You Sow, They Reap: Why Are Your Tax Dollars Lining the Pockets of Wealthy Farm Owners?" *Readers Digest*, March 2007, pp. 46–47.

11. Ibid.

12. "The Farm Bill, Filling the Hoppers," *Economist*, November 3, 2007, p. 37.

13. Center for Responsive Politics, "Agribusiness: Top Contributors to Federal Candidates and Parties," 2007, http://www.opensecrets.org/industries/contrib.php (accessed on September 24, 2007).

14. "The Farm Bill: A Harvest of Disgrace," *Economist*, May 24, 2008, p. 40.

CHAPTER 11

1. "A Preliminary Analysis of the President's Budget and an Update of CBO's Budget and Economic Outlook," Congress of the United States Congressional Budget Office, March 2009, p. ix.

2. "Bush Sought Way to Invade Iraq?" Paul O'Neil interview, *60 Minutes*, CBS News, January 11, 2004.

3. "Overview of President's Fiscal Year 2011 Budget, Table 7.1—Federal Debt at the Year End: 1940–2015," President's Office of Management and Budget.

4. "Budget of the U.S. Government, FY 2009," Historical Tables, President's Office of Management and Budget.

5. "Economy's Focus/Dividing the Pie: To Whom Have America's Productivity Gains Gone?" *Economist*, February 4, 2006, p. 70.

6. Alan Greenspan, "Budget Policy Remarks," speech given to the Policy Forum, Philadelphia, PA, December 2, 2005, http://www.federalreserve.gov/Boarddocs/Speeches/2004/20040113/default.htm (accessed on July 10, 2009).

7. Anthony Faioloa and Zachary A. Gold, "China Tops Japan in U.S. Debt Holdings, Beijing Gains Sway over U.S. Economy," *Washington Post*, November 19, 2008.

8. Ibid.

9. "Bureau of Public Debt's Fiscal Years 2007 and 2008 Schedule of Federal Debt, Report to the Secretary of Treasury, November 2008," fig. 2, United States Accountability Office, http://www.treasurydirect.gov/govt/reports/pd/feddebt/feddebt_ann2008.pdf (accessed on September 15, 2008).

10. "The National Debt," National Debt Awareness Center, November 26, 2008, http://www.federalbudget.com/ (accessed on November 26, 2008).

11. "China Investment an Open Book: Sovereign-Wealth Fund's President Promises Transparency," *60 Minutes*, CBS News, April 6, 2008.

12. Ibid.

13. "America's Vulnerable Economy, Recession in America Looks Increasingly Likely. Can Booming Emerging Markets Save the World Economy?" *Economist*, November 17, 2007, p. 13.

14. "An Old Chinese Myth, Contrary to Popular Wisdom, China's Rapid Growth Is Not Hugely Dependent on Exports," *Economist*, January 3, 2008, p. 34.

15. Jeff Bater, "China Sends $US35bn Message to US as Japan Moves to Top Position in US Treasuries," Dow Jones Newswire, February 17, 2010, http://www.theaustralian.com.au/business/markets/china-sends-us35bn

-message-to-us-as-japan-moves-to-top-position-in-us-treasuries/story -e6frg91o-1225831173392 (accessed on February 26, 2010).

16. Warren Buffett, "Annual Letter to Shareholders," Berkshire Hathaway Inc., Annual Report, March 5, 2005.

17. Paul Volcker, "An Economy on Thin Ice," *Washington Post*, April 17, 2005.

18. Yong Tang, "U.S. Should Adjust Approach to Economic Growth," *People's Daily Online*, China, December 2005, http://english.peopledeaily .com.cn/20051226_230852.html (accessed on February 18, 2009).

19. Steve Forbes and Elizabeth Ames, *How Capitalism Will Save Us: Why Free People and Free Markets Are the Best Answer in Today's Economy* (New York: Crown Business, 2009), p. 169.

CHAPTER 12

1. "Is Wal-Mart Good for America?" *PBS Frontline*, WGBH Boston, produced and directed by Rick Young, written by Hedrick Smith and Rick Young, November 16, 2004.

2. US Census Bureau, *Trade in Goods (Imports, Exports and Trade Balance) with China, Foreign Trade Statistics* (Washington, DC: GPO, 2009), http://www .census.gov/foreign-trade/balance/c5700.html#2008 (accessed on October 4, 2009).

3. "Economics Focus/Dividing the Pie: To Whom Have America's Productivity Gains Gone?" *Economist*, February 4, 2006, p. 70.

4. Michael Mandell, "The Real Cost of Offshoring," *BusinessWeek*, June 18, 2007, pp. 29–33.

5. Ibid., p. 31.

6. Robert E. Scott, "U.S.-China Trade, 1989–2003, Impact on Jobs and Industries, Nationally and State-by-State," EPI Working Paper #270, Economic Policy Institute, January 2005, pp. 7–8.

7. Lou Dobbs, *Exporting America: Why Corporate Greed Is Shipping American Jobs Overseas* (New York: Warner Books, 2004), pp. 73–74.

8. US Census Bureau, *Trade in Goods (Imports, Exports and Trade Balance) with Mexico & Canada, Foreign Trade Statistics*, Table, Trade in Goods with Canada, Trade in Goods with Mexico (Washington, DC: GPO, 2009), http://www.census.gov/foreign-trade/balance/c1220.html (accessed on November 3, 2009).

9. Office of Management and Budget, "Budget of the US Government, Fiscal Year 2009" (Washington, DC: GPO, 2008).

10. "Estimated Costs of US Operations in Iraq and Afghanistan and of Other Activities Related to the War on Terrorism," Committee on the Budget, US House of Representatives, Congressional Budget Office, October 24, 2007 (Washington, DC: GPO, 2007), p. 4.

11. Alan S. Binder, "How Many U.S. Jobs Might Be Offshore?" CEPS Working Paper No. 142, Princeton University, March 2007, pp. 1–44.

12. www.whitehouse.gov (accessed on April 5, 2009).

13. Paul A. Samuelson, "Where Ricardo and Mill Rebut and Confirm Arguments of Mainstream Economists Supporting Globalization," *Journal of Economic Perspectives* 18, no. 3 (Summer 2004): 135–46.

14. Steve Lohr, "An Elder Challenges Outsourcing's Orthodoxy," *New York Times*, September 9, 2004.

15. Michael Regan and Mark Prisloe, "Estimating the Impact of Public Policy and Investment Decisions," Connecticut Department of Labor, *Connecticut Economic Digest* 8, no. 5 (May 2003): 1–5.

16. Swati Prasad, "India@61: From Low-Cost to High Value," Insight India, ZDNet Asia, August 18, 2008, http://www.zdnetasia.com/insight/special reports/india/0,39069 (accessed on September 9, 2008).

17. John Rilbeiro, "India's Offshore Outsourcing Revenues Grew 34.5%," InfoWorld, June 2, 2005, http://www.infoworld.com/article/05/06/02/HNindianrevenu_1.html (accessed on July 15, 2007).

18. "Global Wage Report 2008/09: Minimum Wages and Collective Bargaining: Towards Policy Coherence," International Labor Organization, November 25, 2008, http://www.ilo.org/global/What_we_do/Publications/lang—en/docName—WCMS_100786/index.htm (accessed on May 8, 2009).

CHAPTER 13

1. James Mann, *The China Fantasy: How Our Leaders Explain Away Chinese Repression* (New York: Viking Penguin, 2007), pp. 1–7.

2. Ibid., pp. 7–10.

3. Ibid., p. 17.

4. Ibid., pp. 10–27.

5. David Berratta, "Foreign Policy, Net Effect; How Technology Shapes the World, Pirate Tactics," *Foreign Policy* (July/August 2006), http://www.foreignpolicy.com/story/cms.php?story_id=3478 (accessed December 18, 2007).

6. Justin Lahart, "Undervalued Currency Helps Boost China Growth," *Wall Street Journal*, September 11, 2008.

7. Elisa Gameroni and Richard Newfarmer, "Trade Protection: Incipient But Worrisome Trends," *Trade Notes* 37 (March 2, 2009): 2–3.

8. "China: Alleged WTO Violations and Commodity Prices," STRATFOR Global Intelligence, June 24, 2009, http://www.stratfor.com/analysis/20090624_china_alleged_wto_violations_and_commodity_prices (accessed on November 7, 2009).

CHAPTER 14

1. Jim Mateja and Rick Popely, "Made in America? Hard to Tell," *Boston Globe*, September 24, 2006.

2. "Do China's Abusive Labor Practices Encourage Outsourcing and Drive Down American Wages?" Senate Democratic Policy Committee Hearing, March 29, 2004, pp. 1–2.

3. Lori Wallach, director, Public Citizen's Global Trade Watch, On US Membership in the World Trade Organization, Testimony for the House Ways and Means Committee, May 17, 2005, p. 4.

4. William Greider, *One World, Ready or Not: The Manic Logic of Global Capitalism* (New York: Simon & Schuster, 1998), p. 195.

5. Ross Perot with Pat Choate, *Save Your Job, Save Our Country: Why NAFTA Must Be Stopped* (New York: Hyperion, 1993), pp. 1, 11.

6. Greider, *One World*, p. 137.

7. Mike Allen, "President to Drop Tariffs on Steel," *Washington Post*, December 1, 2003.

8. Ibid., p. 219.

9. Richard W. Stevenson, "Bush to Lift Tariffs on Steel," *New York Times*, December 4, 2003.

10. Gary Clyde Hufbauer and Ben Goodrich, "Steel Policy: The Good, the Bad and the Ugly," *International Economics Policy Briefs*, no. PB03-1 (January 2003): 5.

11. Barack Obama, *The Audacity of Hope* (New York: Crown, 2006), p. 305.

CHAPTER 15

1. Robert J. Ringer, *Winning through Intimidation* (New York: Fawcett Crest Books, 1973), pp. 60–62.

2. Matthew Forney, "Made in China: Here Come the Really Cheap

Cars," *Time*, January 10, 2005, http://www.time.com/time/rintour/
0,8816,1015925,00.html (accessed May 1, 2006).

3. Senator Byron L. Dorgan, "U.S. Oversight Hearing on Trade Policy
and the U.S. Automobile Industry," opening statement given to Democratic
Policy Committee, Washington, DC, February 17, 2006.

4. Joshua E. London, *Victory in Tripoli: How America's War with the Barbary
Pirates Established the U.S. Navy and Shaped a Nation* (Hoboken, NJ: John Wiley &
Sons, 2005), pp. 1–8, 79.

5. Ibid.

CHAPTER 16

1. "New Survey Report Reveals Truth behind Credit Card Debt Explo-
sion in U.S.," Center for Responsible Lending, October 12, 2005,
http://www.responsiblelending.org/press/releases/page.
jsp?itemID=28011726 (accessed on March 7, 2006).

2. Kathy Chu and Byron Acohido, "Why Banks Are Boosting Credit
Card Interest Rates and Fees," *USA Today*, November 14, 2008.

3. Jeanne Sahadi, "Why You Should Pay an Annual Credit Card Fee,"
CNNMoney.com, January 26, 2007, http://money.cnn.com/2007/01/25/pf/
credit_card_senate_hearing/index.htm (accessed on February 12, 2007).

4. David Lazarus, "Banks' Credit Card Bluster Rings Hollow," *Los Angeles
Times*, May 7, 2008.

5. Elizabeth Warren and Amelia Warren Tyagi, *The Two-Income Trap:
Why Middle-Class Mothers and Fathers Are Going Broke* (New York: Basic Books,
2003), pp. 144–52.

6. Rex Nutting, "Paulson Admits Deregulation Has Failed Us All," Mar-
ketWatch, March 13, 2008, http://www.marketwatch.com/news/story/
paulsons-lament-deregulation-has-been/story.aspx?guid={4AEF15AC
-3966-4656-8108-C96712A88D68} (accessed on February 16, 2008).

7. Jessee Westbrook, "Why the SEC Keeps Backpedaling," *Bloomberg BusinessWeek*, January 11, 2010, p. 28.

8. "Secret History of the Credit Card," *PBS Frontline* and *New York Times*,
November 24, 2004.

9. "Bankruptcy Overhaul Enacted—New Rules for Bankruptcy Implemented," CCH Bankruptcy Reform Act Briefing: Bankruptcy Abuse Prevention and Consumer Protection Act of 2005, April 21, 2005, pp. 1–6.

10. "Is Bankruptcy Reform Legislation Working?" *Federal Reserve Bank of*

Atlanta 17, no. 2 (2007), http://www.frbatlanta.org/invoke.cfm?objectid =19422d38-5056-9F12-12E89D9C91AE28DB&method=display_body (accessed on December 18, 2009).

11. Theresa A. Sullivan, Elizabeth Warren, and Jay Lawrence Westbrook, *The Fragile Middle Class: Americans in Debt* (New Haven: Yale University Press, 2001), pp. 6, 9–10, 83, 245–52.

12. Christopher Farrell, "Bankruptcy Reform Bites Back—For Consumers, Debt Relief Is Harder to Come By. And That's Adding to Housing Woes," *BusinessWeek*, October 29, 2007, p. 90.

13. Economic Stimulus Payment Notice, Department of the Treasury, Internal Revenue Service Notice 1377, Catalog Number 15255B, February 2008.

14. Vikas Bajaj and Julie Creswell, "Home Lenders Hit by Higher Default Rates," *New York Times*, February 22, 2007.

15. Richard Benson, "U.S. Subprime Worries Just the Tip of the Iceberg," MoneyWeek.com, February 23, 2007, http://www.moneyweek.com/news -and-charts/economics/us-subprime-worries-just-the-tip-of-the-iceberg .aspx (accessed on March 18, 2007).

16. Cybele Weisser, "Crazy Loans: Is This How the Boom Ends?" *Money*, October 2005, pp. 53–54.

CHAPTER 17

1. Stephen Labtion and Steven R. Weisman, "U.S. Weighs Takeover of Two Mortgage Giants," *New York Times*, July 11, 2008.

2. "Fannie Mae and Freddie Mac, End of Illusions," *Economist*, July 19, 2008, pp. 79–81.

3. Binyamin Applebaum, Carol D. Leonnig, and David S. Hilzenrath, "How Washington Failed to Rein in Fannie and Freddie," Washington Post.com, September 14, 2008, http://www.washingtonpost.com/wp-dyn/ content/article/2008/09/13/AR2008091302638.html (accessed on September 18, 2008).

4. "What Next? Global Finance Is Being Torn Apart; It Can Be Put Back Together Again," *Economist*, September 20, 2008, pp. 19–20.

5. "Paulson: Economy Is in a Fragile Situation," *60 Minutes*, CBS News, September 28, 2008.

6. Deborah Solomon, "Estimated TARP Cost Is Cut by $200 Billion," *Wall Street Journal*, December 7, 2009, http://online.wsj.com/article/ SB12601576439079549.html (accessed on February 10, 2010).

7. Andy Sullivan, "U.S. Bailout Recipients Spent $114 Million on Politics," Reuters, February 4, 2009, http://www.reuters.com/article/politics News/idUSTRE51377B20090204?feedType=RSS&feedName=politicsNews (accessed on February 24, 2009).

8. "Soaring Spillover: Accelerating Foreclosures to Cost Neighbors $502 Billion in 2009 Alone; 69.5 Million Homes Lose $7,200 on Average," Center for Responsible Lending, May 7, 2009, http://www.responsiblelending.org/ mortgage-lending/research-analysis/soaring-spillover-accelerating -foreclosures-to-cost-neighbors-436-billion-in-2009-alone-73-4-million -homes-lose-5-900-on-average.html#print (accessed on June 7, 2009).

9. Jenny Anderson, Vikas Bajaj, and Leslie Wayne, "Big Financiers Start Lobbying for Wider Aid," *New York Times*, September 22, 2008.

10. Cliff Kincaid, "Banking Bill Bails Out China," *Canada Free Press*, October 3, 2008, http://www.canadafreepress.com/index.php/article/5346 (accessed on February 2, 2010).

11. "Madoff Tipster Harry Markopolis Assails SEC," *Los Angeles Times*, February 4, 2009.

12. Jessee Westbrook, "Why the SEC Keeps Backpedaling," *Bloomberg Business Week*, January 11, 2010, p. 28.

13. Jeanne Sahadi, "Senate Passes $787 Billion Stimulus Bill: Senate Votes to Approve the Historic Legislation Aimed at Reviving the Economy. Bill Is Now Sent to President Obama for Signing," CNNMoney.com, February 15, 2009, http://money.cnn.com/2009/02/13/news/economy/house_final _stimulus/index.htm (accessed on February 18, 2009).

14. "The Stimulus Time Machine, That $355 Billion in Spending Isn't About the Economy," *Wall Street Journal*, January 26, 2009, http://online .wsj.com/article/SB123292987008414041.html?mod=rss_topics_obama (accessed on February 2, 2010).

15. Jim Angle, "Lawmakers Worry Whether Obama Tax Cut Will Stimulate Consumer Spending," FOXNews.com, February 16, 2009, http://www.foxnews.com/politics/first100days/2009/02/16/lawmakers -worry-obama-tax-cut/ (accessed February 18, 2009).

16. Matthew Bandyk, "Finding the Pork in the Obama Stimulus Bill: Is Obama's Stimulus Overflowing with Special-Interest Projects?" *U.S. News & World Report*, February 19, 2009, http://www.usnews.com/articles/business/ economy/2009/02/19/finding-the-pork-in-the-obama-stimulus-bill.html (accessed on February 19, 2009).

CHAPTER 18

1. Senator Hillary Rodham Clinton, speech given to the United Auto Workers (UAW) Legislative Policy Conference, Detroit, MI, February 8, 2006, http://clinton.senate.gov/news/statements/details.cfm?id=251414 (accessed on June 16, 2008).

2. Central Intelligence Agency, *The World Fact Book*, 2010, https://www .cia.gov/library/publications/the-world-factbook/ (accessed on February 2, 2010).

3. Ernest D. Lieberman, "Business Forum: Wages and Productivity; Rebuild America by Rebuilding Labor," *New York Times*, January 8, 1989.

4. Rana Foroohar, "China's Economy Stays out of the Red," *Newsweek*, January 19, 2009, p. 38.

5. "Who's to Blame: Washington or Wall Street?" *Newsweek*, March 30, 2009, p. 31.

6. "Fewer Than Half of Eligible Minority and Low-Income Americans Voted in 2006," Vote Trust USA, October 12, 2007, http://vote trustusa.org/index.php?option=com_content&task=view&id=2608&Itemid= 26 (accessed on November 20, 2009).

7. International Labor Organization, *Global Wage Report 2008/09: Minimum Wages and Collective Bargaining: Towards Policy Coherence*, November 25, 2008, http://www.ilo.org/global/What_we_do/Publications/lang-en/docName -WCMS_100786/index.htm (accessed on May 8, 2009).

INDEX

Aaronson, Susan, 83

ABC (TV network), 94, 174

Abramoff, Jack, 40

Afghanistan War, 103, 292, 293

agricultural subsidies, 177–80

    agricultural industry in US would collapse without subsidies: Myth 38, 180

    small family farms receive most federal subsidies: Myth 37, 178–79

Agriculture Department, 177, 179

AIG, bailout of, 271

Air Force Cyber Command, 105

alternative fuels, China excelling in development of, 291

aluminum cartel, 228

American Jobs Creation Act of 2004, 47

American Recovery and Reinvestment Act of 2009, 16, 100, 144–45, 161, 176–78, 187, 279–85

American Society of Engineering Education, 94

America's Recovery Capital (ARC) loan program, 145

Ames, Elizabeth, 196

Arkansas Economic Development Department, 170

ARRA. *See* American Recovery and Reinvestment Act of 2009

Associated Press, 115

Atlantic Council of the United States, 165

Audacity of Hope, The (Obama), 50, 237

Austin v. Michigan Chamber of Commerce, 44

auto industry

    American cars having parts from many other countries, 142, 213, 226, 233

    China developing own markets, 66, 68, 78, 245

    foreign carmakers having assembly plants in US shows free trade works: Myth 56, 246–48

    problems with unions, 31, 142–44

    "legacy costs," 143, 232

    US automakers moving plants abroad, 31, 66–67

    US bailout of, 31, 66, 233

    WTO allowing US and China to put tariffs on cars, 245

Automotive News (newspaper), 31

bankruptcies

    attempt to prevent GM from filing for, 31, 66

    Chapter 7 bankruptcies, 257

    corporate bankruptcies causing job and pension losses, 260

    most bankruptcies are filed by deadbeats: Myth 59, 256–57

    personal bankruptcies, 26, 140, 200, 254–55, 258, 264, 279

    of small businesses, 130, 131, 140, 144–45, 200, 239

    in steel industry, 230

Bankruptcy Abuse Prevention and Consumer Protection Act of 2005, 255–56, 257, 258, 264

Barbary pirates, negotiating with, 247–49

base for political parties, 37, 38, 39

Bernanke, Ben, 252

Berra, Yogi, 271

Binder, Sarah, 40

Bipartisan Campaign Reform Act of 2002, 42, 44, 284, 301

Blackwater: The Rise of the World's Most Powerful Mercenary Army (Scahill), 104

Blinder, Alan S., 204

blue-collar workers, 141–42, 149

blue-collar jobs are being off-shored, but white-collar service jobs are compensating: Myth 29, 139

Borjession, Kristina, 112

Brazil, 22–23, 81, 85, 97, 220, 233

BRIC Summit. *See* Brazil; China; India; Russia

"Bridge to Nowhere," 174

Bringing the Jobs Home (Buchholz), 93–94

Britain, 55, 247–49

on use of corporate funds for political purposes, 46

Broady, William R., 60

Buchholz, Todd G., 93–94, 97

budget deficits. *See* deficit spending

Buffett, Warren, 188, 194, 198

bureaucracy

average federal worker's pay, 107, 140–41

costs of to US economy, 127–31

growth of state and federal employment, 129, 139–41, 269, 280

in India, 57

Bureau of Labor Statistics, 201–203, 204

Bureau of Public Debt, 183

Burma, 214

Bush, George H. W., 197, 247

Bush, George W., 34, 119, 174, 176, 181

approval ratings, 52, 53

belief in Ricardo's Doctrine of Comparative Advantage, 212

Clinton and Bush "ping-pong" trade policy, 227–29

misinformation about 9/11 and Bush, 116

as a Reagonomics devotee on tax cutting, 259–61

and steel industry tariff of 2002, 229–32

Bush administration

Bush bailouts, 187

creating budget deficits, 189, 192

and free trade policies, 203–205

No Child Left Behind Program, 99–101

one-time tax abatement, 268

outsourcing CIA activities, 105

political isolationism leading to loss of support from other nations, 234–35

on relations with China, 215

on takeover of Fannie Mae and Freddie Mac, 271

and TARP, 272–75, 276–79

and tax cutting, 123

trade deficit during, 197

use of private contractors, 103–104

using tactical or crisis management as a style for handling problems, 293–95

BusinessWeek (magazine), 62, 201, 202, 278
"buy American" not saving jobs, 226–28

CAFTA. *See* Central American Free Trade Agreement
CAGW. *See* Citizens against Government Waste
California, 98, 159–61
campaign funding, 40, 50, 259, 278
  average expenditures for House and Senate, 49–50
  Bipartisan Campaign Reform Act of 2002, 42, 44, 285, 301
  in Britain, 46
  and *Citizens United* ruling, 43–46
  and corporations, 35, 44–47, 51, 258, 262, 296
    military and government contractors, 103
    TARP recipients, 274, 278
  expectation that donations buy politicians' votes, 47–48, 49, 300–301
  and lobbyists/special interests, 37–41, 51, 297. *See also* lobbyists
  and the party base, 37, 38, 39
  public financing, 48, 51, 64
  soft money in election campaigns, 42–43, 178
  use of Internet for, 38–39
Canada, 122, 204, 220, 226
capital gains tax. *See* taxes in the US
Caregiver Initiative, 265
Carnegie, Andrew, 229–30
Carter administration, 142
Cartwright, James, 105

Castro, Fidel, 104
Cato Institute, 53
CBO. *See* Congressional Budget Office
CBS (TV network), 191
CBS News (TV show), 51–52, 103, 259, 272, 273
censorship
  of the Internet in China, 65, 111–12
  free press, other countries censor the press, but it will never happen in America: Myth 22, 112–14
  See also free press
Census Bureau, 185, 260
Center for Public Integrity, 262, 278
Center for Responsible Lending, 251
Center for Responsive Politics, 43, 49, 131, 178, 258, 274
Central American Free Trade Agreement, 204
Central California Economic Development Corporation, 161
Central Intelligence Agency, 104–105, 106
CFO Magazine, 133–34, 165
Chapter 7 bankruptcies. *See* bankruptcies
Charlotte Regional Partnerships, 169
Cheney, Dick, 181–82, 259–61
Chery Automobile Company, 245
Chevrolet Spark, 31
Chicago Tribune (newspaper), 99, 110, 113
Child Care Development Fund, 264–65
China, 67–69, 81, 214–16
  antimonopoly law, 220

auto industry in, 31, 66–67
censorship in, 65, 111–12
economy of, 34, 78
  China and India as bubble
    economies are no threat to
    US economic supremacy:
    Myth 6, 33–34
  China and India growing, but
    America keeping pace with
    global economy: Myth 5, 33
  China and US will not harm
    each other's economies:
    Myth 15, 77–80
  China's productivity not as good
    as in America: Myth 10,
    57–58
  studies showing growth of its
    economy, 56
  successfully handling global
    recession, 67, 68, 77–81, 82,
    192, 294–95, 298
  as US main competition, 71–75
education in, 53, 88, 96–97
as an emerging superpower, 55–69,
  78
  demanding apology from
    Mattel, 82–83
  for high-tech industries and
    engineering, 60, 95–101
entrepreneurialism in, 64
financing US budget deficits, 25,
  28, 190–91, 287
  China would never stop buying
    US securities because it
    would hurt China as much
    as US: Myth 41, 191–94
  diversifying out of US assets,
    193
GDP of, 34, 57, 59, 68, 79

  now adding more to global GDP
    than US, 81, 192
  giving aid and comfort to repres-
    sive governments, 213–14
impact of globalization on, 22–23
  bringing China into WTO
    helped US economy: Myth
    44, 203–205
  China's export growth in Middle
    East, 79
  placing restrictions on critical
    raw materials, 220–21
  US trade deficit with China, 72,
    199
importing agricultural products,
  180
infrastructure in, 76, 81, 119, 288,
  292, 294
innovation in, 64–67
  India and China can never sur-
    pass US in innovation: Myth
    12, 58–63
  spending on research and devel-
    opment, 59–60
manufacturing in
  building economy through job
    growth in manufacturing
    and technology, 288
  US manufacturing can never be
    competitive with China and
    Mexico: Myth 30, 151–52
middle class in, 32, 206–207, 209,
  233, 249
as a military power, 71–73
  ability to use cyber attacks, 106
  China will only influence
    America's destiny through
    military power: Myth 14,
    71–75

Nixon administration opening door
to China-US relations, 214
population of, 68, 223, 224
undervaluing currency, 92, 188,
200, 245
keeps Chinese investments in
China, 220
as a way to boost exports,
204–205
yuan vs. dollar, 80–81
US losing jobs to, 17, 119
jobs offshored to China and
India will return to US:
Myth 11, 58–59
China, Inc. (Fishman), 83, 96
China Daily (newspaper), 71, 192, 194
*China Fantasy: How Our Leaders
Explain Away Chinese Repression,
The* (Mann), 214
China Investment Corporation, 191
*China Road: A Journey into the Future of
a Rising Power* (Gifford), 69
Chinese National Bureau of Eco-
nomic Research, 60
Christensen, Clayton M., 117–19
Christian Science Monitor (newspaper),
113
Chrysler. *See* Daimler Chrysler
CIA. *See* Central Intelligence Agency
Cisco Systems, 60, 62, 63, 90
Citizens against Government Waste,
173–74, 176
*Citizens United v. Federal Election Com-
mission*, 43–46
Clinton, Bill, 119, 123, 269
belief in Ricardo's Doctrine of
Comparative Advantage, 212
Clinton and Bush "ping-pong"
trade policy, 227–29

on growth of lobbyists' power, 40
and national debt, 183–84
on need for constant fund-raising,
41
on relations with China, 214
Clinton, Hillary, 25, 28, 204, 215,
287–302
Clinton administration
balancing budget, 184, 187, 192
and free trade policies, 204–205
increase in taxes, 259–61
trade deficit during, 197
using tactical or crisis management as a style for handling
problems, 293–94
Coburn, Tom, 174, 175
Coca-Cola, 220
Colbert, Stephen, 114
College Board, 98
Colorado, 158, 159
Commerce Department, 206
Communist Party in China, 69
Congress, 49, 271, 275, 285, 289, 296
approval ratings, 52, 53
and the auto industry, 144
and bankruptcy law, 255–56, 257
and China, 72–73, 84, 205, 288
Congress writes legislation in the
best interests of Americans:
Myth 8, 40–41
and deficit spending, 182, 185,
187–88, 189, 200. *See also* debt,
federal debt
and the Federal Reserve, 128, 140
and the "Great Recession," 34–35,
252, 255, 270, 273, 275, 294
response to, 145–46, 276, 281–82.
See also American Recovery
and Reinvestment Act

gridlocked government, 40, 265,
284–86

and lobbyists/special interests,
40–41, 47–48, 125, 165, 176,
254, 288, 293, 296, 301. *See also*
campaign funding

congressional members
becoming, 47

Congress too tied to, 51–52, 258

lobbyists outnumbering, 46

and the military, 107–108

and pork-barrel spending, 91, 123,
173–80, 274–75, 282–83, 292

and regulations, 127–29, 148,
253–54, 255, 284, 298–99

Congress will impose regulations to protect economy
from financial collapse:
Myth 63, 277–79

and small businesses, 145, 296

and the tax code, 120–21, 125. *See
also* taxes

and trade, 152, 203, 204, 227, 231,
246. *See also* trade

when housing market collapsed,
Congress promised American
families wouldn't lose homes:
Myth 62, 273–75

Congressional Budget Office, 103,
179, 181, 280

Consumer Credit Protection Act,
258–59

consumer debt. *See* debt, family debt

Consumer Price Index. *See* cost of
living

Cook, Gareth, 40

Coopers & Lybrand, 127

"Corporate Looting and Piracy Act."
See American Jobs Creation Act
of 2004

corporations

benefiting from globalization,
29–30

European views, 23

global corporations not dependent on American markets,
296

US corporations benefitting
from markets in China and
US, 223

and corporate political spending.
See lobbyists

and corporate taxes, 121–23. *See
also* taxes in the US, corporate
taxes

corporate tax rate in other
countries, 122, 123

Japan having highest in world,
26, 122, 125

tax havens, 45, 120–21, 123–24

credit card industry is restricted
on interest rates it can charge:
Myth 58, 251–53

federal government and US corporations will safeguard the
economy and American jobs:
Myth 33, 163–65

free trade should benefit US as
well as corporations, 290

and greed, 16, 252, 275, 292

corporate greed main reason for
offshoring: Myth 4, 31–32.
See also offshoring of jobs;
outsourcing

influencing government trade
agreements, 226, 231, 244–45

not able to self-regulate, 130. *See
also* regulation

what's good for US companies in

international trade is good for the US: Myth 45, 205

cost of living, 207, 262, 284, 285, 302
  as long as cost of living continues to drop, my family stays ahead of the game: Myth 40, 185–89
  See also middle class; standard of living

Council of Economic Advisers, 204

counterfeiting of drugs, 110

creativity. *See* innovation

credit card debt. *See* debt, credit card debt

Credit Cardholder's Bill of Rights Act of 2009, 253

Cronkite, Walter, 113

CRP. *See* Center for Responsive Politics

currencies
  euro as a stable currency, 235
  supremacy of US dollar
    calls for end of US dollar domination of international monetary system, 80
    impact of deficit spending on, 188–89
    potential of foreign investors no longer investing, 190
    undervalued Chinese currency, 72, 188, 200, 204–205, 245
    keeps Chinese investments in China, 220
    yuan vs. dollar, 80–81

cyber attacks, 105–106, 112

Daimler Chrysler, 31, 142–44, 164

Dalai Lama, 214–15

Dateline (TV show), 110

debt

changes in amount of debt middle class can have, 258

credit card debt, 80, 189, 251–55, 299
  credit card industry is restricted on interest rates it can charge: Myth 58, 251–53
  dangers of easy credit, 261–65
  growth of to protect middle-class lifestyle, 24, 32, 260

family debt, 17, 256, 291
  American families better at managing debt than federal government: Myth 57, 251
  tax cuts have helped reduce family debt: Myth 60, 260
  US having largest personal debt, 25

federal debt, 123, 182–83, 189, 200, 275, 285, 294. *See also* deficit spending
  American families better at managing debt than federal government: Myth 57, 251
  China would never stop buying US securities because it would hurt China as much as US: Myth 41, 191–94
  growth of, 25, 32, 105, 140, 181, 183–84, 276, 280, 283
  impact on Americans, 185–89
  interest payments on, 32, 267
  national debt is a nonissue as long as GDP grows faster: Myth 39, 184–85
  paying down, 139
  as a percentage of GDP, 184–85
  supported by foreign governments, 25, 28, 190–91, 193, 276, 287

mortgage debt, 251, 252, 257
  bursting of housing bubble
    could not have been pre-
    dicted by federal govern-
    ment: Myth 61, 269–72
  negative equity, 263
  rise in foreclosures, 26, 279
  subprime mortgages, 252, 257
  when housing market collapsed,
    Congress promised Amer-
    ican families wouldn't lose
    homes: Myth 62, 273–75
  See also bankruptcies
"decoupling" trend, 81–82
defense industrial base, China's
  impact on US, 73, 74
deficit spending. See debt, federal
  debt; federal government, and
  deficit spending
Dell Inc., 60
Dell Theory of Conflict Prevention,
  74–75
DeMint, Jim, 175
Demosthenes, 116
Denso Corporation, 170
Department of Labor, 135, 138, 177
depression. See Great Depression
deregulation. See regulation
derivatives, regulating of. See
  regulation
De Rugy, Veronique, 282
Doctrine of Comparative Advantage,
  211–24, 227, 247
  if all nations supported free trade,
    US economy would grow:
    Myth 49, 222–24
  Ricardo's Theory of Comparative
    Advantage still works: Myth
    48, 216–21

dollar vs. yuan. See currencies,
  undervalued Chinese currency
Dorgan, Byron, 120, 227
Dow Jones industrial average, 21
downsizing. See loss of jobs
Duke University study, 88

earmarking projects. See pork-barrel
  spending
Eaton, William, 247–49
economic development, 153–66
  federal government and US corpo-
    rations will safeguard the
    economy and American jobs:
    Myth 33, 163–66
  ways state and local government
    can be proactive, 170–73
Economic Development Zones,
  147–48
economic migration. See globalization; migration of jobs; offshoring of jobs
Economic Recovery Tax Act of
  1981, 121
Economic Reference (Chinese think
  tank publication), 28
Economic Report Card for the
  United States, 300–303
economic solutions, 267–86
Economic Stimulus Act of 2008, 260
economic warfare, 287–302
  between China and US, 74–75, 84
  China and US will not harm
    each other's economies:
    Myth 15, 77–80
  government has a comprehensive
    plan to keep US as preemi-
    nent economic leader: Myth
    64, 293–97

Index

Economist (magazine), 28, 34, 99–100, 115–16, 144

education
costs of higher education, 291
decline of education at all levels in US, 62, 224, 291
high-tech people can be attracted from overseas: Myth 16, 87–89
importance of to economic development, 85–101
narrowing gap between US and China and India, 59
American children don't do well on tests because we stress creativity: Myth 18, 93–94
American college students are working to meet competition challenges in a global economy: Myth 20, 96–98
American education system has fallen behind, but is rapidly catching up: Myth 19, 94–95
in engineering, 61, 87–88
on production of PhDs, 60, 87–88
reduction in US competitiveness in science and technology, 92
we can train more high-tech people in America: Myth 17, 93
retraining for new jobs, 136, 232, 292
losing jobs to offshoring only requires safety net and retraining for better jobs: Myth 28, 135–36
US educational programs
No Child Left Behind Program, 99–101

Race to the Top program, 100–101
of voters, 53
EEOC. *See* Equal Employment Opportunity Commission
elections
1996 presidential election, 42
2004 presidential election, 37
2008 elections, 38–39, 43–44, 49–50
Citizens United v. Federal Election Commission, 43–46
soft money, 42–43, 178
solutions for reforming election process, 51
system of elections based on who will do best job for Americans: Myth 9, 41–48
"Eleventh Commandment." *See* Doctrine of Comparative Advantage
Embree, Marlowe C., 37
emerging markets, 31, 33, 55, 81–82, 97. *See also* Brazil; China; India
employment multiplier, 206–207
Empowerment Zones, 147
Engineering Trends (journal), 61
Engler, John M., 136
Enterprise Zones in Virginia, 147
entrepreneurialism, 126, 281
no country can surpass US entrepreneurial spirit: Myth 13, 63–64, 224
outside the US, 76–77, 89, 95–122
environmental degradation in US, 291
Environmental Protection Agency (EPA), 129
Equal Employment Opportunity Commission, 129

ERTA. *See* Economic Recovery Tax Act of 1981
Europe, 23, 53, 81–82, 234–35, 249
European Union (EU), 231
  popularity of in the rest of the world, 235–36
  as world's largest market, 235
Exxon Mobil, 164

fair trade. *See* trade, fair trade
families
  changes in amount of debt can have, 258
  family debt, 291
    American families better at managing debt than federal government: Myth 57, 251
    tax cuts have helped reduce family debt: Myth 60, 260
  household incomes, 16, 207–208, 260, 291
    decreasing in US, 22, 185–86
  lack of savings, 262
  most bankruptcies are filed by deadbeats: Myth 59, 256–58. *See also* bankruptcies, personal bankruptcies
  my family can stay ahead if cost of living drops are due to cheaper imports: Myth 40, 185–89
  Obama's suggestions for ways to help, 264–65
  shifting from investing to housing speculation, 262–63
  weak wage growth, 201, 290–91
    international trade causing stagnation of wages, 227
    result of low-cost global competition, 206

wealth in the hands of a few, 178, 186, 201, 208, 227, 252
when housing market collapsed, Congress promised American families wouldn't lose homes: Myth 62, 273–75
See also middle class; standard of living
Fannie Mae, 269–72, 275, 299
Farm Bill of 2007, 178–79
farmers. *See* agricultural subsidies
FastStart program, 161
FDI. *See* foreign direct investment
FEC. *See* Federal Election Commission
federal debt. *See* debt, federal debt
Federal Deposit Insurance Corporation, 128
Federal Election Commission, 42–43. *See also Citizens United v. Federal Election Commission; McConnell v. Federal Election Commission*
Federal Financing Bank, 183
federal government
  best source of funds for federal and state governments is increasing corporate taxes: Myth 26, 121–27
  bursting of housing bubble could not have been predicted by federal government: Myth 61, 269–72
  complicity in financial collapse of Wall Street, 34
  costs of regulation to US, 127–31. *See also* regulation
  and deficit spending, 22, 181–96. *See also* debt, federal debt
    American families better at

managing debt than federal government: Myth 57, 251

China would never stop buying US securities because it would hurt China as much as US: Myth 41, 191–94

countries funding US budget deficits, 25, 28, 188, 190–91, 192, 193, 287

national debt is a nonissue as long as GDP grows faster: Myth 39, 184–85

federal and state governments are helping small to midsize companies: Myth 31, 153–54

federal government and US corporations will safeguard the economy and American jobs: Myth 33, 163–66

government has a comprehensive plan to keep US as preeminent economic leader: Myth 64, 293–97

gridlocked government, 39–40, 52, 146

not representing American people, 167–80

pork-barrel spending, 91, 123, 173–77, 274–75, 292

adding programs to TARP, 274–75

agricultural subsidies, 177–80

in American Recovery and Reinvestment Act, 282–83

See also bureaucracy; state governments; United States; and specific agencies, such as Congress, Environmental Protection Agency, and so on

Federal National Mortgage Association, 128

Federal Reserve, 128, 140–41, 177, 186, 189, 251, 252, 263, 301

congressional oversight of, 128, 140

creating housing bubble, 270–71, 298–299

Feingold, Russ, 42, 44, 285, 301

financial markets and Wall Street

credit card industry is restricted on interest rates it can charge: Myth 58, 251–53

deregulation of lending industry, 16, 26, 35, 253–54, 255, 275, 299

need for regulation of derivatives, 128, 140, 279

S&L deregulation, 255, 271–72

lobbying to restrict consumers' rights to file for bankruptcy, 255–57. See also lobbyists

melt down of, 17, 34, 128, 254, 272–73, 276, 292

Troubled Asset Relief Program, 16, 272–75, 276–79

need for long-term fiscal reform, 284

as one of US biggest growth sectors, 24–25

predatory lending practices, 252

reregulation of, 16

Congress will impose regulations to protect economy from financial collapse: Myth 63, 277–79

US companies operating in India, 62

Financial Panic of 1907, 128

Fisher, Lee, 158–59

Fishman, Ted, 83–84, 96

Flake, Jeff, 176
Food and Drug Administration, 110
Forbes, Steve, 196
Ford Motor Company, 142–44, 164
foreclosures. *See* debt, mortgage debt;
  housing bubble
foreign direct investment, 122
Forrester Research, 62
Fox News (TV network), 38
France, 53, 122
Franks, Barney, 278
Freddie Mac, 269–72, 275, 299
free press
  American press will always protect
    Americans: Myth 21, 108–12
  importance of to a democracy,
    108–109, 114–15
  other countries censor the press,
    but it will never happen in
    America: Myth 22, 112–14
  See also censorship
free speech, 43–46, 108
free trade. *See* trade, free trade
Free Trade Agreement of the Amer-
  icas, 204
Friedman, Thomas L., 74, 93
Frontline (TV show), 198–99
FTAA. See Free Trade Agreement
  of the Americas
"Funding a Revolution: Government
  Support for Computing
  Research" (National Research
  Council), 150

Gans, Curtis, 53
GAO. *See* Government Account-
  ability Office
Gao Xiqing, 191
Gates, Bill, 90, 92, 93

GDP
  consumer spending growing faster
    than, 261
  as a determiner of recessions, 301
  global GDP, 192
  national debt is a nonissue as long
    as GDP grows faster: Myth
    39, 184–85
  "phantom GDP," 185, 201–203
General Electric Company, 90
General Motors Company, 31, 66,
  142–44, 164, 245
Gensler, Gary, 270
USS *George Washington* (warship), 248
Germany, 53, 122
Giddens, Don, 61
Gifford, Rob, 69
Ginsburg, Ruth Bader, 44
globalization, 16, 22–23, 56, 191, 236,
  259
  America's mismanagement of, 24,
    28, 234
  causing reduction in US per-
    capita income, 206
  China and India growing, but
    America keeping pace with
    global economy: Myth 5, 33
  globalization inevitable and
    America will benefit: Myth 2,
    29–30
  US government complicity in off-
    shoring jobs, 26–28
  world's top 100 economies, 164
  See also offshoring of jobs; out-
    sourcing
Global War on Terror, costs of,
  103–104
Godfather, The (movie), 47–48
Goldman Sachs, 34, 56, 62, 252, 273
Google, 111–12, 115

Government Accountability Office, 120

government employment, growth of, 129, 139–41, 280

government-sponsored enterprises, 269–72, 275

Graham, Lindsey, 282

Granholm, Jennifer, 136

"Great Chinese Firewall," 111

Great Depression, 56, 128, 253

Greater Omaha Chamber of Commerce, 169

Great Recession of 2007, 16, 23–25, 26, 28, 113, 128, 194, 233, 279, 290

  bailout efforts. *See* American Recovery and Reinvestment Act of 2009; Economic Stimulus Act of 2008

  caused by deregulating US financial institutions, 252

  effect on states, 151, 157, 158, 159, 160, 239

  Federal Reserve announcing ending of, 301

  slowing growth in credit card debt, 251, 253

  and unemployment, 22, 119, 134–35, 144–51, 199, 205, 290, 301

    America has lost jobs, but this is just like past recessions: Myth 3, 30–31

    growth of federal employment, 139–41

    US and China handling differently, 294–95

    China successfully navigating, 67, 68, 77–81, 82, 192, 294–95, 298

Green, Mark, 41, 51

Greenspan, Alan, 186–87

Greider, William, 227, 228

gross domestic product. *See* GDP

Harkin, Tom, 177

Harris Interactive poll, 94

Harvard University, 122

Hewlett-Packard, 60

high-tech industry

  growth of in India, 57, 60–61, 63, 76

  importance of for status as a superpower, 85

  India and China can never surpass US in innovation: Myth 12, 58–63

  offshoring of jobs to India, 26, 206–207

  US need to stay competitive in twenty-first century, 95–101

  US placing restrictions on China, 74

holding corporations, 163–65

Homeland Security, 103–16

Honda, 144

Honest Leadership and Open Government Act of 2007, 174

household incomes. *See* families, household incomes

housing bubble, 24, 34–35, 252, 262–63, 298–99

  bursting of housing bubble could not have been predicted by federal government: Myth 61, 269–72

  China's avoidance of, 78, 298

  See also debt, mortgage debt

How Capitalism Will Save Us: Why Free People and Free Markets Are the Best

Answer in Today's Economy (Forbes and Ames), 196
HSBC, 30
Huiyuan, 220
Husson, Leon, 62

IBM, 60
Illinois, 160
IMF. *See* International Monetary Fund
import quotas. *See* protectionism
income erosion. *See* families
India
  as economic competition for US, 57, 76–77
    China and India as bubble economies are no threat to US economic supremacy: Myth 6, 33–34
    China and India growing, but America keeping pace with global economy: Myth 5, 33
    GDP of, 76
    growth of entrepreneurialism in, 64
    India and China can never surpass US in innovation: Myth 12, 58–63
    jobs offshored to China and India will return to US: Myth 11, 58–59
    US losing jobs to, 17, 119
  education in, 53
    number of PhDs and engineers, 88
  as an emerging superpower, 55–69
    for high-tech industries and engineering, 60–61, 95–101, 206–207

    for manufactured goods, 60, 76
    freedom of the press in, 108–12
    growth of middle class in, 32, 206–207, 29, 233, 249
    impact of globalization on, 22–23
    importing agricultural products, 180
    infrastructure in, 57, 76, 119
    population of, 223, 224
information technology. *See* high-tech industry
infrastructure. *See* China, infrastructure in; India, infrastructure in; United States, infrastructure in
innovation, 64, 150–51, 284, 291
    American children don't do well on tests because we stress creativity: Myth 18, 93–94
    India and China can never surpass US in innovation: Myth 12, 58–63
    growth of innovation in China, 64–67
Innovator's Solution, Creating and Sustaining Successful Growth, The (Christensen and Raynor), 117–19
Innovest Strategic Value Advisors, 252
Institute for Collaborative Engagement, 165
Institute of Policy Studies, 164
Intel Corporation, 63
intellectual property rights
    need to protect in US, 218, 290
    restriction on flow of intellectual property, 218
    weak Chinese laws, 65, 72, 76, 84, 203
Internal Revenue Service, 120, 126, 129

International Monetary Fund, 81, 263
international relations
  opening US borders to free trade
    has resulted in friendlier rela-
    tions with other countries:
    Myth 55, 245–48
  US losing respect and support in
    international community,
    234–35
international trade. *See* trade, inter-
    national trade
Internet, 39, 61, 217, 284
  censorship of in China, 65,
    111–12, 215
  when newspaper industry col-
    lapses, we can gain informa-
    tion through the Internet:
    Myth 23, 114–16
*Into the Buzzsaw: Leading Journalists
    Expose the Myth of a Free Press*
    (Borjession), 112
InvestNJ Business Grant Program,
    158–59
Iraq War, 103, 120, 292, 293
IRS. *See* Internal Revenue Service
isolationism
  economic isolationism, 233–38. *See
    also* protectionism
  political isolationism during Bush
    administration, 234–35
Italy, 53

Jankowski, John E., 92
Japan, 53, 60, 231, 246
  financing US budget deficits, 193,
    287
  highest corporate taxes, 26, 122,
    125
Jefferson, Thomas, 108–109, 116, 249

job creation, 30–31, 100, 129, 147,
    159, 173, 187, 269, 280, 281. *See
    also* loss of jobs; unemployment
journalism
  American press will always protect
    Americans: Myth 21, 108–12
  handling of Bush administration
    justification for war in Iraq,
    114
  other countries censor the press,
    but it will never happen in
    America: Myth 22, 112–14
  when newspaper industry col-
    lapses, we can gain informa-
    tion through the Internet:
    Myth 23, 114–16
Journal of Economic Perspectives,
    205–206
JP Morgan, 62

Kennedy, Anthony, 43
Kennedy, John F., 53, 281
Keystone Opportunity Zones in
    Pennsylvania, 147
Kim Jong Il, 213
King, Rex (pseudonym), 243–44
King, Stephen, 30
Klein, Naomi, 103
Kose, Ayhan, 81
Krugman, Paul, 276

Lau Naj-Keung, 194
leadership
  American people still control
    political leaders and US won't
    slip as an economic super-
    power: Myth 7, 37–40
  leadership vacuum in US, 51–54,
    297–302

Legacy of Ashes: The History of the CIA
  (Weiner), 104
Levin, Carl, 177
Libertarian Party, 38
Li Changjang, 83
litigation, costs of to US economy,
  131–32
lobbyists
  banking lobbyists restricting con-
    sumers' rights to file for bank-
    ruptcy, 255–57
  constitutional right to petition the
    government vs. lobbying, 51
  and corporate political spending,
    35, 43–46, 47, 51, 258, 262, 296
  and creation of tax loopholes, 163
  efforts to modify TARP, 274–75
  for Fannie Mae and Freddie Mac,
    270
  impact of on applying regulations,
    128–29, 278–79, 299
  impact on Congress, 40–41, 47–48,
    51–52, 125, 165, 176, 254, 288,
    293, 296, 301
    congressional members
      becoming, 47
    Congress too tied to, 51–52, 258
    outnumbering Congress, 46
  impact on elections, 32, 38, 49–51
  impact on president, 51
  influencing government trade
    agreements for corporate
    gains, 228, 231, 244–45
  not as available for small and mid-
    size companies, 153–54
  numbers of in Washington, DC, 46
  push for deregulation, 253–54
  representing groups other than
    corporations, 48
  as a third political party, 41–48
  writing bad legislation, 40, 47, 64
  See also campaign funding
Logistics and Distribution Infrastructure program, 159
Long, Huey P. "Kingfish," 166
Lord, William R., 105
Los Angeles Times (newspaper), 103,
  113
lose-lose negotiations, 239–41
loss of jobs, 15–16, 21, 149–50, 151, 269
  ARRA not adequately addressing
    job creation, 280–81
  blue-collar jobs are being off-
    shored, but white-collar ser-
    vice jobs are compensating:
    Myth 29, 139
  effect of employment multiplier,
    206–207
  effect of investing in infrastruc-
    ture on, 284
  federal government and US corpo-
    rations will safeguard the
    economy and American jobs:
    Myth 33, 163–66
  free trade causing. *See* trade, free
    trade
  isolationism as a reaction to,
    233–38
  "jobless recovery" after Great
    Recession, 301
  in manufacturing, 22, 26, 31, 177,
    199
  retraining for new jobs, 136, 232, 292
    losing jobs to offshoring only
      requires safety net and
      retraining for better jobs:
      Myth 28, 135–36
  reversing job losses, 144–51

slow job growth in twenty-first century, 290

state governments are doing everything possible to save jobs: Myth 34, 167–70

US could solve job loss due to off-shoring, if everyone bought American: Myth 51, 226–27

See also job creation; offshoring of jobs; unemployment

Louisiana, 161

Loveless, Tom, 97

Macpherson, James, 109

Madoff, Bernard, 277–78

Maine, 159

"Main Street Economic Recovery," 282–83

Mandell, Michael, 201

Mann, James, 214, 215

manufacturing, 25, 85

decline of in US, 21, 91, 268

loss of jobs, 22, 26, 31, 177, 199

India's strength in, 76

as a percentage of all nonfarm jobs, 138

US manufacturing can never be competitive with China and Mexico: Myth 30, 151–52

growth of manufacturing in China, 57

Markopolis, Harry, 277–78

Massachusetts, 159

Mattel, Inc., 82–83

McCain, John, 42, 44, 176, 285, 295, 301

on "No Lobbyist Left Behind Act," 47

2008 presidential election, 37

McCain-Feingold campaign finance reform bill. *See* Bipartisan Campaign Reform Act of 2002

McClatchy (newspapers), 113

McConnell, Mike, 106

McConnell v. Federal Election Commission, 44

medical tourism, 61

medicine, narrowing gap between US and China and India, 61

Mercatus Center of George Mason University, 282

Mexico, 68, 85, 202

auto industry in, 31, 142, 226, 233

and NAFTA, 204, 228

US manufacturing can never be competitive with China and Mexico: Myth 30, 151–52

Michigan, 98, 136, 147–48, 160, 213

Microsoft Corporation, 63, 64, 83

middle class

America's strength coming from, 151

Bush tax cuts having little impact on, 260

changes in amount of debt can have, 258

decline of in US, 21–25, 32, 233–34, 244–45

definition of, 207–208

eroding of, 152, 199, 290–91

growth of outside the US, 32, 206–207, 209, 233, 249

household incomes decreasing, 185–86

international battle to keep jobs and standard of living, 24

middle class in US is as strong as ever: Myth 46, 207–209

See also families

Middle East, China's export growth in, 79

migration of jobs. *See* globalization; loss of jobs; offshoring of jobs; outsourcing

military
China will only influence America's destiny through military power: Myth 14, 71–75
comparison of soldier's salary with federal employee's, 141
lack of care for US troops, 107
military spending in US and China, 59
US outsourcing national security, 103–16
growth of mercenary armies in US, 104, 106

Ministry of Propaganda (China), 83

Minnesota, 122, 158, 159

Missouri, 158, 159

morphine solutions to economic problems, 267–86, 293–94

Mortgage Bankers Association, 279

mortgage debt. *See* debt, mortgage debt; housing bubble

MSNBC (TV network), 49

Mugabe, Robert, 213

NAFTA. *See* North American Free Trade Agreement

National Assessment of Education Progress, 94

National Association of Software and Services Companies (NASSCOM), 206

National Bureau of Economic Research, 87

National Center for Public Policy and Higher Education, 98

National Consumers Bankruptcy Coalition, 256, 257

national debt. *See* debt, federal debt

National Defense Research Institute (Rand Corporation), 59

National Research Council report, 150

National Rifle Association, 45

National Science Foundation study, 87

national security, 45, 92, 289
US outsourcing national security, 103–16

NATO, 53

Navarro, Peter, 191

NBC (TV Network), 110

NCBC. *See* National Consumers Bankruptcy Coalition

negotiating
with Barbary pirates, 247–49
intent of achieving a win-win situation in negotiations will make everyone a winner: Myth 54, 242–45
lose-lose negotiations, 239–41

Nelson, Willie, 179

Nevada, 122

New Democrats Coalition, 278–79

New Jersey, 158, 159

Newsweek (magazine), 67

New York Times (newspaper), 51–52, 57, 113, 115, 206, 221, 274

No Child Left Behind Program, 99–101

"No Lobbyist Left Behind Act." *See* American Jobs Creation Act of 2004

Index

North American Free Trade Agreement, 203, 204
  Ross Perot wrong about negative impact of NAFTA on US: Myth 52, 228–29
North Korea, 67, 71, 73, 104, 106, 213
No Worker Left Behind program in Michigan, 136
NPR, 47
NRA. *See* National Rifle Association
"Nuclear Option," 190–92

Obama, Barack
  on *Citizens United* ruling, 44
  on costs of campaigning, 50
  on lobbyists writing bad legislation, 40
  misinformation about, 115–16
  as a pro-union president, 142–43
  suggestions for ways to help families, 264–65
  on taxing offshore corporate earnings, 123–24
Obama administration
  budget for research and development in 2008, 59
  on Chinese imports, 25, 28, 193
  Obama's bailout. *See* American Recovery and Reinvestment Act
  one-time tax abatement, 268
  problems with Congress, 284–85, 289
  on relations with China, 214–15
Occupational Safety and Health Administration, 129
ODNI. *See* Office of the Director of National Intelligence

Office of Advocacy, 129
Office of Federal Housing Enterprise Oversight, 270
Office of Management and Budget, 183
Office of Personnel Management, 140–41
Office of the Director of National Intelligence, 105, 106
offshoring of jobs, 133–52, 199
  American executives supporting, 62–63
  blue-collar jobs are being offshored, but white-collar service jobs are compensating: Myth 29, 139
  claim that it is good for the US, 165
  corporate greed main reason for offshoring: Myth 4, 31–32
  fear of trade retaliation allowing, 247
  federal spending on research and development that is offshored, 60
  globalization inevitable and America will benefit: Myth 2, 29–30
  impact of free trade agreements on, 204
  impact of H-1B visa program on, 89
  increase of in twenty-first century, 21
  job functions sent overseas, 134
  losing jobs in US, 17, 30–31
    jobs offshored to China and India will return to US: Myth 11, 58–59
    losing jobs to offshoring only

requires safety net and
retraining for better jobs:
Myth 28, 135–36
US could solve job loss due to
offshoring, if everyone
bought American: Myth 51,
226–27
more than cheap labor, 117–32, 292
cheap labor causes companies to
outsource jobs offshore:
Myth 24, 117–19
labor costs lower in other countries, but US is most profitable place: Myth 25,
119–20
offshoring of jobs will lead to new
US jobs through relocating
capital in US: Myth 27,
133–35
offshoring of research and development by corporations,
90–92
questioning Ricardo's Doctrine of
Comparative Advantage,
211–24
reasons smaller companies choose,
26–27
US government complicity in,
26–28, 32, 33
See also loss of jobs; outsourcing
Ohio, 159, 160
Ohio Bipartisan Job Stimulus
Package, 159
Ohio University, 116
O'Neill, Paul, 181–82, 259–61
One World Ready or Not: The Manic
Logic of Global Capitalism
(Greider), 227
Oracle Corporation, 60, 63

Organisation for Economic Co-
operation and Development, 57,
59, 60, 121, 136, 218
Osceola, Arkansas, 170
OSHA. See Occupational Safety and
Health Administration
O'Sullivan, Kate, 133
Otrok, Christopher, 81
outsourcing
cheap labor causes companies to
outsource jobs offshore: Myth
24, 117–19
claim that it is good for the US, 165
to companies within the US, 118
labor costs lower in other countries, but US is most profitable
place: Myth 25, 119–20
outsourcing newspaper reporting
to India, 109–12
US outsourcing national security,
103–16

Palin, Sara, 38
PasadenaNow.com, 109
Paulson, Henry, 252, 272–73
"pay to play," 49–51
PBS (television network), 198–99
Peller, Allen, 106
Pelosi, Nancy, 40, 276
Pennsylvania, 122, 147, 160
People's Liberation Army, 72
People's Republic of China. See
China
Perot, Ross, 228
personal bankruptcies. See
bankruptcies
Personal Responsibility and Work
Opportunity Reconciliation Act
of 1996, 269

Pew Center, 23, 115

"phantom GDP." *See* GDP

Philips Semiconductors, 62

Phillips, Charles E., 63

Pig Book, The (Citizens against Government Waste), 173–74

PLA. *See* People's Liberation Army

Pollina Corporate Real Estate, 139, 203–204

    Pollina Corporate Top 10 Pro-Business report, 160

pork-barrel spending. *See* Congress, and pork-barrel spending

Porter, Michael, 177

Prasad, Eswar, 82

Princeton University study, 143

Principles of Political Economy and Taxation, The (Ricardo), 212

productivity

    China's productivity not as good as in America: Myth 10, 57–58

    in the US, 53, 138, 151, 185

        productivity improvement, 142, 149, 163, 201–202, 230, 231

    See also GDP

professional and business service employment, 49, 199, 219

    blue-collar jobs are being off-shored, but white-collar service jobs are compensating: Myth 29, 139

protectionism

    economic isolationism, 233–38

    G-20 pledge to avoid, 220

    if US doesn't continue free trade, it will be called protectionism: Myth 50, 225–26

    import quotas, 71, 218, 225–26

    not a solution to US trade deficits, 234

    tariffs, 218

        and auto industry, 144, 245, 246

        and China, 211, 220, 245

        steel industry tariff of 2002, 228, 229–32, 247

        as a tool to improve trade deficits, 228

Proxmire, William, 258–59

QQ car, 245

quick fix economic policies, 267–86

Race to the Top program, 100–101

RAND Corporation, 59, 165

Rasmussen Reports, 116

Raynor, Michael E., 117–19

Reagan, Ronald, 121, 123, 197, 246, 281

    and deregulation, 253–54, 255

    safeguarding of American workers, 247

Reaganomics

    deficits don't matter, 181–82, 259–61

    tax cuts are self-financing, 259–61

recessions

    Asia's recession, 82

    caused by housing busts, 263

    recession of 2000–2001, 262

    recovery from unemployment after recessions taking longer, 135

    See also Financial Panic of 1907; Great Recession of 2007

regulation

    deregulation of lending industry, 26, 35, 254, 255, 275, 299

Congress will impose regulations to protect economy from financial collapse: Myth 63, 277–79
S&L deregulation, 255, 271–72
effects of over- and under-regulating, 127–32
of Fannie Mae and Freddie Mac, 270
need for long-term fiscal reform, 284
Reagan and deregulation, 253–54, 255
regulating derivatives, 128, 140, 279
reregulation of Wall Street, 35
Renaissance Zones in Michigan, 147–48
Reporters without Borders, 111
research and development
federal incentives for, 121, 148, 150–51, 179, 291
impact of restriction on flow of intellectual property, 218
narrowing gap between US and China and India, 59–60, 81, 90–92
retraining. See loss of jobs, retraining for new jobs
return on assets, 117–19
Reuters, 109, 115
Ricardo, David, 211–24, 227, 247
Rice, Connie, 47
rich-poor gap in US. See families, wealth in the hands of a few
rightsizing, 22
Ringer, Robert, 242
ROA. See return on assets
Roberts, Paul Craig, 221

Rohmer, Christina, 281
Rome Wasn't Burnt in a Day (Scarborough), 49
Roosevelt, Franklin D., 302
Roosevelt, Theodore, 44, 52, 167, 218, 225
"Ruling Class"
American people still control political leaders and US won't slip as an economic superpower: Myth 7, 37–40
definition of, 37
Russia, 56, 68, 80, 81, 97
RWB. See Reporters without Borders

Samuelson, Paul A., 188, 194, 205–206
Saudi Arabia, 287
Savings and Loan industry, deregulation of, 255, 271–72
SBA. See Small Business Administration
Scahill, Jeremy, 104
Scarborough, Joe, 49
Schapiro, Mary L., 254, 277
Scheinman, Daniel, 62
Schieffer, Bob, 259
Schlesinger, David, 109
Schumer, Charles, 43–44, 221
Schwarzenegger, Arnold, 160
science and technology, US competitiveness in, 92
Scripps Howard, 116
Securities and Exchange Commission, 128, 254, 277–78, 299
Selling Out: How Big Corporate Money Buys Elections, Rams through Legislation, and Betrays Our Democracy (Green), 41, 51

Sessions, Jeff, 175
Shih, Willy C., 90
Shirouzu, Norichiko, 170
Simon, Denis, 92
60 Minutes (TV show), 191
small and midsize companies, 296,
    298
  federal and state governments are
    helping small to midsize com-
    panies: Myth 31, 153–54
Small Business Administration, 145
Social Security, 128, 183
soft money in election campaigns.
    See elections
"Soothing Scenario" on dealing with
    China, 214–16
South Dakota, 122, 251
Southern Poverty Law Center, 116
South Korea, 31, 97, 104, 106, 204
  financing US budget deficits, 192,
    194, 287
special interests, 37, 39–40, 50,
    51–52, 54, 84, 101, 218, 224, 282
  *Citizens United v. Federal Election
    Commission*, 43–46
  and national security, 107, 154, 287
  and regulations, 255, 284
  working through lobbyists, 38, 64,
    284–85. *See also* lobbyists
Stahl, Leslie, 191
standard of living, 32, 75, 98, 103,
    186, 227, 289
  decline of in US, 21–25, 33–34, 56,
    181, 185, 199, 201, 205,
    222–24, 225, 236, 268, 287
  middle class in US is as strong
    as ever: Myth 46, 207–209
  need to borrow to maintain, 32,
    200

government has a comprehensive
    plan to keep US as preemi-
    nent economic leader: Myth
    64, 293–97
  as long as cost of living continues
    to drop, my family stays ahead
    of the game: Myth 40, 185–89
  in other countries, 23, 56, 57, 207,
    236
  See also cost of living; families;
    middle class
state governments
  economic development efforts,
    154–62
  examples of failures of, 239–41
  states with economic opportu-
    nity zones, 147, 158
  federal and state governments are
    helping small to midsize com-
    panies: Myth 31, 153–54
  and jobs
    state governments are doing
      everything possible to save
      jobs: Myth 34, 167–70
    states are aggressively pursuing
      efforts for job growth: Myth
      32, 154–63
  not representing American people,
    167–80
  states not having corporate tax,
    122
  top ten pro-business states, 156, 160
steel industry tariffs of 2002, 229–32
Stevens, John P., 44, 46
Stevens, Ted, 174
Stiglitz, Joseph, 273
stimulus packages. *See* American
    Recovery and Reinvestment Act
    of 2009; Economic Recovery

Tax Act of 1981; Economic
Stimulus Act of 2008; Ohio
Bipartisan Job Stimulus Package
strategic planning, need for, 233, 234,
293, 295, 296–97
Strickland, Ted, 158
subprime mortgages. *See* debt, mortgage debt; housing bubble
Sudan, 214
Sun Microsystems, 60
Sun Tzu, 237–38
superpower status
emerging superpowers, 55–69. *See
also* China; India
US as a world leader, 33, 53, 289
American people still control
political leaders and US
won't slip as an economic
superpower: Myth 7, 37–40
government has a comprehensive plan to keep US as preeminent economic leader:
Myth 64, 293–97
losing status by mid-twenty-first
century, 73
needs high-tech industry to continue, 85
US is preeminent global superpower: Myth 1, 21–25
Supreme Court
lifting lid on bank penalty
charges, 251–52
ruling not restricting political
spending by corporations,
labor unions, and other
organizations, 43–46
Sweden, 53, 220

tariffs. *See* protectionism

TARP. *See* Troubled Asset Relief
Program
Task Force on the Future of American Innovation, 92
taxes in the US
ARRA providing tax breaks for
individuals and businesses,
280
best source of funds for federal
and state governments is
increasing corporate taxes:
Myth 26, 121–27
Bush and Obama's one-time tax
abatements, 268
capital gains tax, 125–27, 146, 158,
184, 281
child tax credit, 264
corporate taxes, 26, 121–23, 124,
156, 164, 218, 268, 280–82,
297
best source of funds for federal
and state governments is
increasing corporate taxes:
Myth 26, 121–27
corporate tax code, 120, 125
effect on foreign direct investment, 122
federal tax rate, 122, 123, 218
hurting businesses, 120–27
plugging loopholes, 297
recommendation to cut corporate taxes, 281–82, 297
states not having corporate tax,
122
state tax rates, 122, 147, 157,
160–61, 164
tax havens, 45, 120–21, 123–24
personal tax cuts, 259–61
Tax Code of the US

loopholes in, 123, 124–25, 163, 281, 297
size of, 129
Tax Foundation, 121–23, 160, 218
Tea Party, 38
Tillman Act, 44
Time (magazine), 245
"too big to fail." *See* financial markets and Wall Street
Toyota Motor Company, 66, 144, 170
trade
 calls for protectionism, 152
 fair trade, 197–209, 225–27, 246, 268
 fear of trade retaliation in negotiations, 247–49
 free trade
 bringing China into WTO helped US economy: Myth 44, 203–205
 claims that it results in lower-cost products, 226
 under Clinton and Bush, 205, 227–329, 233
 costs of to US economy, 225–38
 and fair trade, 197–209, 225–27, 246
 foreign carmakers having assembly plants in US shows free trade works: Myth 56, 246–47
 free trade is good for US and stimulates growth: Myth 43, 201–203
 if US doesn't continue free trade, it will be called protectionism: Myth 50, 225–26
 impact of on US, 205–207
 impediments to, 218–20

intent of achieving a win-win situation in negotiations will make everyone a winner: Myth 54, 242–45
 opening US borders to free trade has resulted in friendlier relations with other countries: Myth 55, 245–46
 perpetuating trade deficits, 200
 restriction of trade by G-20 members, 220
 Ricardo's Theory of Comparative Advantage still works: Myth 48, 211–24
 should benefit US as well as corporations, 290
 supposed to bring knowledge jobs to US, 289
 impact of foreign trade, 23
 international trade, 81, 182, 217, 224, 233, 242, 244, 247
 Clinton and Bush "ping-pong" trade policy, 227–29
 Ross Perot wrong about negative impact of NAFTA on US: Myth 52, 228–29
 what's good for US companies in international trade is good for the US: Myth 45, 205
trade deficits, 181, 196, 200
 comparison of Japan in 1981 and China today, 246
 impact on loss of jobs and earnings, 206
 importance of, 197
 isolationism as a reaction to, 233–38
 large trade deficits reflect strong US economy: Myth 42, 198–201

tariffs as a tool to improve
deficits, 228
US has highest trade deficit, 181,
209
US trade deficit with China, 72
trade retaliation, 247–49
unfair trade, 24, 190, 220, 226
what's good for US companies in
international trade is good for
the US: Myth 45, 205
See also protectionism
Troubled Asset Relief Program, 16,
272–75
ramifications of bailout, 276–79
"Truth in Lending Act," 258–59
20/20 (TV show), 94, 174
*Two Income Trap: Why Middle-Class
Mothers and Fathers Are Going
Broke, The* (Warren and Tyagi),
252
Tyagi, Amelia Warren, 252

underemployment, 21–22, 32
unemployment, 21–22, 146
effecting consumer confidence, 261
employment will pick up after the
recession: Myth 3, 30–31
"jobless recovery" after Great
Recession, 301
need for job creation legislation,
269
recovery after recessions taking
longer, 135
unemployment insurance, 128
See also loss of jobs; offshoring of
jobs
unfair trade. *See* trade, unfair trade
Uniform Code of Military Justice,
106

unions, 18, 31, 71, 141, 152, 231
and "legacy" costs, 142–43, 232
political spending by, 43, 44,
45–46, 101
teachers' unions, 94, 99, 101
United Auto Workers, 31, 143
United States
American people still control
political leaders and US won't
slip as an economic superpower: Myth 7, 37–40
and China
China and India as bubble
economies are no threat to
US economic supremacy:
Myth 6, 33–34
China and India can never surpass US in innovation: Myth
12, 58–63
China and India growing, but
America keeping pace with
global economy: Myth 5, 33
China and US will not harm
each other's economies:
Myth 15, 77–80
China as US main competition,
71–75
China's productivity not as good
as in America: Myth 10,
57–58
China will only influence
America's destiny through
military power: Myth 14,
71–75
no country can surpass US
entrepreneurial spirit: Myth
13, 63–64
US manufacturing can never be
competitive with China and
Mexico: Myth 30, 151–52

US trade deficit with China, 72, 199

constitutional right to petition the government vs. lobbying, 51

costs of litigation to US economy, 131–32

cyber attacks on, 106

everyone in the world would rather live in US: Myth 53, 235–38

handling of the global recession, 294–96. *See also* Great Recession of 2007

impact of free trade on, 205–207, 290. *See also* trade, free trade

impact of Great Recession of 2007 on, 78–80

and India

China and India as bubble economies are no threat to US economic supremacy: Myth 6, 33–34

China and India can never surpass US in innovation: Myth 12, 58–63

China and India growing, but America keeping pace with global economy: Myth 5, 33

India as competition for, 76–77

no country can surpass US entrepreneurial spirit: Myth 13, 63–64

infrastructure in, 18, 27, 147, 154, 159, 189, 232, 280, 281–82, 284, 292, 295, 298

largest debtor nation in the world, 181. *See also* debt, federal debt

large trade deficits reflect strong US economy: Myth 42, 198–201. *See also* trade, trade deficits

losing jobs overseas, 119. *See also* offshoring of jobs; outsourcing

US complicity in offshoring, 26–28, 32, 33

not understanding how to work with global corporations, 296

number of PhDs and engineers, 87–88

population of, 223, 224

solutions for economic problems, 267–86

spending on research and development, 60. *See also* research and development

still a world leader, 53

as the twentieth-century superpower, 55. *See also* superpower status

United States Economic Report Card, 300–301

See also federal government; regulation; state governments; taxes in the US

United States Competitiveness in Science and Technology (National Defense Research Institute), 59

United States Conference of Mayors, 282–83

United States Congressional—China Economic and Security Review Commission Annual Report to Congress, 71–73, 74, 75

USA Today (newspaper), 113, 140–41

US Steel Corporation, 230

Vermont, 159–60

Victorville Economic Development Corporation, 161

Volcker, Paul, 188, 194
Volkswagen, 66
voting as an important responsibility,
  300

wage growth, weak. *See* families,
  weak wage growth
Wall Street. *See* financial markets and
  Wall Street
Wall Street Journal (newspaper), 113,
  170
Wal-Mart Stores, Inc., 164, 198,
  260–61
Warren, Elizabeth, 252
Washington, George, 248
Washington Monthly (magazine), 40
Washington Post (newspaper), 107, 113
wealth gap. *See* families, wealth in
  the hands of a few
Weiner, Tim, 104, 105
welfare system as a morphine solution, 269
white-collar jobs compensating for
  offshoring blue-collar jobs:
  Myth 29, 139
Winning through Intimidation (Ringer),
  242
win-win negotiations, fallacy of,
  242–45

World Association of Newspapers,
  109
World Bank, 122, 208, 220
*World Is Flat: A Brief History of the
  Twenty-first Century* (Friedman),
  74
World Trade Organization (WTO),
  65, 204, 231
  and China, 221, 245
    bringing China into WTO
      helped US economy: Myth
      44, 203–205
    US ratification of WTO treaty,
      227
Wyoming, 122

Xe Sevices LLC (aka Blackwater),
  104

Yahoo!, 115
YouGov polls, 99–100, 115–16
yuan vs. dollar. *See* currencies,
  undervalued Chinese currency
Yusuf of Tripoli (pasha), 248

Zakaria, Fareed, 67–68
Zimbabwe, 213